Key Command

Shades of Blue and Gray Series

Edited by Herman Hattaway and Jon L. Wakelyn

The Shades of Blue and Gray Series offers Civil War studies for the modern reader—Civil War buff and scholar alike. Military history today addresses the relationship between society and warfare. Thus biographies and thematic studies that deal with civilians, soldiers, and political leaders are increasingly important to a larger public. This series includes books that will appeal to Civil War Roundtable groups, individuals, libraries, and academics with a special interest in this era of American history.

Key Command

Ulysses S. Grant's District of Cairo

● T. K. Kionka ●

University of Missouri Press   Columbia and London

Copyright © 2006 by
The Curators of the University of Missouri
University of Missouri Press, Columbia, Missouri 65201
Printed and bound in the United States of America
All rights reserved
5 4 3 2 1   10 09 08 07 06

Library of Congress Cataloging-in-Publication Data

Kionka, T. K., 1948–
    Key command : Ulysses S. Grant's district of Cairo / T. K. Kionka.
       p.   cm. — (Shades of blue and gray series)
    Summary: "From his command post in Cairo, Illinois, Grant led troops to
Union victories at Belmont, Fort Henry, and Fort Donelson. Kionka inter-
weaves the story of Grant's military successes and advancement with a
social history of Cairo, highlighting the area's economic gains and the contributions of civilian volunteers through first-person accounts"—Provided by
publisher.
    Includes bibliographical references and index.
    ISBN-13: 978-0-8262-1655-7 (hards cover : alk. paper)
    1. Cairo (Ill.)—History, Military—19th century.   2. Grant, Ulysses S.
(Ulysses Simpson), 1822–1885—Headquarters—Illinois—Cairo.
3. Illinois—History—Civil War, 1861–1865.   4. United States—History—
Civil War, 1861–1865—Campaigns.   I. Title.   II. Series.
    F549.C2K56   2006
    977.3'03—dc22   2006005621

♾™ This paper meets the requirements of the
American National Standard for Permanence of Paper
for Printed Library Materials, Z39.48, 1984.

Designer: Jennifer Cropp
Typesetter: Phoenix Type, Inc.
Printer and binder: Thomson-Shore, Inc.
Typefaces: Palatino, Times, and Snell Roundhand

Frontispiece: First photograph ever taken of Ulysses S. Grant in uniform.
All photos courtesy of the Abraham Lincoln Presidential Library.

For Ted

Contents

Acknowledgments

The research for this book spanned a number of years, and the actual writing evolved from a seminar paper during my master's program, through my dissertation, and, finally, into a book-length manuscript. Many people assisted me throughout the process, and I would be remiss if I did not acknowledge them. First and foremost, I wish to thank the staff, my former colleagues, of the Humanities Library at Southern Illinois University Carbondale: Marta Davis, Kay Biddle, Debbie Cordts, the late Angela Rubin, and Loretta Koch processed many interlibrary loans to acquire needed sources for me. In addition to helping with search requests, they listened patiently to my musings about the organization and scope of the topic and read portions of the manuscript.

First, I wish to thank Beverly Jarrett and Sara Davis at the University of Missouri Press, who understood the intent of this book and gave me extraordinary support. David Koch, Sheila Ryan, and Karen Drickamer of the special collections division at Morris Library, Southern Illinois University Carbondale, supported me via a funded position connected to a grant project that allowed me to inventory and catalog manuscript collections from the Cairo Public Library. Another colleague, formerly with the special collections division at Morris Library, Patty Doolin, read and edited the manuscript more than once. Louise Ogg, director of the Cairo Public Library, assisted me in the same grant project and also in my research conducted at the special collections division of Cairo Public. Louise and her husband, Russell, also took me on walking tours of the historic sites and museums in Cairo, which gave me a more definitive perspective on life in Cairo in the nineteenth century. Following Louise's retirement, director Monica Smith assisted me with documents at Cairo Public Library.

John Hoffman assisted me in retrieving the manuscript collections of soldiers at the Illinois Historical Survey Library at University of Illinois at Urbana-Champaign. Those collections included the very interesting letters of George Durfee and a letter written by John A. Logan in which he put forth the plan of bringing Grant to Cairo to bolster Grant's chances for a third presidential run.

In the manuscripts division of the Illinois State Historical Library, Cheryl Schnirring and her assistants helped me in retrieving many pertinent document collections. Mary Michals and her assistants in the photography division of the Abraham Lincoln Presidential Library in Springfield, Illinois, helped me identify appropriate historical photographs to serve as illustrations.

The history department at SIUC provided me with internships at the Illinois State Regional Archives Depository, which enabled me to become familiar with historical records from Alexander County and the City of Cairo. Also at SIUC, the late Senator Paul Simon of the Public Policy Institute, author of several history books, read and critiqued the initial manuscript and encouraged me to persevere with the project. From the English department, Professor Ken Collins also read and critiqued the manuscript and advised me on stylistic revisions.

As all authors can attest, writing and revising a book manuscript is a very time-consuming, occasionally frustrating, endeavor. My family and friends, especially my husband, Edward Kionka, gave me constant support—financial, emotional, and technical—throughout this project. All of these kind people believed in the project from its inception, and I am very grateful to them.

Key Command

Introduction

During the months leading up to the Fort Sumter crisis, the south-ernmost town in the northern state of Illinois contained a popula-tion plagued by dissension. Some prominent politicians were even planning secession. Sized up as the "key to the West" by Ulysses S. Grant, Cairo reached farther into the South than Richmond, Vir-ginia.[1] The town lay between two great rivers that drained the South, and Union officials believed the importance of securing Cairo could not be overestimated.[2] When the United States dissolved into military conflict, the innocuous little town, laden with unrealized geographic potential, suddenly posed a serious threat to the secu-rity of the North.

With the aftershock of Fort Sumter still reverberating through the nation, Rebel soldiers in the West pushed up to Columbus, Ken-tucky, and would have crossed into southern Illinois had Governor Richard Yates not dispatched volunteer regiments from Chicago to occupy the town of Cairo.[3] Sent to Cairo on April 21, 1861, these four Chicago regiments constituted the first armed force sent out in the western theater of the Civil War. The Cairo base, established by this secret force in the dead of night to defend Illinois against Con-federate invasion, proved to be one of the most important centers of command in the war.

After the Chicago volunteers took possession of Cairo, the first post commanders concentrated mainly on defending the site against the constant threat of Rebel invasion. Purportedly, every Confederate

1. Ulysses S. Grant, *The Papers of Ulysses S. Grant*, edited by John Y. Simon, v. 2.
2. *Annual Report of the Adjutant General of the State of Illinois 1863*, 7.
3. Augustus Harris Burley, *The Cairo Expedition: Illinois' First Response in the Late Civil War*, 5, 15.

general from Columbus, Kentucky, to New Orleans, Louisiana, had designs on the hastily fortified base. Then, six months into the war, an undistinguished Illinois general arrived in town. Assuming his first district command, Ulysses S. Grant decided that more could be done with Cairo than just guarding it.[4]

Struggling against stigmas from the past, both Grant and Cairo hit their stride during the six months when Grant kept his district headquarters at the strategically located town. Favored with an important command, Grant used Cairo's advantageous geography to exercise his naturally aggressive instincts.[5] In bold campaigns that departed from Cairo via the rivers, Grant redeemed his reputation. From his first district headquarters, Grant crafted strategies that allowed him to seek out the Rebels and engage them successfully until he finally pushed the Confederate army out of the West. Grant's victories catapulted Cairo into the national consciousness, delivering the fame and fortune that had eluded the town in its early years. For the twice-failed town of Cairo, the war accomplished what commerce never had.

In its third incarnation, the name "Cairo" became synonymous with wealth and achievement. The *New York Illustrated News* reported that public interest in Cairo, Illinois, rivaled that of Harpers Ferry, Virginia, and Washington, D.C.[6] With a single federal army devouring six hundred tons of supplies a day, opportunity ran rife for enterprising men. As government capital flowed into town "in an unparalleled degree," local speculators found profit more gratifying than the treason they had initially embraced.[7] After the Quartermaster's Department set up shop on the Ohio levee, Cairo entrepreneurs banded together to monopolize supply contracts.

Reminiscing about Cairo during the war years, Mary Simmerson Logan, wife of Gen. John A. Logan, mused, "The most extravagant imagination had never thought that the little city...sitting behind the levees which line the shores of the Ohio and Mississippi Rivers at their junction, could ever be of so much importance in the nation's weal."[8] Accordingly, people who had known Grant before the war

4. Bruce Catton, *Grant Moves South*, 25.
5. Ulysses S. Grant, *General Grant's Letters to a Friend*, 2.
6. *New York Illustrated News*, June 1861.
7. H. C. Bradsby, "History of Cairo, Illinois," in *The History of Alexander, Union and Pulaski Counties, Illinois*, edited by William Henry Perrin, 60.
8. Mrs. John A. Logan, *Reminiscences of the Civil War and Reconstruction*, 49.

never envisioned the greatness that lay dormant in this seemingly unremarkable man.

Grant scholars concede that the general's western commands readied him for his role as commander in chief of all the Union armies. Historian T. Harry Williams concluded that Grant developed his great skills of strategy and campaign management during his campaigns in the West.[9] Using strategic skills he started honing at Cairo, Grant systematically pursued the Confederates with a quiet, contagious confidence that won the trust of his men and restored hope to a disheartened nation.

The time Grant spent with small commands in the first months of the war taught him to be mindful of efficient organization.[10] Forced to deal with disorganization, disloyalty, and dishonesty, Grant's command in southern Illinois shaped his military acumen and coaxed his administrative ability to the surface. Problems with contractors, discipline, sabotage, medical care, Union refugees, and black contraband claimed Grant's time between campaigns. Demonstrating that his intelligent handling of men extended beyond the field, Grant's efficient overall management of his district undergirded his campaigns and stabilized Cairo's society for the first time in the town's history.

This study will examine the most significant dimension of Cairo's history during the Civil War: the relationship between Cairo and Ulysses S. Grant. Both products of the western frontier, Grant and Cairo followed similar but unrelated courses until the American Civil War entwined their histories forever. By the turn of the nineteenth century, the legacy of both Grant and Cairo had diminished in the public consciousness. In recent decades many Grant scholars have revised and elevated the general's reputation. His story has finally been told. But much of Cairo's Civil War history remains obscure. This book will explore Grant's connection to Cairo in the hope that Cairo's Civil War legacy will augment that of Grant and of the war in the West.

The purpose of this volume is to illuminate a long-neglected niche in the history of the war in the West. Many fine biographies of Grant exist; this book will deal with Grant's life only in the context of his experiences relating to his first district command. Exhaustive

9. T. Harry Williams, *Lincoln and His Generals,* 311.
10. Ibid., 290.

military histories of the war in the western theater and Grant's Mississippi Valley campaigns are readily available. This book will not attempt to repeat that history comprehensively. This study will give some cursory discussion of the campaigns that departed from the District of Cairo for the purpose of examining Grant's military evolution and to explore the thoughts and impressions of the soldiers and civilians who participated in his campaigns or had some connection with Grant's command.

In the spring of 1861, with a bloody, fratricidal war on the horizon, people in Cairo faced the future uncertainly. By the last week in April, the Union army had a firm grasp on the town of Cairo, and one other thing was certain. The budding community, still rough around the edges, would be as refined by the conflict raging on its borders as would the general most closely associated with it.

Prologue

Explosions rocked the town of Cairo, Illinois, burning colorful designs into the night sky. Near the Tenth Street music stand visitors from Missouri, Kentucky, and all regions of Illinois mingled in the streets and watched the brilliant display. "Toothsome luxuries" provided by the lady managers of the St. Joseph Catholic Church awaited the general public at the Hibernian engine house, while, far from the downtown, a sumptuous supper had been laid out for privileged ball guests at the St. Charles Hotel on the Ohio levee.[1] On this day, April 16, 1880, Ulysses S. Grant's long—at times elusive—quest for success had finally come full circle. After a sixteen-year absence, the man known to many of the town's leading residents as friend and commanding officer once again walked the streets where his rise to greatness had started.

Homesickness for Cairo had not prompted the visit, but rather, political ambition. After two terms in the White House, followed by a world tour, Grant had finally cultivated a taste for the presidency. His journey abroad had given him a new perspective on the executive office, so, at the behest of former general John A. Logan, Grant started traveling the country to rally support for a possible third term. At a time when robber barons ruled supreme in America, one faction of the Republican Party believed that a third Grant term would quell violence in the South, ensure public safety, and curb "Too much talk of unwritten law when the other laws are disregarded."[2] Logan arranged Grant's appearance in southern Illinois

1. *Cairo Daily Bulletin,* Apr. 16, 1880, Apr. 17, 1880.
2. Ibid.

and then followed his former commanding officer to Cairo from Chicago.

Grant's visit to the site of his first important military command reflected behavior typical of Civil War veterans from every rank. Whenever Union soldiers had spent an appreciable amount of time at one post, they frequently surrounded themselves with simple, innovative comforts and began to feel at home. On the march, they often missed those places where they had left parts of themselves— their naiveté, their fear, and, too often, their fallen friends.

Cairo, Illinois, held a particular nostalgia for Grant. The site of his first district command, Cairo had been designated part of the District of Southeast Missouri until Grant's early victories made it the District of Cairo. Grant headquartered at Cairo from September 1861 to February 1862. From the beginning he had harbored a pride in his Cairo command that verged on incredulity. At times he feared the War Department would realize the great importance of the place and hand it to a more senior officer. The federal government, however, could not have made a better choice for the Cairo command. The site itself seemed to spur Grant's strategic acumen. Perhaps the realization of Cairo's potential, combined with the fear of losing the command, deepened the well-placed aggression and keen strategy that characterized Grant by the time he left the western theater.

Hitting his stride over the course of the months he spent in Cairo, Grant developed a sense of home in his headquarters on the third floor of Alfred B. Safford's City National Bank. If Grant felt nostalgia for Cairo, the town owed him an enormous debt. Kindred souls, Grant and Cairo had both entered the war surviving, but consistently falling short of the success their potential prescribed. The meeting of person and place in 1861 had ushered them both into their glory days. For the remainder of the war, the success of Grant and Cairo increased yearly.

Approaching Cairo aboard the *Junius S. Morgan* in the spring of 1880, Grant heard the firing of a cannon salute as his steamer approached the port at two o'clock in the afternoon. After the boat docked, Grant boarded a train car specially provided by the Illinois Central Railroad for the next phase of his entry into town. Standing on a platform at the rear of the car, the former general acknowledged well-wishers who crowded the levee until the train could hardly proceed.

Beyond the crowd, the landscape of Cairo stretched much farther than it had in 1861. Little remained of the old rough-and-tumble river port possessed of only one main thoroughfare, few social amenities, and no upper-class neighborhoods. Success was everywhere apparent. As the train churned down the tracks, one of Cairo's Civil War landmarks came into view. The St. Charles Hotel, Grant's first "home" in Cairo, had shed its 1860s shabbiness and reflected the new tone of the town.

To the rear of the hotel, on Third Street, stood a building that Grant had promoted but never seen. The Soldiers' Home had been built at Grant's urging and with funds he helped to raise. Hundreds of soldiers had passed through Cairo during the war years on their way home or to the front. Frequently short of cash, the men took refuge in soldiers' homes established by the sanitary commission.[3] The facility in Cairo, built in 1864, could accommodate twelve hundred men per day with palatable food, clean surroundings, and a good night's sleep. Grant, the Illinois Sanitary Commission, and a benefactor from Chicago had worked to make the charitable institution a reality in Cairo.

Carefully navigating the crowds on either side of the tracks, the train finally arrived at the end of the Ohio levee, where Grant and his wife, Julia, transferred to a carriage. Samuel Staats Taylor, former company agent for the Cairo City Property Trust and former mayor, shared the conveyance with the Grants. While Senator Logan focused on escorting the honorable party to their place in the Grand Procession, Taylor worried over the seep water—which had required the appearance of stilted sidewalks all over town—and the possibility that the carriage would be impeded by one of the things every soldier had learned to abhor in Cairo: smelly, pervasive, impassable mud.[4]

Acts of nature and Cairo's ever-present subculture of crime threatened to highlight the most unappealing aspects of Cairo on the day of Grant's visit.[5] The previous evening's torrential rains and a gang of young men who had broken shop windows in the commercial district would have been enough to vex Taylor's mind, but the presidential appearance boosted an even greater concern. Although the

3. Ibid., 1; Mary Ashton Rice Livermore, *My Story of the War,* 131; *Report of the United States Sanitary Commission,* Chicago branch, Oct. 1861, no. 38, 226; William Greenleaf Eliot, "Western Sanitary Commission," *North American Review* (Apr. 1864):6.
4. *Cairo Daily Bulletin,* Apr. 16, 1880, Apr. 17, 1880.
5. Ibid.

local newspaper editor had boasted that Republicans and Democrats, Northerners and Southerners alike, would compete to pay Grant homage, Taylor—a Democrat himself—feared that the editor might have overstated the case.

It was possible that some Cairo residents might resent Grant's presence in their community in 1880 as much as they had in 1861. Already, city officials had found it necessary to issue a request that all citizens of Cairo who could afford to do so should hang flags, banners, and mottos from homes and private businesses. Even so, the editorials in the *Daily Cairo Bulletin* belied a subtle undercurrent of concern that disrespect might be shown the former president through an absence of appropriate patriotic display.

City officials need not have worried. Grant's carriage pulled onto Washington Avenue and, while respect and awe muted a wild outcry, no catcalls arose from the spectators. Throngs of people crowded the streets hoping to catch sight of the great general. Undeterred by the mud, a crush of humanity nearly prevented Grant's carriage from moving. The Illinois Central Railroad had run a special low-fare excursion train from Centralia to Cairo, the Cairo and Vincennes Railroad offered a special run from Mt. Carmel to Cairo, and the Cairo and St. Louis Railroad had run trains at special low fares along all of its routes. The Cairo City Ferry sailed visitors into Cairo from points in Missouri, Kentucky, and Illinois, and steamboats brought hundreds of other people into Cairo. Wagons braved bad roads and traveled overland to bring even more people into the city throughout the day.[6]

Thousands of people from the tristate area watched as the Grand Procession wound its way through Cairo. Ahead of Grant and Julia, a grand marshall on horseback led the parade, followed by the "best orchestra that ever played in Cairo," the Comique band.[7] Immediately in front of Grant's carriage, eye-catching uniforms of military personnel on horseback impressed spectators. Appropriately enough, the committee of arrangements followed directly behind the Grants' carriage, with Mayor Thistlewood and the Delta silver cornet band next in line. Firemen from Cairo's Delta and Rough and Ready firehouses provided more uniformed dash as fashionable civilians marched on foot.

6. Ibid., Apr. 16, 1880.
7. Ibid.

Among the contingent of marching citizens, Samuel Owens served as marshal for a group of black Cairo residents, many of whom had been settled in Cairo by the Union army when Grant decided that a contraband camp should be located at the post. Black residents had also filled one side of the Ohio levee, and their leading citizens—W. T. Scott, J. W. Sides, N. Henry, John Gladney, and T. C. Clarkson—planned a special reception for Grant later in the day. Taking up the rear of the parade, important personages from the tristate area jolted along through the mud in decorated carriages.[8]

As Grant's carriage proceeded on its way from the levee to Washington Avenue and Twelfth Street, then down to the business district on Commercial, he must have found the town dramatically changed. The Union army camps that soldiers, blacks, and Irish laborers had thrown up along the Ohio and Mississippi levees in the first weeks of the war had long since given ground to a business district that stretched from Cairo's waterfront up to the high ground of the prestigious Fifth Addition.[9]

From Washington Avenue the procession turned south to Sixth Street, back again onto Washington Avenue, and then onto Tenth Street, where a public music stand would serve as the platform for Grant's official welcome. Grant's visit sparked the most sumptuous, widely attended festivity in Cairo's history and, perhaps, the most cooperative and all-inclusive. Such an elaborate celebration of their city in the presence of an internationally renowned figure undoubtedly prompted pioneer residents to reminisce on the town's formative years. When the first company of speculators had dreamed of coaxing a settlement at the confluence of the Mississippi and Ohio rivers, the eventual success of the town of Cairo had, perhaps, seemed even less likely than that of Ulysses S. Grant.

8. Ibid.
9. Alexander County Collector Book, 1867, Illinois Regional Archives Depository, Southern Illinois University Carbondale.

One

Company Town

On August 14, 1851, the *Cairo Sun* reported two important events: the third earthquake to rock Cairo in the last four months and the arrival of Samuel Staats Taylor from New York. The earthquake lasted for one minute; Staats Taylor settled into Cairo and lived there for the rest of his life. Taylor, the first resident agent for the Cairo City Property Trust Company, found his new community remarkably different from the metropolis of New York. Reports of an unhealthy atmosphere in Cairo were soon verified for Taylor and his family. Staats and Charlotte Taylor had hardly set up housekeeping when they lost their seventeen-year-old daughter, Mary, to a miasmatic fever.[1] The Taylors' inauspicious beginning in Cairo was only one in the long history of setbacks experienced by people attempting to develop a town at the tip of Illinois.

Illinois' seventeenth township seemed to hold particular appeal for men from the eastern United States. John G. Comegys, the first of three visionaries to imagine a thriving city at the site, hailed from the state of Maryland. During frequent steamboat journeys to St. Louis, Comegys had noticed the point where the Ohio and Mississippi rivers met. In its unsettled state, the site possessed herds of huge black wooly bison, monstrous catfish, and bird-sized, bloodthirsty mosquitoes. Dense forests surrounded by low, alluvial lands

1. *Cairo Sun,* Aug. 14, 1851, Aug. 28, 1851.

provided a bountiful habitat, but Comegys had no interest in agriculture. He envisioned a great river metropolis.[2]

Shortly after the Illinois territory passed into statehood in 1818, Comegys secured a charter of incorporation from the Illinois General Assembly. The City and Bank Company of Cairo listed an impressive roster of company directors that included Shadrach Bond, Illinois' first governor. Sharing explorer Stephen Long's conclusion that a town with as much wealth and importance as any in the United States would develop at the confluence of the Ohio and Mississippi rivers, the shareholders bought a large portion of land at the southern end of Illinois.[3]

The proposed community, located in what appeared to be the most promising region of the new state, looked good on paper but never materialized. Before construction ever got under way, Comegys fell ill. His death killed the project over which he had presided. The Cairo lands passed to Henry S. Dodge and Elias Kent Kane, Illinois secretary of state. In the years that followed, either lack of funds or lack of interest destroyed the whole enterprise, and all the company's lands reverted to the federal government.[4]

The failure of the first land company might have been the end of Cairo's story, but, at about the same time that Jesse and Hannah Grant's firstborn child came into the world at Point Pleasant, Ohio, some signs of settlement appeared at the Illinois confluence. Something about the place appealed to a local man named William Bird. In 1818, the Missourian had purchased approximately three hundred and sixty acres near Comegys's parcel. Bird's tract of land constituted the southeast quarter of section 25 and all of fractional section 36.[5]

During the interim between the failure of the first company and the incorporation of a second company, John and Thompson Bird, sons of William, brought their slaves from Missouri to construct

2. Rueben Thwaites, *Early Western Travels*, 43; Edwin James, *Account of an Expedition from Pittsburgh to the Rocky Mountains*, 43.

3. John Lansden, *History of the City of Cairo, Illinois*, 67; Laws Passed by the General Assembly of Illinois Territory at Their Sixth Session, Held at Kaskaskia, 1817–1818, 72; James, *Account of an Expedition*, 43.

4. Malcolm Comeaux, "Impact of Transportation Activities upon the Historical Development of Cairo, Illinois"; Lansden, *History of Cairo*, 33, 40, 120, 31.

5. Bradsby, *History of Cairo*, 22, 23.

the first buildings on a neglected section of land that later became Cairo.[6] The first African Americans to set foot in Cairo, the slaves altered the primal landscape and put forces in motion that affected Cairo permanently. The first building on the site symbolized the subsequent bane of the town. In 1828 a tavern twenty-five by thirty-five feet pierced the virgin soil of the Ohio riverbank. The first of many taverns on Cairo's waterfront, the Birds' tavern targeted itinerant river men.

A second building constructed by the Birds' slaves established another business tradition in Cairo. A twenty-foot-square structure, placed on piles between the tavern and the river, served as a store from which the Birds sold flour and bacon. Boat stores—or wharfboats—flourished on Cairo's Ohio riverfront throughout the nineteenth century. The Birds' other primitive buildings marked what became the prime commercial area in Cairo during the town's peak development. The prestigious St. Charles, later the Halliday, Hotel would eventually rise at the same location. One section of the land William Bird had claimed remained unimproved and eventually became known as Bird's Point.[7]

In the 1830s, when land in the United States began selling briskly, another transplanted easterner started daydreaming about a city at the confluence. Sidney Breese put together a group of Illinois investors who bought Comegys's defaulted eighteen hundred acres from the federal government. The land stretched from the confluence of the rivers to the Cache River. With the advent of steamboats, Cairo seemed like a promising site. Breese, Thomas Swanwick, and Miles Gilbert started making plans to develop a town.[8]

While all three hoped to devise some scheme for turning a profit on their investment, the ambition and devotion of Breese, a future United States senator, ultimately brought the dream of Cairo to fruition. Descended from the Schuylers and Livingstons of New York, Breese left his native state in the fall of 1818 armed with letters of recommendation from his Congressmen. The young New Yorker found employment as an assistant in the office of Illinois Secretary of State Elias Kent Kane. Believing that he was settling in "Southern Country," Breese became fascinated with the idea of developing

6. Ibid.
7. Comeaux, "Impact of Transportation," 32; Bradsby, *History of Cairo*, 23, 22.
8. Bradsby, *History of Cairo*, 31; Paul Wallace Gates, *The Illinois Central Railroad and its Colonization Work*, 24, 22; Bradsby, *History of Cairo*, 23.

a town at the point where the two powerful rivers joined.[9] The other moving force in the second company had traveled to Illinois from New York in the 1830s hoping to secure manufacturing charters from the state legislature. Darius B. Holbrook succumbed, instead, to Breese's dream of creating Cairo.[10]

The second group of investors proposed to organize a company that would not only build a city at the mouth of the Ohio River, but would also construct a railroad to that city. Breese envisioned a central railroad running through the southern tip of Illinois. Mulling over Breese's projects, Holbrook conceived the idea to form a company that would sponsor both the city of Cairo and the central railroad. Holbrook thought the railroad should connect the prospective city with all of the major cities of the country.[11]

Difficulties surrounded the Cairo project initially, but Breese worked persistently toward his dream. Eyeing the river port as a valuable asset, Breese appealed to a lobby of powerful Illinois politicians who pushed for legislation to support the development of Cairo. The group's first success came on January 16, 1836, when the Illinois General Assembly granted a charter to build a central railroad in the state. However, a year later, the legislature overrode the 1836 railroad charter with the Internal Improvements Act. The act provided for the construction of railroads throughout the state, including a central railroad that would pass through Cairo. With the railroad seemingly assured, the state legislature granted a corporate charter for the Cairo City and Canal Company on March 4, 1837.[12]

The charter authorized the company to buy land on which to build the city of Cairo. The state allowed the company to offer lots for sale and to construct dikes, canals, levees, and embankments. The company also had authority to create banks. The Cairo City and Canal Company partly derived its name from the project outlined in the charter to build a canal that would connect the Cache River with the city of Cairo. But once the town was established, another

9. Morris J. Miller, Letter of Recommendation for Sidney Breese, Oct. 10, 1818, Sidney Breese MSS; Lansden, *History of Cairo*, 31.

10. Morris J. Miller, Letter of Recommendation for Sidney Breese, Oct. 10, 1818, Breese MSS; Lansden, *History of Cairo*, 31.

11. John Lansden, "Cairo in 1841," *Journal of the Illinois State Historical Society*, 5:1:26.

12. Ibid., 26; Incorporation Laws of the State of Illinois, Passed at a Session of the General Assembly, Begun and Held at Vandalia the 6th Day of December, 1836.

waterway leading into Cairo seemed unnecessary, and the company never constructed the canal.[13]

With the struggle for a charter over, Breese returned to the pursuit of a legal and political career, allowing Holbrook to take charge of the company. Breese remained close to the project, working as Holbrook's chief aid and counsel concerning the development of the town and the promotion of the railroad, but Holbrook became president of the company. Between the years 1836 and 1846, Cairo developed under the tight control of the company president. Holbrook threw himself into his job. He authorized the purchase of huge tracts of land at the Ohio and Mississippi confluence, including the holdings of John and Thompson Bird. He traveled to England three times to make arrangements for a $1,000,000 loan with John Wright and Company in London. Having made the investment, Wright and Company sold Cairo bonds in Europe and circulated promotional pamphlets that extolled the glories of the proposed town.[14] One promotional circular touted the Cairo resources: "The advantages which the company possess for building are very great, having their own forests of timber, saw mills, quarries of stone, lime and brick yards, and every other material required is obtainable in large quantities . . . and every kind of labor which can be done . . . by use of steam power and machinery."[15]

The pamphlet neatly summarized the advantages of the site, and Cairo did experience the first improvements on the land during the tenure of the second company. Holbrook funded construction from the sale of bonds and allocations from the general improvements bill. Holbrook authorized the construction of levees to reinforce the site. A levee ran along the shore of each river, joining at the south end of the town to form one continuous embankment at the confluence.[16]

Cairo's Ohio shore attracted all the commercial activity until economic growth occurred during the Civil War. The powerful, erratic current of the Mississippi River required greater restraint than the company could initially provide. But the Mississippi proved valuable

13. Incorporation Laws; William K. Ackerman, *Early Illinois Railroads*, 30; Session 1836.

14. Charles Leroy Brown, "Lincoln and the Illinois Central, 1857–1860," 1: 125; Lansden, *History of Cairo*, 98; Bradsby, *History of Cairo*, 24; Lansden, "Cairo in 1841," 27, 31.

15. Lansden, "Cairo in 1841," 31.

16. Bradsby, *History of Cairo*, 23, 30.

to Cairo's economic and architectural development even without a dock. Abundant forests grew along its entire course. At Cairo, the Mississippi riverbank yielded timber, and in the 1840s, two large sawmills and a planing mill stood near the corner of Eighth Street and Commercial Avenue.[17] Occasionally, the steamboat *Tennessee Valley*, built at Cairo from local lumber milled and planed in the town in 1842, docked on the Ohio riverfront.[18]

The work of the Cairo City and Canal Company turned the Ohio levee into "a little busy city on boats moored to the shore."[19] A three-story machine shop, a post office, and stores spread out along the waterfront. The Union Hotel, built by company laborers, sat on the tip of the Ohio levee.[20] Wharfboats, hotels, stores, houses, and boardinghouses represented the most enduring means of livelihood at the Mississippi and Ohio confluence, but the vice economy thrived right alongside legitimate businesses. Holbrook took no steps to close waterfront saloons, and later maps plainly showed the houses of ill fame traditionally located on the Ohio levee.[21]

While the company did what it could to promote growth in the town, the shareholders continued to focus on building a railroad. Money from the general improvements bill funded an influx of Irish laborers who required housing. Authorization for the construction of all buildings in Cairo came from Holbrook. The company owned most of the structures built in the town. Holbrook lived in a large, long house that dominated the landscape on the Ohio shore, but the laborers who migrated to Cairo lived in modest cottages on the Ohio levee.[22]

Planning to make Cairo their permanent home, the working people organized the first social amenities in the town. In 1838 the Irish Catholic population founded St. Patrick's parish and built Cairo's

17. Ibid., 28; Henry C. Long, Topographical Map of Cairo, Illinois, 1850; Lansden, *History of Cairo*, 115.

18. Bradsby, *History of Cairo*, 28; Long, map; Lansden, *History of Cairo*, 115.

19. Bradsby, *History of Cairo*, 27, 28.

20. Comeaux, "Impact of Transportation," 40; Twelfth United States Population Census Report, Alexander-Bond Counties, Illinois, 1900; D. A. Sanborn National Insurance Company, Sanborn Maps and Publishing Company, 1896.

21. Sanborn, map; Comeaux, "Impact of Transportation," 40; Twelfth United States Population Census Report, Alexander-Bond Counties, Illinois, 1900; Sanborn, map.

22. Long, map.

first church, a small frame building nestled in the woods. A hastily constructed building near the corner of what would be Twelfth Street and Washington Avenue served temporarily as a school.[23]

By the 1840s, new industries were changing the appearance of Cairo. In 1841, Bellews, Hathaway, and Gilbert got a charter to start an ironworks. They imported the necessary machinery from England and opened a business where the Ohio levee met Twelfth Street. The Cairo Iron Works produced the iron parts of the steamboat *Tennessee Valley*. Cairo's soil lent itself to the manufacture of bricks, and two brickyards opened. Ironworks and brickyards, while changing hands, remained constant industries.[24]

Local historians have concluded that the efforts of the second land company stimulated Cairo's development, but the repeal of the general improvements bill, on February 1, 1840, halted railroad construction and caused a slow, general decline in Cairo's economic growth.[25] Nature also played a destructive role. The great natural assets of the site vied for supremacy with significant geographical disadvantages, particularly the flooding of the Mississippi River.

Poor management damaged Cairo's economy. During the approximately three years of the Cairo City and Canal Company's administration, the autocratic Holbrook mismanaged funds and real estate until the entire company floundered. Between the years 1839 and 1841, Holbrook spent $1,250,000 from European investors. Still, Cairo showed little improvement.[26]

Holbrook's refusal to sell lots for private homes led to the characterization of the company as a "monstrous monopoly." The lack of a democratic political system combined with Holbrook's injudicious financial decisions finally resulted in stagnation for the community. Gradually, Cairo's population dropped to approximately one hundred residents, all white laborers from Ireland and the border South. The houses sat empty, and the shops grew idle.[27]

The dilapidated condition of the town led one English investor, author Charles Dickens, to a disparaging description:

23. Bradsby, *History of Cairo*, 31.
24. Ibid., 30, 28, 30.
25. Comeaux, "Impact of Transportation," 37.
26. Bradsby, *History of Cairo*, 30.
27. Ibid., 29; Herman R. Lantz, *A Community in Search of Itself: A Case History of Cairo, Illinois*, 11; Bradsby, *History of Cairo*, 29; Lantz, *Community in Search*, 11.

At the junction of the two rivers, on ground so flat and low and marshy, that at certain seasons of the year it is inundated to the housetops, lies a breeding-place of fever, ague, and death; vaunted in England as a mine of Golden Hope, and speculated in, on the faith of monstrous representations, to many people's ruin. A dismal swamp, on which the half-built houses rot away.[28]

Dickens wrote the passage after an 1842 visit to America.

When Sidney Breese and his partners decided to forfeit the Cairo project, Holbrook deserted the town. Ironically, his absence proved as troubling to Cairo as had his presence. With no company agent and no tradition of self-governance, the small society that existed in Cairo fell into general lawlessness. The company directors, hoping to protect property they had left in the town, sent Miles A. Gilbert to guard their remaining assests. The job nearly cost Gilbert his life.

Arriving at Cairo in 1843, he found a mob of angry laborers threatening violence. Starved and out of work, the men demanded permission to enter the machine shops on the levee and dismantle the expensive equipment and sell it to obtain compensation for their unpaid wages. Gilbert explained that he had no authority to allow the sale of the equipment.[29] Unappeased, the mob left the office and started swarming toward the machine shops. For several hours, the laborers indulged in whiskey and bluster, but in the end, the sight of blood—spouting from the first blow—unnerved them sufficiently that they vacated the building and retreated under cover of night.[30] Gilbert's supervision had abated vigilante violence in 1843, but the incident marked a new tradition in Cairo that survived into the twentieth century.

By 1846 only the auspicious geographic location of Cairo saved the town from total abandonment. Showing tenacity and resilience similar to that possessed by Ulysses S. Grant, residents remained in the village, confident that the town would survive.[31] They appointed town officials from their own ranks who tried to keep peace and

28. Charles Dickens, *American Notes*, 186–87.
29. Bradsby, *History of Cairo*, 9, 30, 32.
30. Ibid.
31. John Y. Simon, "Forging a Commander: Ulysses S. Grant Enters the Civil War," in *New Perspectives on the Civil War*, edited by John Y. Simon and Michael E. Stevens, 50, 64.

restrain rowdy river men.[32] Thus it transpired that while Grant was in Mexico, getting in the habit of taking military strategy into his own hands, the people of Cairo took the law into theirs.

On June 13, 1846, Cairo City and Canal Company transferred all of its assets to Thomas S. Taylor of Philadelphia and Charles Davis of New York. The new owners formed a trust, incorporated as the Cairo City Property Trust Company. They retained Gilbert in the position of company agent until such time as attorney Samuel Staats Taylor, practicing in New York, could move to Cairo and take charge.

At first, Taylor's arrival brought little change to Cairo. The town's economic base remained tied to river transportation. Town residents and the company trustees continued to support river traffic, but they yearned for a railroad in Cairo. Everything in the embryonic community waited on the confirmation of the town as southern terminus for the Illinois Central Railroad. More than hope supported the expectation that Cairo would be designated a railroad depot. Once Illinois had become a state, the battle for a central railroad had worked its way from the Illinois General Assembly into Congress.

In preparation for the railroad, the Army Corps of Engineers sent Henry C. Long to southern Illinois to study the Cairo site. After inspecting the town, Long discovered problems with the levees. However, the site's advantages still seemed to outweigh the flooding problem, and, in the end, Long indulged in the braggadocio adopted by Cairo promoters, stating that if the trustees achieved the objective of protecting Cairo from flooding, the increase in population and wealth would be unsurpassed by that of any other city in the world.[33]

In an addendum he mentioned that, since the date of his report, Congress had donated lands to aid in the completion of a central railroad from Cairo to the Illinois and Michigan Canal with branches to Galena and Chicago. In the same bill, Congress donated an equal amount of land to aid in the construction of a railroad from Cairo to Mobile.[34]

Long referred to a bill that had been introduced into Congress in 1848 by Senator Stephen A. Douglas of Illinois. Although Douglas

32. Bradsby, *History of Cairo*, 97.
33. Henry C. Long, "Report on the Site of Cairo, Illinois," 25.
34. Ibid.

took credit for the idea of the Illinois Central Railroad, Sidney Breese had actually promoted the idea of a central railroad in the state as early as 1835. Elected to the U.S. Senate in 1842, Breese had spent his entire term trying to get federal land aid for the raiload. Unfortunately, his efforts to help his planned community all came to nothing while he served in the Senate.[35]

Breese returned to Illinois, and Stephen Douglas picked up the issue of a central railroad and gave it national significance. Political aid from Cairo shareholders, along with the support of trustees who resided in Massachusetts and New York, helped to pass the federal land grant of 1850.[36] Congress's role ended at that point, and the framing of charters for the specified railroads fell to the legislatures of the individual states through which the road would pass.

Finally, on December 17, 1851, with the help of Breese and Holbrook, the Illinois Central charter named Cairo as southern terminus. As part of the compromise, the state of Illinois agreed to set aside one thousand shares of Illinois Central stock that would not be assessed. From that time on, the two corporations shared responsibility for improving the town, particularly in regard to flood prevention.[37]

In the 1850s the future looked bright for Cairo. On February 10, 1851, in both Cairo and Chicago, construction began on the railroad. The planned route for the line extended between the two towns with a branch to Galena. A promotional Catalog of Lots circulated by the Cairo City Property Trust stated that Cairo was now accessible from all points and at all seasons. The importance of establishing rail lines in Cairo cannot be overstated. The construction of the railroad resulted in the emergence of the river and rail transshipment business that brought the first real prosperity to Cairo.[38] Unquestionably the railroad remedied the most immediate problem with southern Illinois' overall economy: the lack of transportation for

35. Melville W. Fuller, "Biography of Sidney Breese" in *Sidney Breese, The Early History of Illinois from Its Discovery of the Mississippi*, 32, 24; Brown, *Lincoln and the Illinois Central*, 1:125; Fuller, "Sidney Breese," 33.

36. Lansden, *History of Cairo*, 108; Gates, *Illinois Central*, 36.

37. Brown, *Lincoln and the Illinois Central*, 126; Gates, *Illinois Central*, 32–33; Brown, *Lincoln and the Illinois Central*, 126; Gates, *Illinois Central*, 47; *Cairo Sun*, June 5, 1851.

38. *Cairo Sun*, Dec. 25, 1851; Catalog of Lots, July 1853; Cairo City Property Trust MSS; Comeaux, "Impact of Transportation," 42.

shipping products to markets. With that problem solved, Cairo started to grow.

The fact that the adjacent agricultural regions were sparsely popu-lated may have been a general drawback to Cairo's development as a metropolis, but the railroad strengthened Cairo's ties to the North and the East and created a new town psychology. The appearance of progressive technology linking Cairo with larger cities bolstered the inhabitants' confidence in their little village. People began to believe that Cairo had the potential to become an important city. The *Cairo City Times* reported that the railroads and the port opened outlets through which "Cairo might lift Egypt [southern Illi-nois] from the darkness imposed on it by geographic barriers."[39] The reaction of people in the rest of the region to this observation was, apparently, not fit to print.

By 1853, the Cairo trustees acknowledged that "Cairo must be rescued from the rage of the mighty rivers in order to make it com-mercially incomparable," but they decided to start selling residential lots in the town they believed "would render the company worth tens of millions."[40] Staats Taylor and Thomas Davis took the initia-tive to move ahead with the expansion of the town. They wrote the president of the Illinois Central Railroad informing him, "We have advertised and commenced sale of lots with assurance that the work of your company would very soon be resumed at that point."[41] In 1854, the company sold six hundred home lots. The railroad com-pany returned to work in Cairo. By 1855, they had sold $1,100,000 worth of land in the town, and the train was running.[42]

Exhibiting confidence in their investment, the Cairo City Property Trust stockholders formed a building committee in New York City for the purpose of raising funds to construct several entire blocks in Cairo. The building spree included one especially impressive structure: the St. Charles Hotel. Incorporated by the Illinois state legislature in February 1857, the hotel's board of directors included some of the most prominent politicians in Springfield.[43]

39. Lansden, *History of Cairo*, 62; *Cairo City Times*, Nov. 7, 1855.
40. Cairo City Property MSS, Nov. 16, 1853.
41. S. S. Taylor and Thomas Davis to President, Sept. 29, 1853, Illinois Cen-tral Railroad MSS.
42. *Cairo Weekly Times and Delta*, Dec. 12, 1855.
43. Lansden, *History of Cairo*, 236.

Lot sales moved so well that a first addition had been plotted, and residents speculated that the town would soon require a second addition.[44] The local newspaper reported that prominent New Orleans commission merchants had developed an interest in Cairo. One particular resident of the Crescent City, Mr. R. B. Bell, planned to settle in Cairo. Brother to a banker in Pittsburgh, Bell planned to start a bank in Cairo that would be affiliated with his brother's.

It is to be hoped that the Bells were held in higher esteem than a gentleman banker whose obituary appeared in the *Cairo Sun*. The newspaper reported that although the man was a banker, it was generally believed "he died a Christian, and was... respected."[45] While not the most popular group in nineteenth-century American society, bankers were necessary for commercial growth, and the *Sun* finally concluded that the community should welcome these men.

Banking brought Alfred Boardman Safford to Cairo in 1858. A. B. Safford and his sister, Mary Jane, hailed from Hyde Park, Vermont, and came from pre-Revolutionary ancestors. Safford first pursued a legal education but eventually turned from that to engage in business. He spent some time in Shawneetown, Illinois, working as a merchant while Mary Jane taught school. In 1858, the two young people relocated to the new town of Cairo, and A. B. took up banking.[46] At the time the Civil War broke out Safford had become the wealthiest man in town. His unmarried sister served as social hostess.

Light manufacturing followed the brisk business environment to Cairo. The purchase of five lots on the Ohio levee adjoining the Illinois Central freight depot heralded the start of the flour milling industry, one of Cairo's most enduring enterprises. The Dishon, later Cairo City Mills, turned out two hundred barrels a day. Local reporters stated accurately that the mills represented the beginning of manufacturing in Cairo.[47] The possibility of operating flour mills attracted Charles Galigher of Cincinnati, Ohio, to Cairo. Galigher eventually established mills at Cairo and Olive Branch, Illinois.

Growing commerce and increased population started changing

44. Plat maps, First Addition, Special Collections, Cairo Public Library.

45. *Cairo Sun*, May 29, 1851.

46. Le Roy S. Fischer, "Cairo's Civil War Angel, Mary Jane Safford," 54:232; Bradsby, *History of Cairo*, 54–55E.

47. *Cairo Sun*, Oct. 17, 1855.

Cairo's social and professional image. The town attracted four physicians, most notably Daniel Arter. Born in Maryland, Arter moved to
Illinois and resided in Pulaski County. He established auxiliary practices in Cairo and other outlying areas. At the beginning of the
Civil War, President Lincoln appointed Arter to the position of surveyor and collector of the Cairo port. Consequently, the Arters
moved to Cairo, and Dr. Arter became acquainted with other local
men who also held military appointments.[48]

Ten attorneys advertised in the Cairo newspapers. John A. Logan
of Benton and William H. Green of Metropolis opened branch offices
in Cairo. At least two insurance agencies conducted business in the
community, employing some of the town's leading citizens. Henry
H. Candee owned an insurance business, and I. N. Haynie, Charles
Galigher, John W. Trover, and William H. Green directed the Southern Illinois Insurance Company of Cairo.[49]

The combined transportation systems brought another new enterprise to Cairo. In 1858, future general George B. McClellan met with
railroad and steamboat men in St. Louis to organize a mail packet
company that would travel from Cairo to New Orleans. Officers of
the new company designated Cairo as their main terminus. The St.
Louis and New Orleans Packet Company—comprising ten steamers—began operating in 1860. The boats exchanged freight and pas-
sengers at Cairo and transported them to any point touched by
either the steamboats or the Illinois Central Railroad.[50]

As a community of permanent residents continued to multiply
in Cairo, private citizens and businessmen alike felt some degree of
kinship with the South. When the country began to polarize in the
months preceding the war, businessmen hoped that commercial
enterprises such as the Cairo and New Orleans Mail Packet Company would keep regular communications with the South open and
create economic unity between the two regions.[51]

By the end of the decade, new construction had transformed
Cairo's appearance. The most substantial buildings in town represented the company and the business community. By the time serious construction got under way in Cairo, brick had become the

48. Bradsby, *History of Cairo*, 5.
49. *Cairo Tri-Weekly*, Jan. 12, 1856; Isham N. Haynie MSS.
50. Cairo City Property Trust MSS, July 30, 1856; Gates, *Illinois Central*, 275;
Comeaux, "Impact of Transportation," 74.
51. Lansden, *History of Cairo*, 41; *Cairo Tri-Weekly*, Jan. 8, 1865.

material of choice for rising men in America. They believed that brick gave the appearance of efficiency, safety, and financial steadiness. By the 1850s, brick cubes filled the landscape all along the Ohio River Valley.[52] Commercial leaders in Cairo adopted this style in hopes of creating an image of safety for a community traditionally hampered by crime.

In the same way that the architecture in Cairo projected a different material image from that of the surrounding communities, the town also developed a society unique in southern Illinois. Even though the rough element continued to dominate, some degree of refinement surfaced. Amidst violence in bleeding Kansas, Indian uprisings in the West, and a struggle for women's rights in the South, Cairo's society gave birth to a small, tentative middle class.[53]

In 1855, reflecting on the town's growth, the *Cairo City Times* reported, "The change that has taken place in Cairo during the past year consists...more in the consideration which she has acquired abroad than in her actual material progress."[54] Abused and accursed following the failure of the Cairo City and Canal Company, Cairo now found an increasing number of investors. But in order for Cairo to have a bright future, the tone of society in the town still needed improvement.

On the eve of the Civil War, Cairo's society still contained a large lower-class base, a small, emerging middle class, and no upper class.[55] Reports in local newspapers supported the conclusion. Journalists started covering the "fall fights" in November, and the brawling was no respecter of race or gender. Even the bitterly cold winter of 1856—newsworthy in itself—gave rise to stories of frequent fights and much blood spilled on the Ohio levee. Journalists noted: "The extreme cold weather apparently [has] no effect upon the hot blood of some of our citizens."[56] Reporters hesitated to admit that the troublemakers on the riverfront were not all transients. Free fights and knock-down-drag-outs started by Cairo residents constituted a major recurring theme in the local news.

52. Lansden, *History of Cairo*, 432, 439, 431.
53. *Cairo Tri-Weekly*, Feb. 17, 1856, Feb. 9, 1856; *Cairo Weekly Times and Delta*, May 7, 1856; Matthew Josephson, *The Robber Barons: The Great American Capitalists, 1861–1901*, 14.
54. *Cairo City Times*, Nov. 7, 1855.
55. Lantz, *Community in Search*, 27.
56. *Cairo Tri-Weekly*, Jan. 10, 1856.

A particular location, the Taylor House, seemed to draw trouble like a magnet. In a typical incident, one unfortunate man passed out from drink in front of this hotel and someone set him on fire. Journalists reported that the poor man "lost the entire seat of his pantaloons before the fire could be extinguished."[57] One enterprising Cairo physician kept his office at the Taylor House, no doubt to accommodate his patients.

As the village became a town, the absence of a city government plagued Cairo. The vigilante violence that had greeted Miles Gilbert on his arrival in Cairo resurfaced periodically throughout the nineteenth century. Law officials from neighboring cities arrested criminals in Cairo since the town had no police force or city marshal. The arrangement sometimes led to ill feeling, such as in the case against Samuel Hargrave of Union County. The Jonesboro police arrested Hargrave, or from their viewpoint, rescued him, in Cairo.

Jonesboro police charged the offender with Negro stealing and confined him to jail for two days. Reporting the story, a correspondent for the *Jonesboro Gazette* stated that Cairo ruffians had taunted and insulted Hargrave. Not bothering to refute the allegations regarding Hargrave's treatment, the *Cairo Sun* corrected the *Gazette*'s characterization of the citizens involved. The Cairo editor retorted that the alleged "ruffians" were, in fact, the "most respectable, honorable, and enterprising citizens" in Cairo.[58]

Six years before the outbreak of the Civil War, the people of Cairo became incensed when a white man stole money from a black resident of their town. The thief evaded his day in court since a white man could not be convicted on the testimony of a black. Consequently, a Cairo mob hunted down the perpetrator, dunked him in the Ohio River, and banished him to Kentucky. Reporters called this action a dose of "Cairo justice."[59] The term stuck.

Vigilante justice in Cairo sometimes conjured up images reminiscent of the Wild West with men wielding bullwhips and guns and shooting one another in the streets. Alcohol contributed to the aggressive behavior of the rough element in Cairo. Overimbibing existed alongside excessive gambling on the Cairo waterfront. Gam-

57. *Cairo Weekly Times and Delta*, Nov. 7, 1855, Dec. 19, 1855.
58. *Cairo Sun*, May 15, 1851.
59. *Cairo Weekly Times and Delta*, Nov. 7, 1855.

bling, and the crimes related to it, posed such a serious threat that public warnings notified residents and transients of the scams practiced by professional gamblers.[60] When men combined drinking with gambling, deadly brawls frequently followed. Cairo newspapers regularly reported murders on the waterfront.

Less serious crimes may also have been alcohol-related. In one notorious incident, a steamboat deckhand dressed in female attire "promenaded through the suburbs" with a male companion. A string cane band followed them playing "illegant music."[61] The incident amused local folk, but editors of the newspaper construed the stroll as a penitentiary offense. No charges ensued, however, and the couple returned peacefully to their boat.

Circuit court records give further evidence of criminal activity in Cairo. One session in 1856 dealt with murder, kidnapping, receiving stolen property, possession of counterfeiting apparatus, and one offence that recurred regularly throughout the records—public indecency. Saloon proprietors repeatedly violated the tippling laws, statutes that forbade operating a drinking house on the Sabbath.[62]

Crime continued to characterize Cairo, but in 1855, journalists finally brought some measure of law enforcement to Cairo. Before the end of the decade newspaper campaigns stressed the necessity for a jail and a courthouse. Residents raised subscription funds for a jail, which was built in April 1856. People wanted a sturdy structure capable of subduing the unlawful element. The ensuing twenty-by-eighteen-foot building met the need, and editors reported that prisoners in the Cairo jail would not get out except by due process of law.[63]

After the first decade of commercial development, a committee of Cairo City Property trustees from the East finally visited their community for the first time. Trustee Edward Munk, of England, wrote a summary of the city's condition. In the years after the bankruptcy of the Cairo City and Canal Company, Cairo had been a derision in the East—a mere "inert mass."[64] Men were ashamed to say they owned

---

60. *Cairo Tri-Weekly*, Feb. 13, 1856, Jan. 8, 1856.
61. Ibid., Feb. 13, 1856.
62. Alexander County Circuit Court Records, Apr. 28, 1856, May 1, 1856.
63. *Cairo Tri-Weekly*, Jan. 22, 1856, Feb. 1856; *Cairo Weekly Times and Delta*, Apr. 9, 1856.
64. Cairo City Property Trust Company MSS, Jan. 19, 1858.

interest in it. But Munk was convinced that Charles Davis fought for the "embrio [*sic*] city," sinking himself into personal debt.[65]

By 1860, the settlement at the confluence had become a permanent town that stood on the threshold of its golden era. On the eve of the Civil War, Cairo had a population of over two thousand residents, according to the federal population census report. Attorneys, physicians, merchants, bookkeepers, artists, and even a cigarmaker called Cairo home. Migrants from Ohio and the Border South found Cairo attractive, and most worked in its prevalent occupations: tradesmen, railroaders, and servants.

Ethnically, German, Scottish, and Irish immigrants accounted for the largest nonnative groups, with some representation from Holland, Switzerland, and Russia. The native migrants numbered 691 from the Midwest, 237 from the South, 237 from the East, and 103 residents from the territories. Less than a dozen blacks resided in Cairo; all listed their occupations as either housekeepers or laborers.[66]

Soon war entrepreneurs would flock to Cairo to join forces with the town's pioneer settlers in economic enterprises. In 1860 one businessman, gambling that war would come to Cairo, had already positioned himself to benefit from the conflict. Arriving in Cairo from Louisville, Kentucky, forty-two-year-old William Parker Halliday entered the business of grain commissions. In February 1861, Halliday's "mammoth wharfboat" sailed out of port at Mound City, destined to reach Cairo "in a day or two."[67] Journalists predicted that Halliday, Graham, and Company would become the most extensive forwarders in the Mississippi Valley.[68]

In early March the huge wharfboat docked at the Ohio levee, and the owners held a citywide celebration to mark the event. At the river's edge, a low wake lapped gently against the big boat moored to the shore. Lazy waters of the Ohio, slowly moving downstream to disappear into the Mississippi, surrounded the boat. Always considered a bond of union in the past, the rivers would soon mark one of the most important boundaries in the Rebels' struggle against the Union.

65. Ibid.
66. Eighth United States Population Census Report, Alexander-Bond Counties, Illinois, 1860.
67. *Cairo City Weekly Gazette*, Feb. 28, 1861.
68. Ibid., Mar. 7, 1861.

Two

South Illinois

On a crisply cold night in April, Universalist minister Daniel P. Livermore and his wife, Mary, joined a crowd of curious onlookers lining the shore of Lake Michigan. Hats soared, cheers resounded, and hands clapped shoulders in recognition of a momentous occasion. Only six days after Fort Sumter had fallen to Rebel aggressors, thousands of enthusiastic Chicagoans gathered to catch a glimpse of the first Union regiments activated in the western theater of the Civil War.[1] The sight of the citizen soldiers marching through the streets of the city toward the Illinois Central depot stirred feelings of patriotism that had been lying dormant in many Union hearts.

All along the route civilians waved to the volunteers and honored them with salutes. The most prominent families in the city had offered up their young men to fight for the preservation of the Union. Of the four regiments parading to the station, Company "B," the Chicago Zouaves in their flowing red pants, jaunty crimson caps, and open blue jackets, looked particularly dashing.[2] The Lincoln

1. Burley, *Cairo Expedition,* 15; Livermore, *My Story,* 103; John H. Brinton, *The Personal Memoirs of John H. Brinton, Major and Surgeon U.S. V.,* 61.
2. Livermore, *My Story,* 19; Henry H. Miller, "Ellesworth's Zouaves" in *Reminiscences of Chicago During the Civil War,* 30. The Cairo Expedition took place April 21–29, 1861. Infantry units included the Chicago Zouaves, Companies A and B, Chicago Light Infantry Company, Turner Union Cadets, Lincoln Rifles, Houghtailing's Ottawa Company, and the Cairo Sandwich Company. Three artillery companies accompanied the infantry: Chicago Light Artillery, Lockport Artillery, and the Light Artillery Company. General Richard Kellogg Swift commanded the expedition.

Rifles, the Turner Union Cadets, and Houghtailing's Ottawa Company fell in step behind the colorful Zouaves.

Pondering their first encounter with the enemy, the green volunteers halted at the depot and waited to board the train. Just beyond the station, scattered bonfires threw pillars of orange heat flickering into the night sky. Against the halo of the fires, Gen. Richard Kellogg Swift steered 595 soldiers onto a special train. Twenty-six cars, drawn by two powerful engines, would carry the men south to an undisclosed destination.[3]

With no time to wait for guns from either the War Department or the Illinois State Arsenal, the first soldiers in the West drew inspiration from their pioneer forebears and took whatever arms they had on hand: squirrel rifles, shotguns, and antique revolvers. Four six-pound cannon and forty-four horses accompanied the men into southern Illinois. An hour before dawn, the special Illinois Central train, full of untried volunteer soldiers, pulled out of the Chicago station and headed south.[4] Before the sun rose, the band of Union liberators would separate Cairo from Rebels.

After the Parrott guns aimed at Fort Sumter, South Carolina, had finally quieted, and Maj. Robert Anderson had finally surrendered the fort to a fellow Southerner, President Lincoln called for 75,000 volunteer soldiers to put the nation back together again. In towns and cities all over the North, mass meetings attracted thousands of men. Representing a populace that had grown fond of peace, the attendees discussed responses to the aggression of the Rebels at Charleston.

A committee of Chicago citizens met daily at an office on La Salle Street for the purpose of assisting the government in preserving the Union.[5] Chicagoans held a mass meeting at Bryan Hall on April 19. Leaders of the community sat alongside common men paying rapt attention to patriotic speeches. In this city, where many treacherous inhabitants were already threatening sabotage, the meeting produced resolutions to support the federal government and a pledge to raise a $30,000 subscription.

---

3. *Report of the Adjutant General,* 7; Livermore, *My Story,* 103.
4. Burley, *Cairo Expedition,* 3, 4.
5. Ibid., 1, 2.

As men turned out for meetings all over the state, the governor of Illinois learned that the War Department in Washington needed immediate assistance from Chicagoans. Before the committee had even formed, Secretary of War Simon Cameron had requested help from Illinois. On April 15, Cameron wrote to Gov. Richard Yates and asked him to raise six regiments of volunteers to be put into immediate service.

In response to Cameron's urgent request, Yates contacted Swift in Chicago. Four days later, Cameron communicated with Yates once again: "As soon as enough of your troops is [sic] mustered into service, send a Brigadier General with four regiments, at or near Grand Cairo."[6]

In less than a week, Swift had raised four regiments, including an artillery unit, and had it ready to march. In contrast to the South's enthusiasm for war, most Northerners had clung to the hope of preserving peace. Illinois residents had resisted the idea of fratricidal war so strongly that the state arsenal at Springfield held few useable weapons in the spring of 1861. But when the push, or, as Lincoln called it, "the tug," came, Illinois joined the rest of the North in picking up the gauntlet the Rebels had flung down at Fort Sumter. A daring raid by Nathaniel Lyon on the federal arsenal at St. Louis augmented the scant store of weapons in Springfield. Shortly thereafter the Illinois State Arsenal came into capable hands.

The men of Galena, Illinois, had come together for a mass meeting at the courthouse on April 16, determined to rectify what they considered to be the great wrong done to the country by the Rebels. Congressman Elihu B. Washburne and attorney John Rawlins treated the group to some rousing Unionist oratory. Washburne introduced military resolutions, and Rawlins gave a forty-five-minute speech in support of the federal government. The resolutions were received enthusiastically, as was the speech.[7]

After Washburne and Rawlins had yielded the floor, a man who was a stranger to many people in the room addressed the gathering.[8] Although he had resided in Galena for almost a year, Ulysses

6. *Report of the Adjutant General*, 7.
7. Ibid.
8. Grant, *Papers*, 2:7; Ulysses S. Grant, *The Personal Memoirs of Ulysses S. Grant*, 138.

S. Grant had managed to resist the importuning of his wife, Julia, to socialize; hence, he had remained unknown to most of the other residents. A former officer in the regular army with battle experience in the Mexican War, Ulysses S. Grant made remarks that impressed the men of Galena. Grant agreed to help the men of this northern Illinois community raise and organize a military company. Having decided on this positive step, the men of Galena voted to meet again on the eighteenth and then adjourned.

As men separated into small groups following the adjournment, Washburne worked his way through the crowd that had formed around Grant. The Congressman felt somewhat surprised that a Galena resident of Grant's experience should be a stranger to him. Washburne introduced himself to Grant and conversed with him long enough to develop a sustained interest in the man. That fortuitous meeting started a friendship that would bring immeasurable military benefit to the nation. On the basis of two days' acquaintance, Grant had impressed Washburne so favorably that the politician wrote Yates in Springfield recommending a "true man" from Galena for military service. Washburne stated that Grant was ready and anxious to respond to any call.[9]

After the April 16 meeting in Galena, Grant never returned to the family leather goods store where he had been working. Instead, he spent his time drilling the Galena company until it was ready to leave for Springfield. Grant selected the cloth for the regimental uniforms himself, and Julia joined other women in town to sew for the soldiers. Grant supervised the whole process until attractive uniforms distinguished every soldier in Galena. On the day the volunteers left, the entire town turned out to watch their departure. Grant accompanied the volunteers to the state capitol, but loftier ambitions kept him from accepting the captaincy.[10]

At Springfield, the state capitol, he doggedly pursued service for the Union in response to his own innate logic. Considering the national situation, Grant dismissed the idea that the constitution allowed severance of the Union. A Democrat allied through marriage to a slave-owning family from St. Louis, Missouri, Grant articulated

9. Grant, *Papers*, 2:6; Elihu B. Washburne to Richard Yates, Apr. 18, 1861, Yates Family Collection MSS.
10. Grant, *Memoirs*, 138–39.

sound arguments in his personal correspondence that guided his course during the crisis but bore little resemblance to the rhetoric of his in-laws. He expressed a belief that the right to leave the Union had ended with the ratification of the Constitution. Grant's boyhood in Ohio may have accounted for his idea that once Congress had accepted new states forged from the territories, the act of secession became defunct. Grant believed those states that had been formed from territories purchased with funds from the public treasury had no right to leave the Union. They had been bought and paid for by the people of the United States.[11]

Already thinking along the same lines as Lincoln—a fellow westerner—Grant's early writings mirrored the president's thought on secession: the act was illogical as well as impracticable. Grant stated unequivocally that the aggression of the seceded states amounted to revolution.[12] The adjutant-general's office in Springfield was the first military entity to benefit from Grant's sense of duty to the Union cause.[13] Viewing the situation in such concrete terms no doubt strengthened Grant's later drive to destroy the Rebels in the field. Leaving behind the liberal region of his youth, Grant had spent several years farming in Missouri. Residence in the Border South would have given him invaluable insight for his first district command.

In the months after Lincoln's election, southern Illinois newspapers had been keeping their readers apprised of national developments. On February 21, 1861, the *Cairo City Weekly Gazette* reported that seven southern states had seceded. The article predicted the entire South would go out and discussed the need to arouse love of the Union. The editor directed his pleas for staunch Union sentiment toward an audience of readers that was dangerously divided in sentiment.

As much of the Deep South prepared for war, states along the border wrestled with the problem of their geography. The extreme tip of Illinois stretched further into the south than much of the Border South, yet, politically, all of Illinois belonged to the North. Most

11. Ibid., 130.
12. Ibid.
13. Geoffrey Perret, *Ulysses S. Grant: Soldier and President*, 125.

Illinoisans never doubted that their state would remain in the Union. Writing after the war began, one Cairo resident observed, "It had never occurred to me that any party of Illinois could have been in danger from the South or that the Confederacy was such a very near neighbor."[14]

The southern portion of the state, however, had a history and culture that tied it strongly to the antebellum South. Illinois' earliest European roots reached from France to Louisiana and northward along the Mississippi River. Originally known as Upper Louisiana, southern Illinois embraced black African slavery after the French introduced the institution in 1717. Slavery persisted after the French and Indian War delivered Upper Louisiana into the hands of the victorious British. No longer Upper Louisiana, the Illinois Country condoned slavery on condition that slave owners embrace British citizenship.

George Rogers Clark's expedition in the West during the American Revolution pulled the area firmly into the sphere of the United States, and the fledgling country renamed it the Illinois Territory. The name and governing authority may have changed, but the slave system remained. Remnants of the institution festered in dark industrial pockets of Illinois until 1848, just thirteen years before the start of the Civil War.[15]

In 1861, many residents of southern Illinois had recently migrated from the South and still identified strongly with southern culture. Through the early months of the year, Chicago newspapers printed exposés that painted a picture of rampant disloyalty in Cairo. Chicago correspondents reported that citizens of Cairo hunted loyal men, moving in for a kill whenever possible.[16]

Cairo editors refuted the charges, claiming the reports were "horrid slanders."[17] Cairo's leaders, claimed local journalists, disdained associations with one faction or the other. And as for the local citi-

14. Alice Moran to John Lansden, Feb. 15, 1911, John Lansden MSS.
15. Clarence Alvord Walworth, *Governor Edward Coles;* William H. Brown, *An Historical Sketch of the Early Movement in Illinois for the Legalization of Slavery;* Willard Carey MacNaul, *The Jefferson-Lemen Compact: The Relations of Thomas Jefferson and James Lemen in the Exclusion of Slavery from Illinois and the Northwest Territory.*
16. Bradsby, *History of Cairo,* 55.
17. Ibid.

zenry, journalists crooned, "So cosmopolitan were the Cairo people that they were impatient of the bawlings and crocodile tears of the Abolitionists, and the equally idiotic oaths about the divine institution of slavery."[18]

The local media wished to present a picture of Cairo, and southern Illinois, as neutral and unbiased, but actually no consensus existed among southern Illinoisans on sectional issues. As one faction urged loyalty, another pushed for separation. Some people in border areas hoped to achieve neutrality. But political leaders representing southern Illinois failed to stand firm for the Union.

Three months after Lincoln's election, one group of extremist politicians worked covertly to frame a solution to the North/South problem in Illinois. In the belief that they were carrying out the desires of their constituents, the four men concocted a truly divisive plan. Senator Orville Hickman Browning noted in his diary, "A scheme had been set on foot, and about to be perfected by traitors in Southern Ills [*sic*] in confederacy with other traitors in Missouri and Tennessee to seize Cairo—cut of [f] all of the State South of the Ohio & Mississippi rail road—erect it into a state and join the Southern confederacy."[19] Browning fumed over "so diabolical a plot."[20]

Severed from the rest of the state and attached to the Confederacy, the new state of South Illinois would name the political alignment of its leaders. Congressman John A. Logan, Democratic judge William Joshua Allen, attorney William H. Green, and state representative Andrew Jackson Kukyendall were spearheading a movement to promote the secession of southern Illinois.[21] Not unlike the plans to separate western Virginia and eastern Tennessee from the Confederacy, the idea captured the imagination of many inhabitants of the border area. Realizing the significance of Cairo, the quartet envisioned the town as the capitol of their prospective domain.

Logan and Allen had long been the leading Democrats in southern Illinois. The pair had worked tirelessly against the election of Lincoln to both the Senate in 1858 and the presidency in 1860. Early Illinois historians noted that Logan, elected to the Thirty-seventh Congress from the Ninth Congressional District, "contested every

18. Ibid.
19. Orville Hickman Browning, *Diary of Orville Hickman Browning*, 465.
20. Ibid.
21. Arthur Charles Cole, *The Era of the Civil War, 1848–1870*, 302.

inch of ground lost to Republicans in southern Illinois in the 1860 election."[22]

Logan used unorthodox methods in his opposition to Republicanism and sometimes acted outside the law. He earned the nickname "Dirty Work" Logan after he relentlessly persecuted Republicans in his district. Foreshadowing methods used by the South Carolina secessionists, he sometimes organized mob violence to prevent the incursion of Republican ideas into southern Illinois.[23] At some point Logan must have suspected that he was fighting an uphill battle. Perhaps he turned to the idea of secession when he saw that his intimidating acts would not prevent a Republican victory in 1860.

Efforts to homogenize southern Illinois, no matter how strenuous, failed miserably. During the Fort Sumter crisis, Illinois legislators received many letters from downstate residents testifying that Logan cried "Union" in Washington while he worked in his home constituency to promote the idea of a separate southern confederacy.[24] As the postelection crisis deepened, secessionists all over the country realized that the president-elect did not intend to compromise any further with the South. He intended, rather, holding fast to his election platform. With no prospect of gaining further concessions, belligerent southern leaders abandoned all hope of severing the Union constitutionally and started moving toward armed rebellion. Grant referred to the fire eaters as demagogues. He believed these southern men felt comfortable promoting the idea of war because old age protected them against the prospect of actually fighting.[25] In rhetoric inflamed with the same threatening tenor as that of southern radicals, Logan fired the passions of his constituents on February 5, 1861, in a speech delivered before the House. He deprecated the North's coercion of the South.

Cairo newspapers circulated an incendiary speech from one of the town's own propagandists. Concurring with the majority of southern leaders, Logan insisted that Union officials agree to one of the proposed compromises that would allow southern states to leave the Union at will.[26] In his noncoercion speech, Logan went so far as

22. Logan, 13; Cole, *Civil War,* 200.
23. Ibid., 201.
24. Ibid., 75.
25. Grant, *Memoirs,* 133.
26. Appendix to the Congressional Globe 36th Congress, 2nd Session, 178–80; Grant, *Memoirs,* 146.

to state that southern Illinois would never submit its resources to coercing the South to remain in the Union, because Egypt was in the North, but not of it.

Grant himself noted that Logan's constituency consisted mainly of people recently migrated from the South. Many of these people shared Logan's sentiments.[27] At the time, a Union supporter in southern Illinois wrote to inform Governor Yates, "The Democrats of this place have called a meeting, and have passed a resolution pledging to prevent an invasion on the South by the North."[28]

From February through March of 1861, speculation concerning the possibility of creating the new state of "South Illinois" ran rampant in Egypt. During the last week of February, the efforts of the separatists appeared on the verge of coalescing. Seeking to gain legitimacy for their proposed state, prominent men from southern Illinois introduced a resolution into the legislature of Louisiana, Illinois' sister state. The resolution stated that the people of southern Illinois would "hail with joy a division of their state, and the establishment of a new state south of the Ohio and Mississippi Railroad."[29]

Proponents of the new state claimed that people on Illinois' southern border regarded their political connection with northern Illinois as unnatural. Perhaps many residents in the southern section of the state saw little value in fighting a war with the South over a system they would gladly have adopted, or at least, did not object to strenuously. Then, in an abrupt about-face, the southern Illinois separatists displayed a desire for neutrality: "We will stand between extremists North and South, as an impassable barrier, and partaking of the animosities of neither section, become the great mediators in our country."[30]

The country might well have benefited from great, impartial mediators. In March, however, the rhetoric of the southern Illinois extremists devolved into inconsistencies concerning whether "South Illinois" would remain part of the Union or would fight to be attached to the Confederacy. At least four reports in the *Cairo City Weekly Gazette* in February and March testified that southern Illinoisans intended to leave the Union. Logan's February speech had

27. Grant, *Memoirs*, 146.
28. A Unionist to Richard Yates, Apr. 22, 1861, Yates Family MSS.
29. *Cairo City Weekly Gazette*, Feb. 28, 1861.
30. Ibid.

echoed the sentiments of Union County residents, who objected so greatly to the action of the state legislature in pledging Illinois' resources to the federal government that they warned, "People of Egypt will take up arms for the South, if it comes to a fight."[31]

Another article predicted that if the legislature refused to grant statehood to "South Illinois" peaceably, the residents of that area would secure it through revolution. In county meetings, the people of Johnson County drafted a resolution at Vienna petitioning for the division of Illinois with the southern portion annexed to the Confederacy. A subsequent article explained more particularly the sentiment underlying the draft. Reminiscent of articles in the popular southern publication *De Bow's Review*, Egyptians saw themselves as a distinct people, a people who did not favor free-love societies, women's rights associations, temperance unions, or abolitionism.[32]

A few days later, deviating from the objectives stated in the Johnson County resolution, southern Illinoisans insisted that they wished to maintain friendly relations with the South but remain in the Union. At the time, however, that sentiment did not appear to dominate public opinion throughout the region. Residents of Williamson County met on the day of Lincoln's call to arms. The group adopted resolutions stating that the Republicans caused the rebellion and that if Illinois did divide, people in Williamson County wanted the southern part of the state to be attached to the Confederacy.[33]

Evidence suggests that Logan gave his personal approval to the Williamson County resolutions. Grant himself stated that people in Logan's Congressional district terrorized Union supporters in southern Illinois. They were the very people Lincoln and Cameron were targeting. Republicans from Williamson County had informed Governor Yates "the property & lives of your friends are threatened in this part of our FREE state, especially those that took an active part in the campaign of 1860 in favor of President Lincoln & the Republican ticket."[34]

One Republican resident, Griffith Garland, declined to give a complete enumeration of the secessionists' activities in Williamson

31. *Jonesboro Weekly Gazette*, reprinted in *Cairo City Weekly Gazette*, Feb. 28, 1861.

32. Ibid; *Cairo City Weekly Gazette*, Mar. 7, 1861.

33. Ibid., Mar. 21, 1861, Apr. 25, 1861.

34. Grant, *Memoirs*, 146; Griffith Garland to Richard Yates, Apr. 1861, Yates Family MSS.

County but decided that there was one thing the governor should know: "they say they will divide the state and join on to Kentucky, but their favorite plan is to form a separate state of this part of Ills & secede with the south."[35] Other evidence shows that the secessionists were not planning a peaceful departure: "They say that all the Republicans & union men shall leave this part of the state & they threaten their [Republican] leaders with death."[36]

The advent of war unleashed militant activity along the borders, where Unionists and secessionists were struggling for ascendancy. Letters poured into the Illinois governor's office tutoring him on the state of affairs. One letter from Nashville, Illinois, read: "All the Civil officers are more or less tainted with secession.... We are expecting disturbances on this account."[37] Another correspondent urged Governor Yates to take notice of the Rebels in the southern end of the state: "They say they're going to help Jeff Davis, going to hang, cut throats, shoot every Republican in Egypt.... [They] Say it Will be sport if [they are] killing the Republicans as they are scatiring [*sic*]."[38]

A letter from Shawneetown, Illinois, deplored the fact that "we have received information that Fort Sumter has been surrendered to the Rebels. At Uniontown, Kentucky on the Ohio River twelve miles from here they this morning were firing cannon in *Honor* of the victory of the C.S.A."[39] John Olney then emphasized to the governor, "Our people are for the Union . . . Captain Michael K. Lawler . . . requests a battery of artillery. He knows how to use the guns and drill men."[40] Michael Lawler had, in fact, fought gallantly in the Mexican War and eventually made a name for himself as a tough Union general.

Loyal citizens, both in Illinois and in other northern states, addressed the issue of Cairo's ambiguous location. Writing from Pittsburgh, Pennsylvania, T. L. Rodgers informed Governor Yates, "A great many of our citizens think Cairo is the most important point on the Mississippi."[41] The concerned citizens in Pittsburgh thought

35. Ibid.
36. Ibid.
37. A Unionist to Richard Yates, Apr. 22, 1861, Yates Family MSS.
38. Ibid., Anonymous Letter to Richard Yates, Apr. 16, 1861.
39. Ibid., John Olney to Richard Yates, Apr. 15, 1861.
40. Ibid.
41. T. L. Rodgers to Richard Yates, Apr. 1861, Yates Family MSS.

Cairo should be occupied immediately and made the base of operations in the "Southwest."[42] They believed the movement should be made in as much secrecy as possible. Another letter addressed to Governor Yates demonstrated a deep level of concern about southern Illinois. Coinciding with Secretary Cameron's call for Illinois volunteers to move on Cairo, an urgent note had reached Governor Yates from Chicago: "We have had some talk here today [of] arming men of all parties in relation to the necessity for the immediate occupation of Cairo . . . to keep it out of the hands of the traitors."[43] Dr. Charles H. Ray, co-owner of the *Chicago Daily Tribune,* accurately concluded that Cairo represented the most important military position in the West. He exhorted Yates to look on the map and see that Cairo extended farther into the South than any other western point.

Ray explained to Yates that Cairo commanded the commerce of the upper Mississippi River as well as that of the Ohio rivers on which Kentucky's commerce depended. Ray emphasized, "The line [of rivers] is a fortification in itself."[44] Ray believed that five hundred men hostile to the federal government could "play the devil" if they destroyed the bridges forty miles up. Predicting that Kentucky would secede and Jefferson Davis would send companies of soldiers full of organized secessionists into Kentucky, Ray lamented, "I shall not be surprised any day to hear that they have Cairo in their hands."[45]

As a waning sun disappeared into the Mississippi River in southern Illinois on April 21, the self-appointed soldiers of the Cairo Guard finished their evening drill on the commons. Four days prior to the passage of the Williamson County Resolutions, the Cairo newspaper ran an article on the formation of the Cairo Guard. Prominent men in town had organized the militia for the ostensible purpose of local protection, due to "the peculiarly exposed condition of Cairo."[46]

After the drill, the group dismissed as a militia unit and then reassembled at Bill Schuter's restaurant on Commercial Avenue for

42. At the time of this correspondence, Illinois was considered the western frontier, and southern Illinois was viewed as the "southwest."
43. Dr. C. H. Ray to Richard Yates, Apr. 16, 1861, Yates Family MSS.
44. Ibid.
45. Ibid.
46. *Cairo City Weekly Gazette,* Apr. 25, 1861.

a mass meeting.[47] At the meeting the men entered the debate over coercion and disunion. With two slave states on their borders, men from Cairo wanted to consider all of the issues carefully before declaring allegiance to one section or the other. It seemed readily apparent that if the states bordering Illinois' southernmost town seceded, Cairo could become a corridor of battle between the two warring sections. Alarming events indicated that the allegiance of Missouri and Kentucky was not settled. Events in Kentucky would soon demonstrate that efforts to remain neutral only invited invasion from both armies. Neutrality had never figured largely in public sentiment at Cairo.

On a visit to St. Louis, Grant saw a large force of Missouri state militia camped on the outskirts of the city. Grant believed the secessionist Gov. Claiborne Fox Jackson intended to use the militia to take the arsenal at St. Louis, a strike that would give Confederates control of the only federal arsenal in the entire northwest.[48] Due to the foresight of Captain Nathaniel Lyon in Missouri, those arms ended up under Grant's control in Springfield. Grant commended Lyon's daring, "But for the little piece of stratagem used to get the arms out of the [St. Louis] arsenal . . . they would have fallen into the hands of the Secessionists."[49]

Many of the Cairo men sitting in the mass meeting at Bill Schuter's had friends and kinfolk who had already left for Tennessee, a place where Northerners could enlist in the Confederate army. Other residents of the town harbored loyalty toward the Illinoisan occupying the White House. In the 1860 election, for the first time, the Republican Party had drawn an appreciable number of votes from southern Illinois.[50] After lengthy debate, cool heads prevailed. Members of the Cairo Guard voted to adopt a temporary policy of what they termed "armed neutrality."[51]

The group intended to watch developments along the border and maintain their nightly drill. Their meeting over, the men of the Cairo Guard secured their weapons in the village armory and then drifted off to various saloons along the Ohio riverfront. By the time these minutemen finally tumbled into their beds in the wee hours

47. Bradsby, *History of Cairo*, 59.
48. Grant, *Memoirs*, 140.
49. Grant, *Papers*, 2:16.
50. Cole, *Civil War*, 200.
51. Bradsby, *History of Cairo*, 59.

of the morning, volunteer soldiers from Chicago were just pulling into southern Illinois.

Southern Illinoisans of secessionist persuasion had made little effort to hide their intent to aid the Rebels. Sixty miles above Cairo, General Swift halted the train and detached a company to guard the Big Muddy Bridge in Carbondale. Based on intelligence from loyal citizens, Union officials had feared that traitors would destroy the bridge before it could be fortified. James L. Cage of St. Louis had received a letter from his son, James Cage of Carbondale, stating that "at a meeting last week the people [of Carbondale] agreed to tear up the rails and burn the bridge above here."[52] Carbondale, a stop on the Illinois Central Railroad, appeared to be a hotbed of secessionism. One resident had even mounted a loaded blunderbuss near the train depot and threatened to fire on any train attempting to travel to Cairo carrying war matériel.[53]

The arrival of the Chicago regiments in southern Illinois sealed Cairo's fate. After securing the crucial Big Muddy Bridge, the rest of the Chicago soldiers continued south. Throughout the early morning hours of April 22, trains carrying Illinois volunteer soldiers continued to arrive in Cairo. Men of the Cairo Guard awoke to find the streets of their town, and even the surrounding woods, full of Union soldiers ready to shoot anyone who threatened the sovereignty of the federal government in southern Illinois. The Cairo Guard never met again.[54]

The timely action of Governor Yates and the Chicago volunteer soldiers ended viable discussion on the issue of dividing the state of Illinois. The Cairo Expedition secured southern Illinois for the Union, but loyalties along the Illinois border remained divided. The occupation of Cairo by Union troops ended schemes to attach the town to the Confederacy, but the men who had hatched the plot pursued their treacherous activities for many months afterward.

A benevolent interpretation of the sentiment in Cairo during the first days of the war suggests that, initially, men on the border regarded the conflict as an aggressive war started by a new president. Apologists claim that this factor made southern Illinoisans

52. James Cage to Richard Yates, Apr. 23, 1861, Yates Family MSS.
53. *Chicago Daily Tribune*, Apr. 23, 1861.
54. Bradsby, *History of Cairo*, 59.

reluctant to take up arms against the South. Other historians believe that, after the war started, people along the border demonstrated a deep, mystical feeling for an undivided country. Men who held no serious objections to slavery willingly fought to preserve the Union.[55]

A more plausible explanation for the emergence of Union sentiment in Cairo appeared in the *Providence Journal:* "There were plenty Secessionists at Cairo, Ill., but the Chicago soldiers came, and brought their artillery."[56] A farmer from the confluence area commented, "tell you what it is, them brass missionaries has converted a heap of folks that was on the anxious seat."[57] On Illinois' southernmost border, the presence of the Union army and fear of Confederate invasion finally overshadowed constitutional debates and sectional loyalties. With Federal soldiers camped at the edge of town, and Rebels bivouacking just across the rivers, Cairo and its hinterlands declared for the Union.

55. Bruce Catton, *This Hallowed Ground: The Story of the Union Side of the War,* 63.

56. William A. Pitkin, "When Cairo Was Saved for the Union," 51:297.

57. Ibid.

Three

Ready for the Scratch

On April 23, in the city that had launched to the Cairo Expedition, headlines screamed:

CHICAGO TROOPS IN CAIRO![1]

Chicagoans read about the military occupation of Cairo even as Governor Yates called a special session of the Illinois General Assembly to retroactively authorize the actions of General Swift and the volunteer regiments. Perhaps in response to the news of Chicago's participation in one of the first movements of the war, so many local men volunteered that Illinois' quota in the first call could almost have been filled from Chicago's response.[2]

Throughout Illinois, so many men volunteered that Governor Yates feared the state might look a little too eager to go to war.[3] While the first army camps were taking shape at Cairo, Grant traveled the state, mustering in volunteer regiments. Taking time from his work to write a letter to his sister, Mary, Grant exultantly informed her, "The enthusiasm through this state surpassed anything that could have been imagined three weeks ago. Only six Regiments are called for here while at least thirty could be promptly raised."[4]

1. *Chicago Daily Tribune*, Apr. 23, 1861.
2. *Harper's Weekly Journal of Civilization*, Apr. 27, 1861; Grant, *Papers*, 2:18.
3. Grant, *Memoirs*, 139.
4. Grant, *Papers*, 2:13.

In an earlier letter Grant had expressed the hope that all Union sympathizers in the border areas would "remain firm."[5] However, during the early weeks of the war, the southern counties of Illinois showed no signs of organizing companies that would fight for the federal government.[6] Letters written to state legislators explain the lack of enlistment activity in southern Illinois. At the very time state legislators were assembling for the special session, a Mason, Illinois, Unionist wrote to Governor Yates, "since the ICRR has been carrying Soldiers to Cairo, the cloven-foot of Secession has manifested itself right in our midst."[7]

By far, the majority of the state's population chose loyalty to the Union and approved Yates's decision to authorize the Cairo Expedition. But state legislators received many letters written by loyal southern Illinoisans warning of treachery—planned or ongoing—in their region. In the midst of the special session, State Representative A. J. Kuykendall, still in dissension, protested the presence of Federal soldiers in southern Illinois and introduced a resolution that called for Governor Yates to explain the occupation of Cairo by Union troops.[8]

Even as Kuykendull spoke, Yates was reinforcing the four companies stationed in Cairo with seven additional companies that had been raised in Springfield. Col. Benjamin M. Prentiss commanded the new force. On arrival, Prentiss relieved General Swift. The April 25 edition of the *Chicago Daily Tribune* reported that Union companies continued to arrive rapidly in Cairo. Many people in the ambivalent border town greeted the occupying Federal forces with surprise and rage. Some families, fearing recriminations for having displayed their southern sympathies too boldly, fled before the Federal troops.[9]

Following the attack on Fort Sumter, pleas for quick action to keep Cairo in the Union had reached beyond Springfield and surfaced in Washington, D.C. Many people believed the retention of Cairo was vital to the North. Grant's own department, the Illinois' adjutant general's office, believed the safety of the Union depended

5. Ibid., 2:14.
6. "Lyman Trumbull Papers," 2:44.
7. G. Wright to Richard Yates, Apr. 23, 1861, Yates Family MSS.
8. Ibid., Apr. 25, 1861.
9. Ibid., 7; Logan, *Reminiscences of the Civil War*.

on possession of the strategic point at the confluence of the Mississippi and Ohio rivers.[10]

The adjutant general's office had rightly assessed the situation. Union soldiers were not safe in southern Illinois. The quick response of the War Department and Governor Yates had foiled the secession plot of the southern Illinois separatists; the group turned to a default plan. They began raising men to drive the Chicago Zouaves away from the Big Muddy Bridge. Union officials then sent fifty heavily armed soldiers to reinforce the regiment guarding the bridge. That regiment kept a constant vigil, even sleeping outside in the rain.[11]

Besides failed efforts to sabotage Federal troops, news reports coming into Cairo on April 26 discouraged southern sympathizers. During the first week of the war, Attorney General Edward Bates had started pushing members of the cabinet to blockade the Mississippi River at Cairo.[12] Two days after Kuykendall's failed resolution in the Illinois General Assembly, residents of the occupied town read that Bates's idea had succeeded: Cairo would become the base of operations for the Union on the Mississippi River; the federal government planned to blockade the mouth of the Mississippi River. Cairo secessionists found the last sentence in the article particularly jarring: "Federal troops will be quartered among us."[13]

Apprised of the blockade even before residents of Cairo, Confederate Col. M. C. Galloway—stationed at Memphis—had sent a message to Confederate Secretary of War L. P. Walker regarding the proposed Union blockades. On April 18, 1861, Galloway wrote, "It was telegraphed from Washington to Cairo [actually, Springfield] to-day that Cairo will be made base of operations on the Mississippi River, and several Southern ports will be blockaded."[14] The following day, President Lincoln issued his Proclamation of Blockade that bottled up the South's eastern seaports.

After the blockade went into effect, a local newspaper carried an article explaining the situation, "No provisions headed for the South

10. *Report of the Adjutant General*, 8.
11. *Chicago Daily Tribune*, Apr. 25, 1861, Apr. 26, 1861.
12. John D. Milligan, *Gunboats down the Mississippi*, 3.
13. *Cairo City Weekly Gazette*, Apr. 25, 1861.
14. *The War of the Rebellion: A Compilation of the Official Records of the Union and Confederate Navies* (hereinafter, OR Navies), I:22, M. C. Galloway to L. P. Walker, Apr. 18, 1861, 786.

can pass through Cairo. All steamers leaving Cairo for insurrectionary ports will be examined. Any arms, munitions of war, or other
supplies will be taken off."[15] Following these developments with
interest, recruit George Durfee of Decatur, Illinois, described the
scene at Cairo to relatives at home: "This fort was blockaded last
Monday at 4 oclock [sic] since which time there has no boats gone
by here without being stopped and examined which makes the
Capt. of the boats swear some."[16] Another Illinois soldier explained
to his family that boats were not allowed to pass down the Mississippi River. Soldiers did observe boats arriving at the Cairo port,
but they were only allowed to pass because additional recruits filled
their decks: "A boat come down the Ohio river [sic] yesterday
loaded with union [sic] soldiers. The boat was decorated with flags.
There was great cheering for them."[17] As additional troops arrived,
the volunteer soldiers in Cairo kept busy throwing up entrenchments
to protect the site. Working in rotating shifts around the clock, soldiers learned the meaning of hard labor. Men in the Ninth Illinois
considered the time they spent building the Cairo fortifications the
hardest work of their military careers.[18]

The federal government hired one hundred Irish laborers to aid
in the construction, but each army regiment worked on the fort
every ninth day, digging and setting cannon.[19] Recruits watched
Camp Defiance rising between the edge of the Mississippi River
and the town of Cairo.[20] The threat of the enemy just across the
rivers helped to move the project along.[21] Soldiers tore up railroad
tracks and demolished an old brick distillery at "the southern point
of Ill."[22] George Durfee told his uncle that the army planned to build
a fort on the site. He added optimistically, "It begins to look like
doing something don't you think?"[23]

15. *Cairo City Weekly Gazette,* May 16, 1861.
16. George S. Durfee to H. B. Durfee, May 16, 1861, George S. Durfee MSS.
17. William McLean to Father and Son, May 6, 1861, William McLean MSS.
18. *Chicago Daily Tribune,* Apr. 25, 1861; Marion Morrison, *History of the
Ninth Regiment Illinois Volunteer Infantry,* 10.
19. William McLean to Friends, May 23, 1861, William McLean MSS; Andrew
to Katy, May 30, 1861, Andrew MSS.
20. Morrison, *Ninth Regiment,* 10.
21. W. Y. Jenkins to Mr. McLean, June 20, 1861, William McLean MSS; Brinton, *Memoirs,* 45.
22. George S. Durfee to H. B. Durfee, May 21, 1861, George S. Durfee MSS.
23. Ibid.

The emerging fortifications caught the attention of Rebel officers keeping an eye on Federal movements in the West. In one assessment, Confederate spies speculated on the Union troops amassing at Illinois' confluence, "so great a force can have but one object—to descend the Mississippi."[24] During another reconnaissance, Josiah Gorgas, Confederate commander in charge of ordnance, wrote to the Confederate secretary of war, "Assume that they [Union forces] are concentrating at Cairo . . . what can be the object of assembling so formidable a force?"[25] Within months Grant would provide the Rebels with an answer to that question, fulfilling their worst imaginings.

May brought spring to its full expression in southern Illinois, and activity along the riverbanks increased. Wooden barracks rose along half a mile of the Ohio levee, and a frame building twenty feet by fifty feet appeared near the St. Charles Hotel. The sizeable structure housed the Commissary Department.[26] A neighboring building accommodated the Quartermaster's Department. Before the end of the month, soldiers mounted cannon on the levee in front of the St. Charles.

Heavy enlistment for the Union would not begin in southern Illinois until the summer of 1861, but in May, Grant traveled to Cairo, where he managed to muster in one regiment.[27] At that time, he dismissed what he called the prevailing opinion of people in the North that "people of Egypt are ignorant, disloyal, intemperate, and generally heathenish."[28] Grant assessed the regiment formed in Cairo as equal, if not superior, to any regiment in the state. Grant's conclusions concerning the residents of southern Illinois undoubtedly applied to a significant portion of the population, but secessionists continued to plague the area, threatening the Union's security.

While Grant worked to recruit regiments in southern Illinois, the Chicago soldiers worked hard to secure Cairo against attack. The Confederates were devising several strategies for attacking southern Illinois, and public officials in the state spent the early months of the war filtering out disloyalty. Unable to see any of his family members save those in St. Louis, Grant also dealt personally with

---

24. *Official Record of the War of the Rebellion: Union and Confederate Navies* I:22, J Gorgas to Secty of War, CSA, Apr. 29, 1861.

25. OR Navies, I:22, J. Gorgas to Secretary of War, C. S. A. Apr. 29, 1861.

26. *Cairo City Weekly Gazette,* May 9, 1861.

27. Grant, *Papers,* 2:32.

28. Ibid., 2:33.

the stress of dissension. Writing to Julia from Mattoon, Illinois, where he was mustering in the Twenty-first Illinois Volunteer Regiment, Grant stated, "I hope by this time you feel as loyal to the Union as Aunt Fanny does."[29]

Julia's father, Frederick Dent—a Missouri slaveholder—repeatedly displayed secessionist sentiments to his son-in-law during Grant's visits to the Dent family plantation. Following in his father's footsteps, John Dent, Julia's brother, sought a colonelcy in the Confederate army at the time Grant was mustering in Union regiments in southern Illinois.[30] Julia had always been close to her father, and the prospect of disagreeing with him on so important an issue must have been difficult.

As Grant continued traveling around the state in his work for the adjutant general's office, the site of his future headquarters became stronger with each passing day. Once completed, the main camps at the Cairo base extended one-half mile along the inner banks of the Mississippi levee. On the Mississippi side, three miles above the confluence of the rivers, Camp Smith materialized. One company of artillery, one company of infantry, and six guns completed that camp. The Chicago Light Artillery and the Lincoln Rifles called Camp Smith home. Reportedly, the men in that location enjoyed the best of health and spirits.[31]

A Chicago correspondent reported in May, "Chicago can be proud of its citizen soldiers at Cairo."[32] Despite unavoidable discomforts in the Cairo camps, the volunteer soldiers felt "in fine spirits and full of fun and fight."[33] The journalist concluded that the recruits from Chicago compared favorably with soldiers in the East, except that they displayed the free, frank, determined demeanor that was characteristic of the West.

After settling into their camps, the Chicago troops decided they were "an interesting crowd in an interesting place," even though a Chicago correspondent, commenting on the mud—as everyone who visited Cairo did—noted, "Cairo is the color of oversteeped tea with a little milk in it."[34] Soldiers in the West got used to mud, and

---

29. Ibid.
30. Ibid., 2:26.
31. *Chicago Daily Tribune*, May 25, 1861, May 16, 1861.
32. Ibid., May 25, 1861.
33. Ibid.
34. Ibid., May 25, 1861, Apr. 26, 1861.

the troops at Cairo ultimately came to view the levees as a natural breastwork.

For some recruits, patriotic fervor cooled a little under the torments of camp life. Calling Cairo "one of the last places in the world," one Illinois soldier noted that the men had no place to sleep and had built shanties for shelter.[35] The first companies of volunteer soldiers stationed in Cairo slept on the ground without even tents. Graduating from canvas, the men slept in empty railroad cars, old sheds, and any place that would shield them from the elements until permanent barracks appeared.[36]

After initiates experienced the ordeal of setting up housekeeping for themselves, they had to learn the art of soldiering if they wished to survive their tour of duty.[37] In one of his regular missives to his uncle, Durfee described the daily routine of camp life: "In the morning the reveille beats at 5 oclock [sic] when we all turn out of bed to roll call. We then drill 1 hour after which we get breakfast. After breakfast we draw our rations. we [sic] then have drill from 8 till 10 after which we have officers drill from 11 to 12 when we get dinner."[38] Company drill followed the dinner hour and lasted from one o'clock until three o'clock.

William McLean, a central Illinoisan, followed a similar schedule. McLean mentioned that the soldiers in Cairo got plenty to eat and even had ice water to drink. Generally, in the early weeks of the war, soldiers found the food at Cairo satisfactory. Some even spoke of getting fat. But the Ninth Illinois complained of insufficient food and clothing and found life pretty hard at the southern Illinois base.[39]

Soldiers spent part of each day attempting to master the manual of arms, which proved difficult even for officers. When the drill hour ended at three o'clock, soldiers were free until half past five. Roll call brought the men into parade formation, and they marched into dress parade at six o'clock.[40] In their daily regimen, after dress pa-

35. William McLean to Sisters, May 2, 1861, William McLean MSS.

36. George S. Durfee to H. B. Durfee, Apr. 29, 1861, George S. Durfee MSS.

37. Logan, *Reminiscences of a Soldier's Wife*, 107.

38. George S. Durfee to H. B. Durfee, May 21, 1861, George S. Durfee MSS.

39. William McLean to Friends, May 9, 1861, William McLean MSS; William Onstat to Sister, Sept. 11, 1861, William Onstat MSS; Morrison, *Ninth Regiment*, 10.

40. George S. Durfee to H. B. Durfee, May 21, 1861, George S. Durfee MSS.

rade, soldiers spent some free time strolling wherever they pleased so long as they didn't leave their camps. Durfee emphasized: "we are in the point that is made by the Ohio and Mississippi and are not allowed to leave the ground without a pass from the Capt."[41] Edwin Loosley of Du Quoin, Illinois, a baker who received favors from many officers, explained to his wife, "I have got a pass and go to town when I like which is a great privilege."[42] Soldiers who left camp without a pass would be put in the guardhouse or lose two or three months' pay.[43]

Chicago had sent a drum corps under the direction of drum major William Nevans to Cairo with the first regiments that took the town.[44] Soldiers quickly learned to respond to the sound of a drum. Drum beats called the soldiers to quarters at nine o'clock, and at ten, the lights went out. Adherence to the daily routine produced a semblance of military order.

Initially known as Camp Union, the name of the Cairo base changed to Camp Defiance in the first week of May. On May 10, 1861, Union soldiers completed the massive earthworks crowned by heavy artillery at the point of land between the rivers. The Cairo fortifications controlled the passage of steamboats from the Missouri side of the Mississippi River.[45] As one soldier writing from Cairo expressed it, "We are now in readiness to meet our enemy which is said to be only 6 miles distance both on Kentucky and Missouri shores. . . . We are prepared to give them a good Reception."[46]

But before any genuine campaigning could get under way, federal officials needed to hammer out an overall strategy for both theaters of the war, and the Mississippi Valley did not command top priority. Although national leaders came to consider Cairo second only to Washington, D.C., in strategic importance, their first concern focused on the East, where Rebels were threatening the nation's

41. Ibid., Apr. 29, 1861.
42. Edwin Loosley to Wife, Sept. 18, 1862, Edwin Loosley MSS.
43. Hiram T. Fite to Father, Abraham, Nov. 12, 1862, Hiram T. Fite MSS.
44. Sherman Lee Pompey, "Muster Lists of the Drum Corps," Lincoln Illinois Rifles and the Light Artillery Company on the Cairo Expedition; "Illinois during the Civil War."
45. George S. Durfee to H. B. Durfee, May 7, 1861, George S. Durfee MSS; John W. Allen, *Legends and Lore of Southern Illinois*, 288–89.
46. Joseph Dietschy MSS, Apr. 1861, Illinois State Historical Library, Springfield, Illinois.

capitol. Initially, Lincoln and his military advisors thought only of occupying and holding Cairo because they had not framed a strategy that included operations in the Mississippi Valley.[47]

Then a strategy that had been as much ridiculed as had the early attempts to settle Cairo changed Lincoln's overall perspective. Gen. Winfield Scott proposed a plan to move an army of sixty thousand men, accompanied by gunboats, down the Mississippi River. Working in conjunction, the army and navy would seize and hold ports from Cairo to the Gulf, thus severing the Confederacy and cutting it off politically and economically. Scott believed the federal government could then wait for Union sentiment to take over in the South and end the conflict. After studying Scott's plan, the president eschewed the notion that the strategy could work as designed. Lincoln did not believe the war could be won by strangling the South. He did think, however, as did Grant in the early weeks, that if the South suffered one decisive defeat in the field, the Rebels would give up.[48]

At that time Lincoln adopted the idea of controlling the Mississippi River along the perimeters of the Confederacy, a strategy that focused his attention on Cairo. Lincoln's strategy for the West would take time to implement, however, and the first commander of all the armies, Gen. George McClellan, made no arrangements to coordinate movements between the eastern and western theaters. Until Grant took command of all the western armies, no all-encompassing, coordinated strategy existed among various movements, even in the West.[49]

During the first five months of the war, the western commanders occupied themselves with training and waited for directives from Washington. While the War Department worked to bring the Department of the West into being, Col. Benjamin Prentiss took command at Cairo, claiming that the confluence area could be "held against all that can be brought against it."[50] But to others, who were observing operations at the base, Prentiss's boast seemed hollow. Despite the strong Union presence at the Illinois post, soldiers and citizens alike feared Confederate assault.

47. *Report of the Adjutant General*, 7; Williams, *Lincoln and His Generals*, 16.
48. Williams, *Lincoln and His Generals*, 18, 20.
49. Ibid., 18, 46.
50. *Harper's Weekly*, June 1, 1861.

Even Grant believed the Rebels capable of plotting against Cairo. When journalists claimed that Rebel troops from Missouri, Kentucky, and Tennessee, under the command of Gen. Gideon J. Pillow, planned to attack Cairo, Grant, who was recruiting in southern Illinois, did not question the validity of the report.[51] However, instead of worrying over it, he informed his father, Jesse Root Grant: "There is no doubt but the *valiant* Pillow has been planning an attac [*sic*] on Cairo, but as he will learn that . . . point is well Garrisoned."[52]

With no military campaigns to analyze, local journalists and state politicians contemplated possible strategies against Cairo. Journalists sensationalized the most obvious option for the Rebels: running steamboats up the Mississippi River to Illinois. By early summer this route seemed least probable of all. The approach in question would require that the Rebels run past the guns at Cairo, which were already formidable.[53]

Another possibility for entering the Union through Illinois involved landing Rebel troops above Cairo to cut off the railroad and then waging a land assault against the Federal base. Journalists decided this tactic could only work with the assistance of secessionists operating inside Cairo, and they heartily recommended that "strict watch should be kept upon all who are known or suspected to be traitors."[54]

An incident at the St. Charles Hotel early in May 1861 demonstrated that traitors did lurk in the town. The St. Charles sat on the line of the military camps. Late one evening, four men left the hotel by way of a special passage that exited to the street through a back door. The men tried to pass the picket guards, but the guards ordered them to halt. Disregarding the order, the men continued walking. The guards asked if they had the countersign. One of the men answered, "Yes, this is my countersign."[55] On the last word, he drew a revolver and, as the quartet ran for the river, gave a cheer for Jeff Davis.

A Union sentinel raised his musket and fired at the traitors' legs, trying to cripple them, but the men escaped. Telling the story in camp

51. *Cairo City Weekly Gazette,* May 16, 1861.
52. Grant, *Papers,* 2:22.
53. *Harper's Weekly,* June 1, 1861.
54. Ibid., June 22, 1861.
55. George S. Durfee to H. B. Durfee, May 10, 1861, George S. Durfee MSS.

later, the Union guards joked that when the muskets discharged in the direction of the secessionists, the sound scared them to death. Soldiers in Cairo thought that if all the Rebels were so "pusillanimous" it wouldn't take much time to clean out the whole South.[56]

The guardhouse at Cairo held further proof of surreptitious treachery in southern Illinois. On June 6, buried in an obscure section of a Cairo newspaper, a report appeared that a "member of the state Legislature was brought to Cairo on charges of high treason."[57] After the recruitment of the first volunteers, the federal government authorized commanding generals, in proper cases, to suspend the writ of habeas corpus. At their discretion, post commanders could arrest questionable people and detain them without due process of law. Colonel Prentiss deemed William Green to be a person "dangerous to the public safety."[58]

Although some military historians of the western theater have concluded that "peace sentiment was rife in southern Illinois" and that Logan and his colleagues were peace men, the documented actions of Logan and his friends belie this conclusion.[59] William H. Green, one of the South Illinois conspirators, and one of John A. Logan's law partners in Cairo, had given a fiery speech in the Illinois General Assembly four days after the Cairo Expedition brought Federal soldiers to Cairo. Warning Unionists against coercing the South, Green had declared: "Should you of the North attempt to pass over the borders of our State to subjugate a Southern state... you shall not shed the blood of our Southern brethren, until you had first passed over the dead bodies of the gallant sons of Egypt."[60]

The *Golconda Weekly Herald* ran the speech in which Green advised southern Illinois men to "get ready your rifles and flintlocks to fire on the Black Republican army marching over the soil of Egypt."[61] The editor referred readers to the remarks of the "noble, brave, and

56. Ibid.

57. *Cairo City Weekly Gazette*, June 6, 1861.

58. Abraham Lincoln, "Special Message to Congress, July 4, 1861," in *Speeches and Writings of Abraham Lincoln*, edited by Roy P. Basler.

59. James Pickett Jones, *Black Jack: John A. Logan and Southern Illinois in the Civil War Era*.

60. *Chicago Daily Tribune*, Apr. 25, 1861, reprinted from the *Golconda Weekly Herald*.

61. Ibid. The term *Black Republican* referred to white men in the Republican Party who favored abolition.

patriotic" William H. Green. Green's outspoken support of the Confederacy following the occupation of Cairo placed him under serious suspicion. In an attempt to avoid arrest, Green attested his innocence in a public loyalty oath, stating: "I am a Union man and will stand by my country under all circumstances. I deny that any of my constituents are secessionists or traitors."[62] Something about the declaration did not ring true with Prentiss. He had Green arrested, and the Democratic politician spent the early months of the war in the guardhouse at Cairo.

While Green languished in the guardhouse, stories of John Logan's complicity in the secession attempt continued to circulate. Finally, Republican newspapers demanded a statement of loyalty from Logan. Initially reluctant to declare allegiance to the Union, Logan found himself facing charges of acting in concert with the Rebels and furnishing aid and comfort to the Confederacy.[63] According to oral tradition, General Prentiss told Logan at Cairo in June 1861 that he had but one step further to take to commit actual treason.

In Jackson County, site of John Logan's ancestral home, the "Home guard" drafted resolutions against him and demanded his resignation from Congress. Logan reviled the Jackson County group for not signing individual names on the resolutions.[64] For many weeks Logan declined to publish an oath of loyalty. Kuykendull and Allen also remained at large, proclaiming their innocence.

A meeting with Grant in Springfield brought Logan's dilemma to a head. When Grant received his commission as colonel of the Twenty-first, his regiment was waiting in the state capitol to be mustered into the United States service. Two Democratic state legislators asked to speak to Grant's men to encourage all the volunteers to remain in the army. Grant felt hesitant to let Logan speak, having read about his treacherous activities, but John A. McClernand's loyalty had never been questioned.[65]

Grant must have sensed the quality of leadership lurking in Logan when the two men met face to face for he consented to both speeches. Logan spoke with particular fervor, perhaps hoping to convince state officials at Springfield of his proclaimed patriotism.

62. Ibid., May 2, 1861.
63. *Cairo City Weekly Gazette*, June 27, 1861.
64. Ibid.
65. Grant, *Memoirs*, 145.

He definitely convinced Grant's men of the noble duty before them. They all reenlisted and, by the end of summer, Logan himself had entered the Union army, assigned to McClernand's brigade.[66] Listening to the two politicians orating from the steps of the state capitol that day, Grant could not have foreseen the significant role each would play in his western campaigns.

In the summer of 1861, as Grant pursued Confederates through Missouri, conflict between secessionist and Union troops guarding that state gave rise to more panic in Cairo. Newspaper stories outlined a third possible strategy for attacking the base. Journalists, soldiers, and citizens began to fear that the Rebels could mount batteries on the Missouri and Kentucky shores and shell the Cairo camps. The terrain of Kentucky's shore actually prohibited the positioning of batteries aimed at Illinois, but Missouri's shoreline could accommodate batteries at the water's edge near a place called Bird's Point.

From that location, the Rebels could shell the camps at Cairo and use rifled cannon to cut away the levee and flood the camp and the town. When Cairo soldiers read reports of this plan in the *Mobile Register*, they retorted that if the Rebels tried to carry it out, Confederate throats would be cut rather than the levee. Ironically, in the midst of the invasion hysteria, soldiers at Cairo wrote to relatives at home, assuring them there was no sign of the enemy in southern Illinois.[67]

As the fortification of the confluence area continued to develop, it became apparent that the defense of the southern Illinois base depended on a point of land in Missouri. Bird's Point, Missouri, worried Governor Yates. The governor feared that if Confederates succeeded in taking the Missouri sites of Bird's Point and New Madrid, along with the Kentucky sites of Columbus and Hickman, all that the Union soldiers had done in Cairo would be undone. Yates told Lincoln that the enemy could bring the war into Illinois unless the government fortified those places.[68]

After visiting the base, Senator Lyman Trumbull concluded that Bird's Point offered the only practical site to place batteries for the defense of Cairo. Bird's Point lay just across the rivers' confluence

66. Ibid., 146; Grant, *Papers*, 3:88.
67. *Cairo City Weekly Gazette*, May 9, 1861; George S. Durfee to H. B. Durfee, May 21, 1861, George S. Durfee MSS.
68. Richard Yates to Abraham Lincoln, May 16, 1861, Yates Family MSS.

in Missouri, a few miles north of Belmont. The Union army placed heavy guns manufactured in Pittsburgh along with several guns from Indiana at Camp Lyon on Bird's Point. Pvt. Lemuel Adams recorded that Union soldiers initially complained about black laborers who were hired to work on the fortifications at Bird's Point. Once the soldiers were assigned to help with construction themselves, they welcomed assistance from these men.[69]

A Union regiment from St. Louis, composed mainly of Germans, occupied the site, "the only available point of attack on Cairo from the Missouri shore."[70] Following Yates and Trumbull's recommendations, the steamer *Louisiana* brought fifteen hundred Union troops to guard Bird's Point.[71] Sentries stood watch for twenty miles up the Mississippi side of the levee. With forts and soldiers in place, Senator Lyman Trumbull informed Governor Yates that Cairo could be defended against anything but an attack from large guns, which could throw shell beyond the reach of the Union cannon. Yates acted on Trumbull's observations and replied that he was telegraphing, writing, and sending messages to the War Department in Washington to hurry up the big guns. As a further safeguard against sabotage in southern Illinois, General Prentiss detailed a regular force, comprising mainly Cairo natives, to patrol the streets of the town. Local journalists concluded that Prentiss's patrols kept men sober better than temperance societies.[72]

After the soldiers had spent two months drilling, they had their first brigade parade at the Cairo base. Uniforms had arrived in May after some difficulty with the first contractor. Both the blue and the gray could be found in early Union uniforms, hence the difficulty of distinguishing between friend and foe on the field of battle. The Illinois volunteers at Cairo wore bluish gray uniforms, more gray than blue. The ensemble consisted of blue pants and a jacket topped by a jaunty blue Zouave cap.[73] Decked out in the blue and the gray, the Cairo regiments dazzled admiring journalists.

69. Trumbull Papers, 10; *Cairo City Weekly Gazette*, May 16, 1861; Lemuel Adams, diary, n. p.

70. *Harper's Weekly*, June 15, 1861.

71. *Cairo City Weekly Gazette*, May 30, 1861.

72. Trumbull Papers, 10; *Cairo City Weekly Gazette*, May 9, 1861, May 16, 1861.

73. Grant, *Papers*, 2:42; *Cairo City Weekly Gazette*, June 13, 1861; George S. Durfee to H. B. Durfee, May 27, 1861, George S. Durfee MSS.

Correspondents for the *Cairo City Weekly Gazette* considered the brigade parade the "most thrilling and absorbing spectacle ever witnessed."[74] Troops at Cairo became proficient at dress parade. Once established, the Cairo base merited a visit from Gen. George Brinton McClellan, the man whose ineptitude would eventually open the door to Grant's advancement. Positioned in front of Prentiss and his staff, McClellan presided over the first brigade parade ever held at the southern Illinois base.[75] As row after row of volunteer soldiers passed before him, six thousand men in all, McClellan saw "a vast, moving sea of union men with thousands of bristling bayonets glistening above them."[76]

The visiting general pronounced Cairo's review the "finest and best drilled body of troops he had seen since he had been in command of the Western Division of the army."[77] Prentiss gave an able address, and that evening, the St. Charles Hotel hosted a ball in honor of McClellan. In attendance were Cairo's commanding officers with their ladies, friends, and several notable residents of Chicago who had traveled south to enjoy the gala affair.[78]

Grant had been rejected by McClellan early in the war and was soon to replace Prentiss at Cairo; no pomp or glamour attended Grant in the summer of 1861. On a visit to Galena in the midst of his mustering-in duties, Grant confessed to a nagging intuition that seemed prophetic in retrospect, "During the six days I have been at home I have felt all the time as if a duty was being neglected that was paramount to any other duty I ever owed."[79]

The fulfillment of Grant's pressing duty began with his commission as colonel of the Twenty-first Illinois Volunteer Regiment, which Governor Yates conferred on him in his absence from Springfield. With June's balmy warmth slipping into the dog days of July, Grant led his soldiers from Illinois into Missouri, doling out "regular army punishment" to encourage discipline. In the same month, Gen. John C. Frémont arrived in Missouri to take command of the Department of the West. Recently returned from Europe with ten thousand Enfield rifles and several batteries of rifled cannon, Frémont

---

74. *Cairo City Weekly Gazette,* June 13, 1861.
75. *Chicago Daily Tribune,* June 14, 1861; *Cairo City Weekly Gazette,* June 13, 1861.
76. *Cairo City Weekly Gazette.*
77. Ibid., June 14, 1861.
78. *Chicago Daily Tribune,* June 14, 1861.
79. Grant, *Papers,* 2:37.

harbored visions of glory.[80] By the time Frémont reached St. Louis, the whole tri-state area teemed with secessionists.[81] Throwing himself into his duties, the Pathfinder discovered that he "had to assume responsibility, act without orders and even borrow money to get along."[82]

Confident that he was up to the task of dealing with treacherous Missourians, Frémont entrenched himself in his St. Louis headquarters surrounded by pomp and rigid protocol. One soldier seeking an interview with the general recalled, "I doubt whether there was as much difficulty and ceremony displayed in gaining an audience with any emperor or king as there was in order to be ushered into the presence of Frémont at St. Louis."[83]

Soldiers at Cairo had no such difficulty seeing the department commander. Laboring on entrenchments at the rivers' confluence, enlisted men noticed a long string of smoke descending down the Mississippi River. Gradually, eight steamers came in sight. The boats were carrying General Frémont and reinforcements to Cairo. Frémont rode on the flagship *City of Alton*. Prentiss met him at the wharf and escorted him to the St. Charles Hotel.[84]

Soon after Frémont's arrival, a crowd gathered outside the hotel and called the general out on the balcony. Prentiss introduced Frémont as the commander who would lead the Union to victory, and Frémont delivered a few remarks. His speech made scant impression on the soldiers gathered below, but his appearance drew their attention, "a short man and looks as though he had seen servis [*sic*] his hair and beard is iron grey and his countenance very much resembles the portraits that I have seen of him."[85] Frémont never led Union troops to victory. His resistance to official policy caused Lincoln to remove him from command of the Department of the West, and, for a time, from any command at all.[86]

In Cairo, the scorching heat of summer descended on the Union camps, and soldiers waited impatiently to face the enemy. Batteries

---

80. *Harper's Weekly*, June 22, 1861.
81. Cole, *Civil War*, 262.
82. Trumbull Papers, Aug. 31, 1861.
83. Julian Kune, *Remeniscence of an Octogenarian Hungarian Exile*, 111.
84. Lemuel Adams, "Memoirs"; George S. Durfee to H. B. Durfee, Aug. 5, 1861, George S. Durfee MSS.
85. George S. Durfee to H. B. Durfee, Aug. 5, 1861, George S. Durfee MSS.
86. Ibid., 2:42, 44, 48; Grant, *Memoirs*, 145.

commanded the river, artillery horses fed in rows along the levees, harness hung over the fences, tents popped up everywhere, squads and companies drilled constantly, pickets guarded the whole length of the levees and a general hospital had been established. Chicago troops announced to their war correspondent, "We are all ready for the scratch."[87] The man who would lead them to it was just across the river, steadily working his way to Cairo.

87. *Chicago Daily Tribune,* June 14, 1861.

Four

This Awful Sickly Place

A month after volunteer soldiers set up the Cairo camps, Pvt. Hiram T. Fite from Wabash County, Illinois, suffered a typical bout of soldierly illness: "I have been taking some medecine [sic] from the doctors at the hospital. I have not been so bad that I had to go to the hospital to stay."[1] Illustrating the common occurrence of camp disease in Cairo, Fite stated, "there is about half of our regiment sick."[2] Soldiers learned from personal experience that Cairo deserved its reputation for disease. In the spring of 1861 typhoid fever stalked soldiers in the southern Illinois camps.[3] A few weeks after Fite recovered from his first bout, he succumbed to illness again and lamented, "I expect we will have to stay here all summer in this awful sickly place."[4]

At the time Fite was complaining to friends and family in letters, the national media reported, "Out of so large a force [at Cairo] but twenty-three men are reported upon the sick list."[5] The reality was much grimmer. Illness was running rampant through the camps. A month after the Cairo Expedition brought Chicago troops to southern Illinois, doctors from Chicago had organized a hospital department at the base. Reportedly, adequate supplies, good ventilation, and clean beds made the hospital a "perfect gem."[6] The *Daily Tribune*

1. Hiram T. Fite to Father Abraham Fite, May 26, 1862, Hiram T. Fite MSS.
2. Ibid.
3. George S. Durfee to H. B. Durfee, May 24, 1861, George S. Durfee MSS.
4. Hiram T. Fite to Father Abraham Fite, May 26, 1862, Hiram T. Fite MSS.
5. *Harper's Weekly*, June 1, 1861.
6. *Chicago Daily Tribune*, May 25, 1861.

stated that women from all over Chicago had donated supplies that kept the dispensary well stocked, and medical personnel at the base even supplied patients with ice water. The Chicago correspondent's glowing description of the post hospital at Cairo comforted relatives at home but did not coincide with actual conditions. Although the Cairo base did have one of the few military hospitals built in the early months of the Civil War, newspaper correspondents exaggerated the positive condition of both the medical facilities and the soldiers' health in the Cairo camps.[7]

Since general hospitals had not existed at army bases prior to the Civil War, organizing and operating medical facilities at military bases proved to be a challenging task for commanding officers all over the North, none of whom had much experience with administration and organization. Until the civil conflict, the military had never perceived care of the sick and wounded as one of its responsibilities. No plan existed for treating soldiers in hospitals, for collecting wounded from the battlefield, or for transporting casualties to the rear. In the United States, the army had not trained surgeons or nurses, did not keep a supply of medicine, and had little knowledge of proper nutrition. Nurse Mary Livermore recalled that in the early months at the Cairo base, inexperienced, ignorant commissaries and quartermasters caused intense suffering among soldiers, who experienced deprivations of every sort.[8]

Living conditions in the camps increased the risk of contagious disease. Crowded quarters, poor sanitation, and exposure to hundreds of strangers in army camps left soldiers even more vulnerable. Adding to the usual crowding in military encampments, the group that Mary Logan referred to as the "other army" in Cairo doubled the potential for the spread of disease.[9] Because the Civil War was a regional conflict in which camps and battlefields were often close to home, friends and relatives found military sites within easy traveling distance.

Lonely soldiers encouraged loved ones to visit them in camp. Carriages, wagons, and other vehicles brought a constant stream of

7. Louis C. Duncan, *The Medical Department of the United States Army in the Civil War,* 98.

8. Williams, *Lincoln and His Generals,* 5; Sister M. Eleanore, *On the King's Highway,* 235; Brinton, *Memoirs,* 99; Emmett F. Pearson, "Historic Hospitals of Cairo" 77:23; Duncan, *Medical Department,* 17; Livermore, *My Story,* 125.

9. Logan, *Reminiscences of the Civil War,* 109.

people to the town, which had insufficient housing to accommodate the thousands of visitors. The new breed of camp followers pitched tents and made brush houses near their men.[10] Referring to the extraneous campers, a correspondent for the *New York Times* satirized Cairo as a place "fast becoming a . . . fashionable resort for the local society of Illinois."[11]

By autumn, many of the soldiers stationed in Cairo were battling disease rather than grappling with the enemy, and visiting relatives suffered from the same conditions that plagued soldiers.[12] Newcomers to the area learned that partaking of the most basic necessities could be problematic. Within days of arriving at Cairo, several soldiers wound up on the sick list as a result of drinking river water. William Onstat informed his sister that he had been unwell and was taking medicine, "Day before yesterday I had a high Fever [*sic*] was as sick as I want to be."[13] Onstat mentioned, "Alex Boggs attends to all my necessary wants."[14] Onstat referred to the standard practice early in the war of allowing convalescent soldiers to serve as nurses.[15] Onstat's medicine failed to cure his ailment, and he spent two days in the post hospital.

When they first arrived at Cairo, men from rural areas had not been exposed to ordinary childhood diseases. Those diseases spread freely through the camps.[16] Measles, especially, plagued the soldiers at Cairo. Smallpox also came calling. As life-threatening as the plague during the first year of the war, smallpox frightened soldiers even more than the enemy. They had no defense against the disease. With such large numbers of men living together in very close quarters, doctors could hardly be expected to prevent the spread of contagious disease.

Soldiers learned, however, that death came through many channels. Officers strove to put an end to casualties that resulted from carelessness and human error. William Onstat described an unfortunate accident that occurred in his camp. Returning from drill, one of the men walked into his tent and threw his loaded gun onto

10. Ibid., 104, 109.
11. *New York Times*, June 8, 1861.
12. Eleanore, *King's Highway*, 244.
13. William Onstat to Sister Lizzie, Oct. 3, 1861, William Onstat MSS.
14. Ibid.
15. Fischer, "Cairo Angel," 54:229.
16. Brinton, *Memoirs*, 61.

the floor. The gun discharged, and the bullet passed through a soldier in a nearby tent. The victim died the following day.[17]

William McLean's regiment suffered a similar tragedy. The picket guard erroneously shot and killed a soldier in McLean's regiment. The victim had rowed a boat into the river in order to wash his clothes. From the levee, the guards mistook him for an enemy intruder and fired on him.

The funeral, attended by the entire regiment, made a lasting impression on the men. Soldiers of McLean's Ninth Illinois Infantry Regiment formed a line at the hospital, where the chaplain read scriptures and prayed. A detail then placed the casket on a bier that was hitched to a white horse. The long procession of uniformed soldiers solemnly followed the hearse to a cemetery seven miles above Cairo. Fifes and muffled drums accompanied the marchers. At the cemetery, the soldiers buried their comrade.[18]

Recruits in Cairo lived with the constant threat of illness and accident, but the prospect of falling into the hands of the camp's medical establishment seemed to inspire particular dread. When illness overtook William McLean, one of his cousins reassured his family by telling them that McLean had not gone to the hospital and was still well enough to perform his duties.[19]

Only one general hospital existed in Cairo when the volunteers first arrived. Located in the same block as the St. Charles Hotel, the facility consisted of two small dwellings and a large ward. The space could accommodate about one hundred patients. Solid construction and good ventilation characterized the building, but whitewashed walls created a stark atmosphere for patients. In fact, the walls hurt one's eyes. Correspondents reported that the administration in the Cairo camps had a penchant for whitewashing. In the hospital buildings, glaringly white walls made a startling contrast to the crimson blood that decorated them after battles.[20]

Named the Bulletin, the general hospital in Cairo evoked disturbing reminiscences from women who had worked there. During Mary Livermore's first stay, the general hospital in Cairo overflowed with sick and wounded. Substandard as the facility was, Livermore concluded that the Bulletin—which she referred to as the Brick Hos-

17. William Onstat to Sister, Oct. 20, 1861, William Onstat MSS.
18. Ibid.; W. Y. Jenkins to Mr. McLean, Jane, Lis, Abi and Jimmy, June 8, 1861.
19. William McLean MSS.
20. *Chicago Daily Tribune*, May 25, 1861; Eleanore, *King's Highway*, 238.

pital—represented progress in military medicine. Previously, the army had offered only post hospitals, which contained forty beds.[21] At the Cairo post, smaller military hospitals eventually existed at Bird's Point and Paducah.

At all of the bases, regimental officers improvised medical facilities to care for their own men. When soldiers fell ill, they disliked being separated from the familiarity of their regiments; any indisposition could prove fatal. Whenever possible, soldiers wished to stay with relatives and friends in their own company. So, officers confiscated houses, carriage houses, and sheds to serve as infirmaries.

All the women working as nurses at Cairo characterized the regimental hospitals as places where filthy conditions prevailed.[22] Following her first visit to the base's general hospital, Livermore made an inspection of the regimentals. Housed in small, stifling buildings, these places were "never very attractive institutions."[23] Despite the appalling conditions of these facilities, soldiers overwhelmingly preferred them, and a constant stream of patients passed through these private infirmaries. Miraculously, many recovered.

At the outbreak of the war, the *Chicago Daily Tribune* advised women to practice brave self-sacrifice by telling their men, "Go."[24] Northern women exceeded the recommendations of the *Tribune*. Many worked as clerks, planted gardens, and managed farms. Some sent boxes of comfort items, such as pillows and newspapers, to soldiers at the front. But women did more than tend the home fires and send comfort to their men. Women of the West made the supreme sacrifice of encouraging their men to go, and then, they followed. The medical examination given by army physicians to recruits was so superficial that many women managed to disguise their sex and pass undetected. This lapse in military medical practice allowed some women to actually enlist in the army and fight. But by far the most important contribution of women during the Civil War occurred in the field of medicine.

Illness and injury in military medical camps aroused civilians. Before the first year of the war wound to a close, the desire of women to provide fighting men with the comforts of home combined with a true need for greater medical expertise in the army

21. Eleanore, *King's Highway*, 235; Brinton, *Memoirs*, 99.
22. Livermore, *My Story*, 204.
23. Ibid., 203.
24. *Chicago Daily Tribune*, Apr. 25, 1861.

gave rise to organizations that filled the gaps in the military's medical establishment. In the early days, physicians at the Cairo post found that they alone could not handle the demands of caring for patients. At first, convalescing soldiers acted as nurses in both the general and regimental hospitals. These men did little in the way of providing sound medical care and frequently did much harm. Consequently, doctors turned to women for assistance, or, in some instances, had the ministrations of women forced upon them.

As interest in the southern Illinois military base spread throughout the state, Unionists who were unable to fight devised other means of aiding the cause. Many Christian congregations, some far removed from the theaters of war, offered matronly members for service as nurses. The day after the Illinois General Assembly voted to appropriate funds for the Cairo base, the Rev. Robert B. Tuttle of Chicago wrote Governor Yates, offering the services of thirty ladies of high character and reputation to act as nurses to the troops. Tuttle himself volunteered to serve as a chaplain.[25]

Most of these novice nurses lacked appropriate qualifications and harbored unrealistic expectations regarding camp life. Church-supported women who volunteered for nursing required living quarters that proved costly to the Federal army. Some of these women indulged in romantic notions about nursing men at the front. Military doctors and officers had little patience with these largely incompetent women, but the general public saw camp nurses in a sentimental way. Writing from Decatur, Illinois, a friend teased George Durfee, "I suppose you wish you were in Decatur sometimes. You ought to have taken some of the gals with you to nurse you."[26] But romantic fantasies about medical duties with the military vanished once women encountered the actual conditions in the camps.

In Cairo, a few of the women volunteers turned into very competent, efficient caregivers. One of the most capable nurses in the western theater had followed the first regiments of volunteer soldiers from Chicago to Cairo. After working as a governess on a Virginia plantation, Mary Livermore harbored a deep hatred for slavery. She left the South and moved to Boston, where she met and married

25. Robert B. Tuttle to Richard Yates, Apr. 24, 1861, Yates Family MSS.
26. Cy to George S. Durfee, May 2, 1861, George S. Durfee MSS.

Daniel Livermore, a Universalist minister. The couple migrated to Chicago, and Daniel started the *New Covenant* newspaper.[27]

In the Cairo hospitals, Livermore gained renown for her competent, compassionate care of soldiers. Another well-respected female nurse hailed from the highest level of Cairo's own prewar society. The most prominent woman in town, despite her youth, Mary Jane Safford undertook the direction of a group of Cairo women who had come together in the first weeks of the conflict to perform hospital work. Drawing on a family tradition, Safford began working as a nurse as soon as Union troops occupied the town. She is believed to have been the first woman in the West to undertake nursing in an army camp. Her brother, Alfred Boardman Safford, donated money to fund several of the regimental hospitals. When all of the base camps reached completion, Mary Jane traveled between Cairo and Bird's Point ministering to the ailing soldiers and assessing their situations.[28]

A frail woman about the size of a twelve-year-old child, Safford brought order out of chaos in the Cairo hospitals. The townspeople of Cairo readily volunteered to assist with a project so important to the wealthiest man in town and his self-taught sister-nurse. The twenty-six-year-old's uncanny ability to perceive the needs of ailing men and provide these patients with appropriate care set her apart from other amateur nurses. Safford collected items for individual patients and visited the wards every day with magazines, newspapers, games, and letter-writing materials. A. B. Safford supported his sister's medical work by covering the cost of the many items Mary Jane handed out to soldiers in the Cairo wards.[29]

Soldiers' letters testify to Safford's compassionate treatment of the sick and wounded. During the two weeks that William Onstat stayed in his regimental hospital he met Mrs. Bluford Wilson of Cairo and Mary Jane Safford. He perceived Safford to be an exceptional young woman, "I think the latter [Mary Jane Safford] is quite an accomplished Lady. She visits the various Hospitals in town regularly."[30] Seeing the desperate need for hospital space, Safford also

27. Nina Brown-Baker, *Cyclone in Calico: The Story of Mary Ann Bickerdyke*, 56.
28. Livermore, *My Story*, 206; Pearson, *Historic Hospitals*, 24, 479.
29. Fischer, "Cairo Angel," 232; Livermore, *My Story*, 208; Fischer, "Cairo Angel," 234.
30. William Onstat to Sister Lizzie, Oct. 17, 1861, William Onstat MSS.

turned her Cairo mansion into a convalescent center.[31] Although she gave the appearance of a fragile-looking product of the Victorian Cult of Domesticity, Safford would exhibit an iron will during Grant's western campaigns when battle casualties required triage and immediate care.

Yet another Mary left a mark on the Cairo hospitals. In Galesburg, Illinois, Dr. Edward Beecher, brother of the famed Henry Ward Beecher, pastored the Brick Congregational Church. That congregation decided to sponsor Mary A. Bickerdyke on a nursing mission to Cairo. No amateur in the field of healing, Bickerdyke—nicknamed Mother—had been trained in botanic medicine at Oberlin College in Ohio. Shortly after the Cairo camps appeared, Mother Bickerdyke joined Mary Jane Safford in Cairo, and the two women waged a campaign to improve the squalid regimental hospitals. Mother Bickerdyke came to Cairo with her own medical supplies.[32]

Like Grant, she possessed good organizational and administrative skills as well as a great measure of confidence in her own ability. Bickerdyke approached her work aggressively. If necessary, she would turn a sharp tongue on doctors and officers alike until the men at Cairo learned to obey her directives. In addition to improving the regimental hospitals, Bickerdyke reorganized the wards in the general hospitals at Cairo and Mound City and changed the methods of caring for patients.[33] Bickerdyke worked to address the problems of the medical establishment at Cairo until after the battle at Belmont, Missouri.

At Cairo, female nurses provided soldier-patients with good care, clean surroundings, and wholesome food. The dedicated service of these women saved lives and brought the comforts of home to young men who had left that place far behind. They could not, however, meet all of the pressing medical needs of the soldiers. Providing efficiency and innovations in military medical care in the West would require the contributions of many more private citizens working in conjunction with military officers and the federal government. More than anything else, medical progress required a commanding general with good management skills and an eye for efficiency in every aspect of the district. Such a man was on the way.

---

31. Brown-Baker, *Cyclone in Calico*, 52.
32. Fischer, "Cairo Angel," 230; Pearson, *Historic Hospitals*, 24.
33. Agatha Young, *The Women and the Crisis*, 466.

Five

Lively Times in Cairo

In the early hours of September 6, 1861, officers of the Kentucky State Guard gazed through the slats of a moving cattle car, watching the landscape of home fade from view. After loading their men onto the only available train at the depot, Simon Bolivar Buckner and Lloyd Tighlman had helped other militia officers secure the rolling stock at the station. Having done all they could to deprive the Federals of booty, they accounted for their men and jumped into the nearest passing car.[1]

When West Point graduate Lloyd Tighlman had learned that Grant was landing troops at the Paducah riverfront, he had hurried to the home of another West Pointer, Simon Bolivar Buckner. Grant's offensive movement spurred the secessionist-minded men to take their unit of the Kentucky State Guard out of Paducah and join the Confederate army. Even a poignant correspondence with his brother-in-law, Maj. Robert Anderson, during Anderson's siege inside Fort Sumter had not altered Tighlman's rebellious inclinations. As the surrounding countryside swallowed every trace of the Rebel train, Grant's troops spread out through the streets of Paducah.[2]

Arriving in Cairo without fanfare on September 4, Grant had entered district headquarters in the City National Bank building and inadvertently inflicted one of life's most embarrassing moments on Acting Commander Richard Oglesby. Listening to petitions from

1. Agatha Young, *The Women and the Crisis*, 466.
2. Grant, *Papers*, 2:196.

local businessmen, Oglesby mistook Grant, unadorned by regulation dress uniform, for an interloper. Oglesby consequently ignored Grant, as he would have any stranger. Never one to draw personal attention unnecessarily, Grant simply passed a note to Oglesby informing him that he was taking command.[3] Once Oglesby understood that the short, unshaven, average-looking soldier before him was the new commander of the District of Southeast Missouri, he directed Grant to his office. Grant settled in and quietly went to work, writing Julia, "We are likely to have lively times here."[4]

With fifteen years' experience in the army at the time the civil conflict erupted, Grant had appreciable military experience and a measure of important perspective. Though he had opposed the war with Mexico, the same sense of duty that led him to enlist in 1861 had pulled him into the Mexican War.[5] Tending to articulate a love/hate relationship with the army, Grant at times appeared to desire nothing more the pursuit of a private, civilian existence. Then he would contradict himself with statements such as "I do not think that I will ever [be] half so well contented out of the Army as in it," and "Soldiering is a very pleasant occupation generally."[6] Whatever his true feelings, the fact that Grant acted out of a sense of duty rather than pure political ambition may have been a great benefit to him.[7]

Before embarking on his Civil War career, Grant had already experienced the fire of battle. The first sounds of artillery near the Rio Grande had left him wishing that he had not enlisted. And yet, he showed no fear of dying, only regret.[8] The fearlessness faded somewhat over the years, and by the time Grant was marching through Missouri twenty years later, the prospect of facing the enemy filled the happily married father of four with a particular dread.

Perhaps demonstrating the deeply disturbing effects of war, even on those devoted to it, Grant could still recall at the end of his life the first casualty he witnessed. He described a gruesome scene at the battle of Palo Alto in which a cannonball decapitated an enlisted man. Not only did that man die, but his bones and brains flew into

3. Grant, *Memoirs*, 157.
4. Grant, *Papers*, 2:214.
5. Simon and Stevens, *Forging a Commander*, 50; Grant, *Papers*, 1:74.
6. Grant, *Papers*, 1:47, 1:64.
7. Simon and Stevens, *Forging a Commander*, 54.
8. Grant, *Memoirs*, 58; Grant, *Papers*, 1:83.

two or three other soldiers, injuring and horrifying them. Grant's early military education in the Mexican War coaxed out a tendency to occasionally act without orders, when opportunity presented itself in the absence of a commanding officer, and to volunteer for dangerous duty when he saw a workable strategy.[9]

With all the lessons of West Point and the Mexican War stashed into his highly organized brain, Grant began his first district command. Grant's new command included Cape Girardeau and Bird's Point, Missouri; Cairo and Mound City, Illinois, and—by the middle of September—Fort Holt, Kentucky. Coveting such a command, Grant had come to Cairo convinced that Federal troops could do more than just occupy and defend the place. Cairo, Grant believed, might be used as a point of departure for reclaiming the Mississippi Valley. With this strategy in mind, Grant considered that his new command was third in importance in the Union's entire theater of war.[10]

In fact Grant placed so much importance on Cairo, he worried initially that the War Department might replace him with an officer of higher rank. Consequently, Grant moved quickly on Paducah when he saw an opportunity to initiate an aggressive strategy. Having learned to separate rumor from truth in the short time that he had been campaigning in the West, Grant concluded that Rebels were indeed marching through Kentucky. He reasoned that the objective of the force of four thousand Confederates could only be to wrest Kentucky from the Union.[11]

Officials in Washington had been following a wait-and-see policy with the Blue Grass State on the advice of General Scott, who had informed them, "many of the wisest & best Union men in Kentucky have strongly intimated that thrusting protection upon their people is likely to do far more harm than good."[12] But Grant was not a wait-and-see kind of general. So, on September 4, after sizing up the situation and requesting permission to move, Grant decided he would transport troops across the Ohio River at ten-thirty the following night.[13]

---

9. Grant, *Memoirs*, 60, 68, 92, 95.
10. Catton, *Grant Moves South*, 25; Grant, *Papers*, 2:214.
11. Grant, *Memoirs*, 158.
12. General Scott to Governors Yates, Dennison, and Morton, May 29, 1861, Yates Family MSS.
13. Grant, *Memoirs*, 158.

Grant's departure for Paducah coincided perfectly with government policy. Confederate Gen. Leonidas Polk had taken it upon himself to violate Kentucky's neutrality, thereby opening the door for
Grant's move against Paducah. After Union troops had occupied
Cairo, Polk countered by moving into Columbus, Kentucky, and
scattering Confederate troops throughout other parts of the officially
neutral state.[14]

If Kentucky could have remained neutral, the state would have
served as a natural barrier, keeping each army from the other's territory.[15] But when Polk moved into Columbus, loyal state legislators petitioned Congress for federal intervention. In an attempt to
move Kentucky into the Confederacy, Polk had sent Gen. Gideon J.
Pillow marching through the state. Grant gladly took action to foil
Pillow, an officer he considered totally inept.

The Paducah campaign showed the first evidence of Grant's character as a fighting general. Without waiting for orders, Grant sent
three steamers carrying volunteer soldiers to their first concerted
movement against the enemy. The entourage included the Ninth
Illinois Volunteers under Gen. E. A. Paine, the Twelfth Illinois Volunteers under Col. J. MacArthur, and a battery of light artillery under
Capt. James Smith. In an early example of Grant placing his faith in
the element of surprise, he ordered that the gunboats drop anchor
in the Ohio River until he gave the command to move forward.
The movement commenced at dawn, even though the boats had
arrived before Paducah in the middle of the night.[16]

Early on the morning of the sixth, Union troops from Cairo took
Paducah without firing a shot. To prevent the Confederates from
reentering the town, Grant also occupied Smithland. Grant left two
gunboats on the Kentucky waterfront and placed soldiers at all
roads leading into the city. Gen. E. A. Paine stayed in Paducah with a
directive from Grant that he should take care not to harm inoffensive
citizens of the city.[17]

The federal government's fears that western Kentucky would be
attached to the Confederacy if the Rebel army reached the site

14. *Cairo City Weekly Gazette*, Sept. 12, 1861.
15. E. B. Long, *The Civil War Day by Day*, 115.
16. Grant, *Memoirs*, 158.
17. Bern Anderson, *By Sea and by River: The Naval History of the Civil War*, 43;
Grant, *Memoirs*, 158; Grant, *Papers*, 2:195.

unopposed had not been misplaced. Citizens of Paducah extended no welcome to Grant's troops when they arrived. The general himself reminisced, "Men, women and children came out of their doors looking pale and frightened at the presence of the invader. They were expecting rebel troops that day."[18]

In an effort to allay the fears of the citizenry, Grant addressed the people of Paducah in a printed proclamation. The proclamation contained no declaration of policy, just an assurance of safety to the civilians in the city. Grant told the people that his soldiers had only peaceful intentions. He observed privately that "the majority would have much preferred the presence of the other army."[19]

In camp at Cairo two days after the campaign, George Durfee sent his uncle a description of the movement on Paducah. He stated that troops from Bird's Point and other points up the river had been passing Cairo ever since E. A. Paine's regiment left for Paducah on Thursday night. After Federal forces under Grant had secured the city, a separate squad of Union officers crossed over to the Kentucky shore to find a place for an encampment.[20] With Paducah securely under his control, Grant ordered that secession flags flying over the city be replaced with the Stars and Stripes.

A fort that would guard the fifth point of federally controlled territory in the vicinity of the Ohio/Mississippi confluence began to materialize shortly thereafter. Instructed by General Frémont to name the Kentucky site Fort Holt, Grant sent Col. Joseph Webster to Paducah to direct the construction of the fortifications. Grant informed Frémont on September 7, "have been pushing the work of fort Holt for three or four days."[21]

A week later Grant telegraphed to say that the Union army had placed the first gun in position at Fort Holt. The Kentucky fort showed its worth almost immediately. William Onstat told his sister, Lizzie, "Rebel gunboats appeared at the bend of the river last Sunday evening, a few shots from Fort Holt sent them back to Dixie."[22] While the guns at Fort Holt kept the Rebels from getting too close to Cairo, Col. John Turchin's Chicago regiment, the

18. Grant, *Memoirs*, 136.
19. Ibid., 158.
20. George Durfee to H. B. Durfee, Sept. 8, 1861, George S. Durfee MSS.
21. Grant, *Papers*, 2:191, 203.
22. William H. Onstat to Sister Lizzie, Dec. 6, 1861, William H. Onstat MSS.

Nineteenth Illinois, stayed busy on the Kentucky side chasing Confederates away from Paducah.[23]

Perhaps Grant's victory at Paducah has been minimized because it pales in comparison to his subsequent victories in the West. In the eastern theater, however, McClellan made a similar accomplishment in early June when he successfully routed Rebels at Rich Mountain and the Cheat River Valley in western Virginia. This very small victory gained McClellan the command of the Army of the Potomac. Pondering the move, Lincoln concluded that McClellan's minor offensive showed an aggressive assumption of risk to win battles.[24] Grant's Paducah campaign had actually arisen from the mentality Lincoln erroneously attributed to McClellan.

The Paducah victory evidenced the early manifestation of many other remarkable qualities in Grant that would mature over the next two years. Based on information from his scouts, Grant believed that the Rebels were moving on Paducah; he thought he could thwart an enemy advance. In a matter of hours, he turned thought into action. His decisive action allowed him to surprise the enemy forces and overpower them without firing a single shot.[25]

Military historians interpret Grant's instinct for acting without hesitation as evidence of a sense of public and personal morality since anticipating the enemy's movements allows for surprise attacks. Other Union generals, notably McClellan, appeared to be dogged by hesitancy, a characteristic of a siege mentality that could result in heavy losses.[26]

Another important military tactic—targeting a place in a defensive strategy—can be seen in Grant's move on Paducah. He perceived that he was preventing a Rebel attack on Cairo. The information he gathered told him that an enemy army was on the march, and not knowing what he might encounter, Grant moved toward the logical objective of that army. Acting on instinct and common sense, Grant realized great success in his first campaign out of Cairo. The movement was flawed only in that the Federals failed to destroy the Rebel force.[27]

23. Grant, *Papers*, 2:214.
24. Donald, *Lincoln*, 42.
25. Grant, *Papers*, 2:196.
26. Herman Hattaway and Archer Jones, *How the North Won: A Military History of the Civil War*, 149.
27. Donald, *Lincoln*, 30.

As with most of Grant's western campaigns, through success in Paducah he managed to raise the spirits of his own troops and demoralize the enemy. Rather than face Grant, Tighlman and Buckner fled before him. He captured their matériel and kept them from assisting the Confederate army to invade Union territory. As for Tighlman and Buckner, they managed to avoid capture by the commander of Cairo during the occupation of Paducah, but the two Rebels would not escape a day of reckoning with Grant.

Grant had accepted his commission as colonel of the Twenty-first believing that "a few decisive victories in some of the southern ports will send the secession army howling."[28] If Grant had followed his ego into the kind of illusory imaginings that seemed to plague some of his rivals, the easy victory at Paducah could have reinforced his mistaken perception. But Grant had the objectivity and sense to realize that, even though the Confederates ran from him at one site, they were formidably entrenched at other nearby locations.[29] Grant did not delude himself into thinking that the war could be won in only one theater without bloodshed and aggressive, relentless pursuit. Under Grant's capable command, the uncertain borders around Cairo began to look a little more secure.

When Grant returned to his headquarters after the Paducah campaign, he saw that Frémont had given him permission to move on Paducah.[30] It was not the last time Grant would leave Cairo, on the offensive, without specific orders from the department commander. And it represented only the first of many victorious campaigns Grant would lead out of Cairo. In the aftermath of Paducah, Grant turned his attention to the business of creating a competent fighting force with which he hoped to conquer the Confederates in the West.

28. Grant, *Papers*, 2:28.
29. Williams, *Lincoln and His Generals*, 24.
30. Ibid., 2:211–21.

Six

Mischief

As fall burst into glorious color in southern Illinois, Col. G. Waagner, chief of artillery, assessed the strength of the fortifications along Cairo's waterfront. Anticipating a Confederate attack at any time—a constant state of mind along the borders—Waagner wrote to the new post commander, John A. McClernand, requesting two additional artillery regiments. At the time of Waagner's request, the Cairo correspondent for *Harper's Weekly* had reported, "Heavy cannon are mounted and ready for mischief."[1] During Grant's early days at Cairo, mischief abounded, but the Rebels had little to do with it.

Turning from campaign strategy to administration, Grant started addressing a variety of problems in the camps. In his memoirs, he reminisced, "From the occupation of Paducah up to the early part of November nothing important occurred with the troops under my command."[2] No fighting occurred during that period, but Grant performed important tasks that greatly affected the troops and impacted the success of his later campaigns.

Lack of proper military discipline topped the list of serious problems in Cairo.[3] Working with a staff that included Capt. John A. Rawlins, assistant adjutant general; Capt. Clark B. Lagow, aide-de-camp; Capt. William S. Hillyer, aide-de-camp; and surgeon James Simon, medical director, Grant went to work.[4] He adjusted to the

1. *Harper's Weekly*, June 29, 1861; John A. McClernand MSS, July 20, 1861.
2. Grant, *Memoirs*, 160.
3. Ibid.
4. Grant, *Papers*, 2:206.

dearth of experienced officers on his staff by handling the responsibilities of several positions himself. Grant assumed his first district
command already familiar with the discipline-resistant soldiers of
the West. Prior to his assumption of command of the Twenty-first,
the regiment had earned the name "Governor Yates' Hellions."[5]
Grant managed to turn those soldiers away from habitual intoxica-
tion, infighting, stealing, and molestation of private citizens.

Contrary to journalists' predictions, Illinois volunteers at Cairo
had overwhelmingly remained in the army after their first three
months of service, but they continued to resist discipline. For the
Paducah campaign, Grant had selected the fullest, best-armed, and
best-equipped regiments at Cairo.[6] Whipping the other regiments
into proper shape to meet the enemy presented Grant with a task
as challenging as that of transforming the Twenty-first.

In the area of tactics, Grant had long since discarded Hardee's
manual—a translation of Jominian strategy—and come to rely more
and more on his own instincts and common sense.[7] Creating a system for getting the Cairo soldiers ready to implement battle strategy tutored Grant in the little-practiced military arts of administration and organization. His natural inclination for sound discipline
prompted him to address threats from his own men as decisively
as he had pursued the Rebels' challenge.

In the temperate autumn months, soldiers in Cairo worked at
perfecting their drilling and anticipated their first engagement.
Being so near the Rebels yet unable to strike created some frustration, but most officers struggled to obey the orders they were given
and strove to get their regiments battle-ready. Unfortunately, one
officer at the Cairo base, chafing at inaction, lost control of his men
before campaigning ever began. Despite the fact that a friendship
had ripened between Grant and Col. Bill Schuter, Grant took swift
action against the incompetent officer once he realized that serious
problems existed in Schuter's regiment. Grant and his commanding
officers decided that Schuter could not be trusted. The colonel was
arrested before his regiment went on the march.[8]

In another troubling incident, soldiers at Bird's Point learned
in October that they were under Grant's watchful eye. Some of

5. Hattaway, *How the North Won*, 54.
6. Grant, *Papers*, 3:30.
7. Grant, *Memoirs*, 151.
8. Joint Committee, 93.

Oglesby's men burned a local steam ferry. Upholding Lincoln's policy against the wanton destruction of private property, Grant dealt harshly with the perpetrators. He ordered the guilty men to come forward or force their entire command to reimburse double the cost of the ferry from their pay. The culprits did not surrender, and Grant showed his mettle by deducting the money.[9]

Grant confronted more common breaches of discipline as well. Chafing under the military yoke, enlisted men escaped the confines of camp as often as possible. Drunken sprees landed them in the guardhouse, and abuse of alcohol sometimes led to even more serious consequences. A guard report from the first week of September 1861 showed that of fourteen arrests, nine stemmed from drunkenness.[10] Under the influence of alcohol, soldiers committed crimes against local citizens and became victims of crime themselves.

George Durfee wrote his uncle of the circumstances surrounding a case that involved a man in another company from Decatur. While intoxicated, the soldier had committed murder. Durfee explained, "Dave Tucker will be tried by the civil authorities and in all probability be hung as it was nothing less than a wanton murder."[11] Durfee judged that even though Tucker had committed the crime under the influence, he had known what he was doing.

Hoping to curb drunkenness, Col. Harry B. Smith, a Cairo native, wrote General Frémont in September 1861 to discuss the problem of liquor in Cairo: "I would like to call your attention to the Great Number of Drinking Saloons in this City Most of which are of the Lowest Order."[12] Colonel Smith attributed rows, fights, and murders of an almost daily occurrence at all hours to drunkenness. He finally begged, "Can you not issue orders, entirely close them or restrict them."[13]

Whether Frémont never saw the letter or simply chose to ignore it is not known. The problems persisted. The *Chicago Daily Tribune* echoed Smith's complaint: "Every other house on the levee is a saloon, and every one has a guard stationed at the door to preserve order."[14] The guards proved to be largely ineffective, and the

---

9. Grant, *Papers*, 3:29.
10. Guard Report, Camp Defiance, Sept. 2–3, 1861, John McClernand MSS.
11. George Durfee to H. B. Durfee, May 24, 1861, George S. Durfee MSS.
12. John McClernand MSS, Sept. 3, 1861.
13. Ibid.
14. *Chicago Daily Tribune*, May 25, 1861.

waterfront establishments remained a danger to both soldiers and civilians.

Liquor went hand in hand with other vices that tended to undermine discipline in the Cairo camps. During the years when Cairo was an active river port, many gaming houses had sprung up along the riverfront. After the military established control over the rivers, gambling continued. Enlisted men became quite familiar with the gaming tables. William Onstat informed his sister, Lizzie, that he had not gambled a cent or played a card since he got to Cairo, boasting, "Of course I have not used a bit of Liquors or Tobacco."[15] A lament followed the boast, "Very few of our Company I am sorry to say can give as good an account of themselves as I can in this particular. . . . I am constantly surrounded by men who gamble."[16]

Even the twin vices didn't cause as much discord among the ranks as one other breach in moral conduct. Journalists habitually described Cairo in glowing hyperbole, in one instance touting the Union camps as "romantic locations, being fairly embowered in trees, rendered musical by the deliciously-tuned voices of birds and myriads [sic] of mosquitoes." The locale under description went unrecognized by soldiers stationed at the site.[17]

When soldiers at Cairo felt romantic, they sought female companionship in the town. One particular establishment had adapted especially well to the desires of soldiers. Enlisted men and important military and political leaders from all over the Union patronized the St. Charles Hotel. The hotel's registers from April 15, 1861, to April 15, 1865, showed a list of distinguished names that would be exceeded only by those in the registers of hotels in Washington, D.C., in the same time period.[18]

By the time Grant had arrived in Cairo, however, many of the visitors to the St. Charles had no intention of signing the register. One eighteen-year-old, Pvt. James Swales, gave an account of a Sunday afternoon adventure far from the everyday routine of camp. After first decrying the lack of respect shown the Sabbath in Cairo, Swales confessed to his brother that, on a recent Sunday afternoon, he had succumbed to the charms of a young woman who leaned out of a third-story window at the St. Charles Hotel. She seduced

15. William Onstat to Sister Lizzie, Nov. 27, 1861, William H. Onstat MSS.
16. Ibid.
17. *Chicago Daily Tribune*, May 25, 1861.
18. Lansden, *History of Cairo*, 137.

the young man by winking at him in a way he could not ignore. He bragged to his brother that, "she was as good looking a woman as you could wish to look at" and then stated simply, "the rest you know if you can guess good."[19] Satisfied with the encounter, Swales noted that the woman was "'newly enitiated' [*sic*] and didn't cost a cent."[20]

Some of the first businesses that had appeared on the Cairo waterfront, houses of prostitution had long attracted gamblers and sailors and plagued the town's emerging middle class. Despite efforts by the town's respectable citizens to bring prostitution under control, the war only made it more profitable. To an eighteen-year-old away from home for the first time, such an enticement was, perhaps, irresistible. But soldiers' attitudes toward the available vices in Cairo varied as much as the men's individual personalities.

Not all enlisted men engaged in morally destructive pastimes, and the enlisted men who did indulge could not be judged too harshly since many of their officers set a poor example. Commenting on this issue, George Durfee explained to his uncle that some of the best soldiers in his company wanted to stay in the army but did not want to continue serving under their current officers. Durfee discussed the grievance against his first lieutenant: "perhaps you think we [the soldiers] are hard on him, but it don't look well to see a man, especially a married man to be the biggest [*sic*] whore master in the company."[21]

Durfee's description coincided with remarks made by Henry Adolph Kircher from Belleville, Illinois. Kircher complained to his father, Joseph, about the lack of well-educated people at Camp Defiance, including the army officers. Officers at the Cairo base gained popularity with the men by telling dirty jokes and making lewd gestures, behavior that Kircher did not wish to imitate.[22]

A stickler for discipline, Grant did not hesitate to come down hard on the flourishing vice industry at Cairo. He intended to do more than commiserate over the unacceptable situation. When he came into possession of the information that had been sent to Frémont by

19. James Swales to David Swales, Sept. 8, 1861, James Swales MSS.
20. Ibid.
21. George Durfee to H. B. Durfee, June 5, 1861, George S. Durfee MSS.
22. Henry Adolph Kircher, *A German in the Yankee Fatherland,* edited by Earl J. Hess, 4.

Harry Smith, Grant acted decisively. What became the "infamous" Order No. 5 stated: "It is with regret the Genl Comdg sees and learns that the closest intimacy exists between many of the officers and soldiers of his command; that they visit together the lowest drinking and dancing saloons."[23]

General Order No. 5 closed all drinking houses and all houses of prostitution in Cairo. The document demonstrated further that District Commander Grant took action when necessary. Lest any of his subordinates should misunderstand the intent of the order, Grant emphasized that discipline would be maintained in his military district even if it cost the commissions of all officers who stood in the way of attaining that end.[24]

To add teeth to his program, Grant also decided that McClernand should appoint a provost marshal to "entirely suppress drinking saloons or put them under wholesome regulations."[25] As early as September 8, McClernand had felt compelled to write Grant to disclaim responsibility for the lack of discipline at the Cairo post. The note is, perhaps, the first evidence of the deep sense of rivalry McClernand felt toward Grant. Later in the war, the rivalry would mature into a full-blown rift. Explaining that he had only been in Cairo for four days himself, McClernand declared that he could not be held responsible for the misbehavior of the soldiers.[26]

Stating further that his particular regiment had not participated in any rowdy behavior, McClernand, in his pompous, political manner, informed both Grant and Frémont that "it is my determination, while in command, to enforce, if necessary, with a strong hand, the observance of both [discipline and duty]."[27] McClernand then proceeded to demonstrate his poor judgment of the men at the post by appointing a fellow Democratic politician, A. J. Kuykendall, to the position of provost marshal general for the District of Cairo.[28]

In the same week that Grant had taken command of the District of Southeast Missouri, journalists noted that John A. Logan finally had a regiment of Egyptians camped in Cairo. With the Rebel army

23. Grant, *Papers*, 2:208.
24. *Cairo City Weekly Gazette*, Oct. 19, 1861; Grant, *Papers*, 2:208.
25. Ibid., 2:210.
26. Ibid., 2:211–12 n.
27. Ibid.
28. *Jonesboro Weekly Gazette*, Jan. 11, 1862.

nipping at their heels, men from southern Illinois began volunteering in excessive numbers in the fall of 1861. Logan's brush with arrest and incarceration had convinced his followers to seek safe harbor in the Union blue. Following Logan's lead, the "Cairo boys" all enlisted. Many of them gave valuable service to the Federal cause and rose to prominent positions. Joseph Skipworth, groom to John A. Logan, noted in a letter to his wife that Colonel Logan was "satisfied with his boys and the boys are satisfied with him."[29]

Assigned to McClernand's brigade, John A. Logan had recruited many of the southern Illinois secessionists for his Thirty-first Illinois Regiment. A. J. Kuykendall appeared as the second in command in the Thirty-first. In her reminiscences, Mary Logan boasted that the provost marshal of Cairo belonged to her husband's regiment. Major Kuykendall, lately associated with the plan to attach Cairo to the Confederacy, was indeed one of Logan's boys. Under McClernand's orders, he directed the work of implementing military discipline in the rowdy town. In September 1861, Allen alone among the Cairo conspirators remained immune from the prosecution of federal officials or the protection of enlistment.[30]

Hardly a military enthusiast during his early days at Cairo, Logan eschewed drilling his troops and instructing his officers. Instead, he left those jobs to Lt. Col. John H. White and Pvt. Robert N. Pearson, respectively. Logan and Kuykendall spent their time searching for equipment. Kuykendull's duties as provost marshal general created further diversions for the pair. His appointment not only dried up the saloons, but also drained the resources of local businessmen.[31]

The activities of Kuykendall's dishonest force gave rise to tales of ruthless provost marshals in Cairo, and, in truth, the marshals' policing of the city frequently ended in acts of wanton violence toward private citizens. Working under McClernand's direction, Kuykendall used the same overzealous tactics reminiscent of his brigade commander but with a more mercenary objective. At this time, Grant reprimanded McClernand for searching individuals who were not

29. Bradsby, *History of Cairo,* 66; Joseph Skipworth MSS, Oct. 18, 1861.
30. Grant, *Papers,* 3:88; Logan, *Reminiscences of the Civil War,* 111; Following a court martial in Cairo in August 1862, Allen would endure house arrest in Washington, D.C.
31. Nathaniel Cheairs Hughes, Jr., *The Battle of Belmont: Grant Strikes South,* 16. *Jonesboro Weekly Gazette,* Jan. 11, 1862.

under suspicion. He ordered McClernand to stop threatening people with violence for failure to comply with his searches.[32]

Kuykendall sent soldiers out to pressure businessmen into paying for protection. The unconscionable force required a "contribution" of at least five dollars to discourage molestation of their businesses.[33] Before Kuykendall's abuse of power required Grant's intervention, relief came through the workings of the democratic process: Kuykendall won Logan's vacated seat in Congress.

Secessionists outside of Cairo also troubled Grant's forces, but they offered diversion, too. Campaigning in Missouri early in the war, Grant had forbidden his men to hunt down southern sympathizers and bring them into camp. He still believed that most Missourians wished for the preservation of the Union.[34] After a few weeks at Cairo, Grant adopted a different policy, a reflection of his changing attitude toward Missouri dissenters. By the time he assumed his first district command, Grant knew that his soldiers needed to sharpen their animosity toward the Rebels because the enemy literally resided in their midst.

At the Bird's Point post, Oglesby's men kept busy hunting the enemy. At Cairo, between daily drills and evening dress parade, soldiers spent some part of every day "hunting Secessins [*sic*]."[35] Hunting parties caught six to eight "traitors" daily. The prisoners were treated to the hospitality of the guardhouse. Col. Robert Kirkham led one special hunting party in pursuit of men from Hamilton and Jefferson counties. The southern sympathizers planned to form companies and go South to fight for the Confederacy.[36] As a result of Kirkham's hunt, the rebellious Illinoisans spent the war being guarded by Federals instead of shooting at them. Union men saw the inside of Rebel jails as well.

The practice of exchanging prisoners rather than feeding and housing them had already begun in the West. But Grant's keen understanding of government policy and his natural loyalty kept him from participating in this process while he was still organizing

---

32. Richard L. Kiper, *Major General John M. McClernand: Politician in Uniform*, 37.
33. Bradsby, *History of Cairo*, 66.
34. Catton, *Grant Moves South*, 13, 14.
35. Joseph Skipworth MSS, Sept. 27, 1861.
36. Grant, *Papers*, 3:119.

his new command. In response to Polk's request to make an exchange, Grant informed the Rebel general that he could not take such a step on his own authority, "I recognize no Southern Confederacy."[37] He subsequently referred the issue to his superiors at St. Louis.

Although the Rebels often characterized Yankees as cowards, their own courage appeared to fail them upon capture: "Hecker's boys have just caught a secesh and sent him over to this side . . . our boys say he is pretty badly scart [sic] and pale as a ghost."[38] The Federals also vacillated between great courage and honest fear. In spite of the many Confederates confined in the guardhouse, one private from De Soto, Illinois, confessed to his wife, "The soldiers are expecting an attack . . . every day."[39]

The strong defensive fortifications at Cairo and the aggressive pursuit of Rebel scouts prevented the anticipated attack. In October, Grant's initial apprehension on arriving at the post turned into confident calm. He informed his wife, "Our Pickets had a little skirmish with some Rebels killing three or four probably. These things are so common that they are hardly noticed."[40] This casual acceptance of fatal encounters with the enemy evidenced the growing preparedness of the soldiers at Cairo.

In the long months before full-scale campaigning began, Grant allowed his soldiers to vent pent-up energy in skirmishes and expeditions. He sharpened his soldiers' taste for battle even further by organizing expeditions to capture his arch foe, Jeff Thompson. Trailing the Rebel marauder into southeast Missouri, Grant had noticed that Thompson moved light and had no static headquarters, a tactic that made an enduring impression on him. Relying once again on the tactic of surprise, Grant hoped to catch Thompson in the act of raiding on the Missouri side of the Mississippi River. September brought only aggravation in the search for Thompson, but in October, Grant's forces had some measure of success. Col. Joseph B. Plummer, post commander of Cape Girardeau, attacked and routed Thompson on the Greenville Road near Jackson, Missouri. Grant wasted no time in writing to congratulate Plummer and his men.[41]

37. Ibid., 3:39.
38. George S. Durfee to H. B. Durfee, Sept. 8, 1861, George S. Durfee MSS.
39. Joseph Skipworth MSS, Sept. 27, 1861.
40. Grant, *Papers*, 2:300.
41. Grant, *Memoirs*, 156; Grant, *Papers*, 2:212, 3:80.

Feeling his way in his first district command, Grant developed some unorthodox methods of curbing Rebel activity. Under his auspices women continued to aid the Union cause, occasionally in a clandestine capacity. Two women turned out to be soldiers as good as the volunteer recruits. The *Memphis Argus* reported that Confederate officers discovered two Cairo women of ill fame traveling by train to Memphis. The women confessed to their captors that military officers in Cairo had sent them to the Confederate base to see if the Rebel forces were really planning an attack on Cairo.[42]

The Confederate officers informed the Memphis Committee of Safety of the women's mission. After due consideration, the committee decided to return the girls to Illinois. In the wake of poor communications, and the lack of directives from either departmental headquarters or Washington, spies figured largely in Grant's movements at Cairo. He frequently requested additional funds to pay spies, since he had no other means of gathering information and the services of such people came at a high price.

While Grant was implementing policies that transformed the recruits in Cairo from men who fought against one another into soldiers who were itching to fight the enemy, he also got ideas that better prepared the troops and the district for battle. At the end of October, soldiers in Cairo started moving into wooden barracks designed by Grant. The new quarters were set up like box houses. The men found their new accommodations—rats and lice notwithstanding—more comfortable than the old makeshift quarters. In the same month, Grant ordered Quartermaster Reuben Hatch to build storehouses on the Ohio waterfront for the Quartermaster's and Subsistence departments at the base. Telegraph lines had also appeared by order of the district commander, running all along the Illinois side of the Ohio River.[43]

As the natural surroundings faded from crimson and gold to drab brown, soldiers in the Cairo District had adequately fortified all the posts and spent some time adjusting to the environs around Cairo. The Eighth Illinois thought if they had to stay long in a camp, they

42. *Cairo City Weekly Gazette*, May 9, 1861.

43. Grant, *Papers*, 3:30; Illinois Infantry, 31st Regiment, 27; William H. Onstat to Sister Lizzie, Oct. 27, 1861, William H. Onstat MSS; Joseph Skipworth MSS, Dec. 11, 1861; Edwin Loosley MSS, Sept. 26, 1862; Grant, *Papers*, 3: 53, 2:326–27.

would prefer to be at Camp Defiance. The men were happy with their quarters "and with things in general and Cairo particularly."[44] A short stay at the St. Charles Hotel had suited Grant, but he began to enjoy the Cairo base after moving his lodgings from the St. Charles to his headquarters at Safford's bank: "Cairo is not half so unpleasant a place as I supposed it would be. I have a nice office and live with the members of my staff immediately back of it."[45]

Finally able to relax somewhat by late fall, soldiers spent some time visiting with relatives who ventured down to Egypt. Missing his wife and children, as he invariably did throughout the war, Grant longed for them to visit the post. At first he feared that his wife, sister, and father would "make poor soldiers."[46] Then, considering the constant skirmishing between Cairo pickets and advancing Rebels, Grant worried about his family's safety. When the fear of attack lessened at the end of October, Julia and the children came to visit.[47]

Distracted by "such an undertaking" of packing for and traveling with four small children, Julia Dent Grant left no detailed impressions of Cairo.[48] She and the children stayed at Grant's headquarters during their visit. Commenting on the geography of the region, Julia remembered that the rivers seemed high and threatening to her and the building where she stayed resembled a great barracks.[49] In spite of the drawbacks of the camp, the presence of family members elevated the spirits of military men.

Grant's father also visited in October, and the families of Grant's staff officers spent time in Cairo as well.[50] Children found Camp Cairo just as stimulating as had the Chicago soldiers, especially when the children received "commissions" from the district commander. In a lighthearted moment, Grant conferred on Master Willie S. Hillyer, son of Grant's aide-de-camp, an appointment as "Pony Aid de Camp."[51] The stable boys were all obliged to obey him.

Soldiers whose family members could not visit Cairo sought other forms of relaxation between thrusts into enemy territory. Barred, for

44. Edwin Loosley MSS, Sept. 4, 1861.
45. Grant, *Papers*, 2:290.
46. Ibid., 2:237.
47. Ibid., 3:77.
48. Catton, *Grant Moves South*, 105.
49. Julia Dent Grant, *The Personal Memoirs of Julia Dent Grant*, 92.
50. Grant, *Papers*, 3:23.
51. Ibid., 3:102.

the most part, from indulging in the dissipated activities that took place indoors, soldiers engaged in outdoor recreation and games that gave them as much exercise as drilling. Camp play helped men to pass the time in a generally positive way. William McLean and his friends enjoyed swimming as well as boating. The men found a good swimming hole about one mile from their camp. On one outing, they capsized a canoe, drinking in more of the scenery than anticipated.[52] The soldiers also organized team sports such as baseball and horseshoes.

For some soldiers, free time gave rise to philosophical reflection. The rivers prompted deep metaphorical thought. One southern Illinois soldier felt drawn to the natural beauty of the Mississippi and Ohio confluence. He wrote of the "dazzling white sand" at the riverfront.[53] The rivers suggested a symbolic image of war and peace in his mind; the dark and angry Mississippi representing war, and the calm, peaceful Ohio representing the country as he remembered it before war had torn it apart. The rivers at Cairo fascinated men who had always lived inland on farms. They spent some time at the rivers every day watching steamboats.[54]

Hunting traitors and going out on expeditions occupied only a small portion of the soldiers' time. During idle times in camp, homesickness crept over the men like a canker. Some civilian groups came into military towns for the express purpose of organizing activities that counteracted the "debasing tendencies of camp life."[55] The United States Christian Commission opened a station at Cairo that maintained reading and writing rooms. Many soldiers took advantage of these amenities.

Middle-aged family men were well represented in the volunteer army in the West. These men tended to be well-read people who spent time writing letters and keeping diaries. Civil War soldiers particularly enjoyed reading news from home. Many western towns and counties had been settled by a small number of families who socialized in close circles and tended to intermarry. Consequently, soldiers in a particular company frequently shared ties of kinship. The men often shared letters from home because hometown gossip touched every soldier in the company. Just as frequently, soldiers

52. William McLean to Friends, June 20, 1861, William McLean MSS.
53. Edwin Loosley to Wife, Sept. 1862, Edwin Loosley MSS.
54. William McLean to Sisters, May 4, 1861, William McLean MSS.
55. Cole, *Civil War*, 283.

destroyed letters to protect a friend or relative from reading unpleasant news about loved ones at home.

As the weeks passed by without action, soldiers started to miss the riotous pastimes that Grant had curbed. Already harboring fears that they might be in a position "where neither service can be seen nor glory won," Cairo soldiers boasted that "we are ready to go for it at any time if they will only [send us] where there is some fighting to be done."[56] Volunteer soldiers in Cairo would shortly discover the antidote to drunkenness and monotony in the West. Soon they would undertake the sobering experience of campaigning with Ulysses S. Grant.

56. William McLean, July 4, 1861; George Durfee to H. B. Durfee, Sept. 4, 1861, George S. Durfee MSS.

Seven

Comfort for Our Boys

After spending a short time at his southern Illinois headquarters, Grant commented to Julia, "Cairo does not appear to be particularly sickly at this time. It is usually considered to be an unhealthy place and looks as if it must be so."[1] Appearances were not deceiving; soldiers in the camps suffered many maladies. The post's remote location, far from the nerve center of Washington, tended to exacerbate the struggle against sickness and poor sanitation.

In between planning and executing the first major Union victories in the Civil War, Grant began addressing the problems. Lacking a competent professional staff to organize and manage the medical facilities, Grant felt compelled to share this responsibility with his medical directors.[2] Overcrowded hospitals, insufficient medical personnel, contagious diseases spread by poor sanitation, and shortages of medical supplies challenged Grant, his medical director, James Simon, and the assistant medical director, John H. Brinton. Working with Simon and Brinton, Grant forged very successful solutions.

Five days after establishing his new headquarters, Grant sent Simon on a mission to Springfield. Grant's willingness to part temporarily with his medical director stemmed from conditions in the regimental hospitals. Acknowledging that devoted women such as Mary Jane Safford, Mary Livermore, and Mother Bickerdyke had made improvements in the quality of some of the Cairo hospitals,

1. Grant, *Papers*, 2:3; Brinton, *Memoirs*, 35.
2. Hattaway, *How the North Won*, 103.

Grant nevertheless realized that health care in the regimentals still fell far short of any acceptable standard. Deciding that Governor Yates needed to understand the urgency of appointing surgeons and assistant surgeons to the regiments at Cairo, Grant chose Simon to plead his case.[3]

Innovation as well as standardization characterized Grant's medical reforms at the Cairo bases. On September 10, the day after Simon left for Springfield, Grant wrote an order creating what was arguably the first hospital ship in the western theater. During the Crimean War, hospital ships had transported casualties to medical facilities, but the boats had lacked surgeons and medicines. Consequently, most of the soldiers died en route. Envisioning a new role for naval vessels, Grant ordered Quartermaster Hatch to engage the steamer *Swallow* to be used as a hospital for the troops housed at Fort Holt. Hatch was to have the boat towed to Paducah at once.[4] Grant conceived the idea of using a steamer for a floating hospital before it occurred to anyone in the War Department. He was even a step ahead of the volunteer organizations that pushed for progressive reforms in military medicine.

Grant displayed a deep concern for the men under his command. In the established hospitals of the district, Grant noticed much suffering. The health of the Second Iowa Regiment had deteriorated so alarmingly, Grant thought they should go to hospitals in St. Louis to recuperate.[5] Then, particular problems in the post hospital at Bird's Point called for action that foreshadowed the general's crackdown on discipline in the Cairo camps. Reports indicated that private citizens were selling alcohol to incapacitated soldiers. Upon learning that the consumption of beer was impeding the recovery of patients—which was difficult enough at the substandard facility—Grant took charge. Overruling the surgeons at Bird's Point, Grant directed post commander W. H. L. Wallace to drive beer merchants away or place them under restrictions.[6]

Maintaining the soldiers' physical health posed problems enough, but Grant looked beyond the body to the mind. At the district hospi-

3. Grant, *Papers*, 2:223.
4. John S. Haller, *Farmcarts to Fords: A History of the Military Ambulance, 1790–1925*, 19; Grant, *Papers*, 2:231.
5. Grant, *Papers*, 3:78.
6. Ibid., 3:32.

tals Grant began to notice that several patients were suffering from emotional strain. He believed that unsettling emotions, if neglected, could fester into physical illness. Grant did not view the soldiers' depression as cowardice. Homesickness immobilized even soldiers who desperately wanted to fight for their country. In the West, many recruits had never before been away from home for any appreciable amount of time. Grant, a man whose own yearning to be near his family had brought him to the point of physical impairment at times, understood that separation from family could make a man ill.[7]

Following his problem-solving instincts, Grant decided that men whose homesickness rendered them physically ill should be given three or four days' leave of absence. Most of the soldiers would be able to make brief trips home to see their loved ones and return to camp refreshed and ready to resume their duties. Grant believed this course of action would be less expensive than the cost of draining valuable medical supplies to treat men whose ailments lay beyond the reach of pills and powders.

Hopelessness ravaged men worse than loneliness. The lingering ill—men with no hope of recovery—also drew Grant's attention. For men who were in danger of dying without ever seeing their families again, Grant espoused an unprecedented course. He notified departmental headquarters in St. Louis that he intended to discharge such patients, explaining that human kindness required such action. Grant learned that compassion for the dying didn't sit well with officials in St. Louis. They quickly informed him that he had no authority to sign medical discharges. As always, Grant complied with official policy. However, throughout his campaigns in the West, he worked quietly to see that dying soldiers were reunited with their loved ones.[8]

In Simon's absence, Grant appointed John H. Brinton acting chief surgeon. In September 1861, Brinton had arrived at Cairo to serve as assistant medical director under Simon. Together, Brinton and Grant departed from tradition and remedied another deficiency in the medical community at Cairo. Brinton spent one month trying to work with untrained female nurses at the base and then dismissed them all. The media criticized him for sending away the women he

---

7. Ibid., 3:74.
8. Grant, *Papers,* 3:47, 3:51; Eleanore, *King's Highway,* 243.

referred to as the "old hags," but he remained adamant; he had already formed an alternate plan by the time he sent the charitable ladies packing.[9]

Many soldier-patients rested more comfortably due to the efforts of the three Marys (Safford, Livermore, and Bickerdyke), but a few able nurses in Cairo could not bring the hospitals up to the level of competency that would be required to care for battle casualties. Desperate for efficient nurses, Brinton and Grant turned to a system that had originated in France. After consulting with Grant, Brinton. sent to Indiana for Catholic nuns from the Sisters of Immaculate Conception and Notre Dame. Although untrained in nursing, the first group of sisters learned so quickly and worked so capably that the War Department requested subsequent groups for service at the Cairo hospitals.[10]

As with any change in established practices, the sisters met with some opposition. The freewheeling, free-drinking Dr. Burke, still working at the Bulletin, harbored jealous feelings toward Grant's medical directors. The nuns added fuel to his well-primed fire. Acting on a strong prejudice against Catholicism, Burke refused to accept the Indiana nuns. Evidence suggests, though, that Burke's resistance to Grant's management was not just rooted in bigotry. Prior to Grant's arrival the good doctor had benefited from lax hospital administration. Burke had made a practice of looking the other way as his staff stole supplies intended for patients. Even worse, he systematically removed any liquor contained in soldiers' boxes and locked that commodity in the doctors' lounge. In a move that was sure to infuriate Grant, Burke and his aide indulged in nightly drinking binges.[11]

At a time when crucial supplies were hard to come by, Burke's staff was diminishing essential commodities at the Cairo base. Burke's head nurse, a convalescent male, had tapped into the very profitable business of removing articles from the boxes of donated goods and selling them to anyone willing to pay his price. The kitchen staff followed Burke's unethical lead in routinely eating food that had been provided for the patients.[12] Grant and Brinton quickly rooted

9. Grant, *Papers*, 3:74, 2:206; Brinton, *Memoirs*, 44, 45.
10. *Report of the Western Sanitary Commission*, 3; Eleanore, *King's Highway*, 237.
11. Livermore, *My Story*, 204; Brown-Baker, *Cyclone in Calico*, 64; Brinton, *Memoirs*, 48.
12. Ibid., 64.

out the corruption and set the Bulletin to rights. With Burke protesting loudly, Brinton issued orders assigning the Catholic nurses to the Cairo hospitals, and the sisters settled in to work.

Perhaps the effects of overimbibing had clouded Burke's perception of the care offered at his hospital, since he seemed to find it acceptable. The truth surfaced, however, in descriptions left by the Indiana nuns. On entering the hospital for an initial inspection, one of the new nurses found the place in very bad condition. Sister Eleanore observed that many patients had undergone surgery but received little follow-up care. Human limbs littered the floors, and blood stains splattered the walls. Mary Livermore, who was revisiting the Cairo hospitals in the fall of 1861, recorded, "It was by no means a lovely place at the time."[13] These eyewitness reports explain the dread soldiers felt when facing the prospect of a stay in the post hospital.

In short order, the sisters started changing the image of the Bulletin. Almost as soon as they started caring for patients, they renamed the facility St. John's Hospital of Cairo. The sisters thought the name of a saint would be more appropriate for an institution that housed men who were dying for their country.[14] Peacemakers themselves, the sisters nevertheless viewed their patients as martyrs and worked diligently to bring healing and comfort to the incapacitated soldiers.

One set of problems in the district usually revealed deeper problems, occasionally in the chain of command. Grant and Brinton's new system of placing female nurses in the Cairo hospitals took several months to complete. In the interim, an incident concerning the convalescent male nurses revealed John A. McClernand's poor administrative judgment. When duty called Grant to St. Louis he left McClernand as acting commander. Hampered by the initial naiveté possessed of most regular Union generals in regard to political officers, Grant believed the Cairo post could not be in better hands during his absence.[15]

But McClernand—in a move that foreshadowed his signature behavior—seized the opportunity to exercise his authority to the detriment of the troops. Reappraising the situation in the hospitals, McClernand ordered Brinton to return all convalescing able-bodied

13. Eleanore, *King's Highway*, 237; Livermore, *My Story*, 201.
14. Eleanore, *King's Highway*, 239, 247.
15. Grant, *Papers*, 3:67.

soldiers to their regiments, regardless of the duties the men were performing in the hospitals.

Brinton feared the consequences of reactivating these men, who were giving valuable assistance to the female nurses. Short of committing mutiny, Brinton believed he had no choice but to comply with the order. Then, chafing at the prospect of losing all his nurses, Brinton saw a way out. He jumped at the chance to exploit McClernand's oversight of military protocol. McClernand had sent the order to Brinton by way of a chaplain. Realizing that chaplains only had authority in their own departments and couldn't carry out any other orders, Brinton simply disregarded McClernand's missive. In Brinton's professional opinion, to obey would have immobilized all the hospitals in Cairo. To McClernand's consternation, Grant stood fully behind Brinton's decision.[16] It was the first of many injudicious orders issued by McClernand and later remedied by Grant.

Only a few weeks after assuming command, Grant had been able to alleviate the suffering of many soldiers, petition Springfield and Washington for additional medical necessities, and resolve the problem of providing competent nurses for the hospitals. Other problems still loomed over the Cairo camps, but Grant once again showed his capacity for embracing visionary solutions. When members of civilian volunteer organizations began visiting the bases to work in conjunction with the general, Grant welcomed their contributions. Throughout the Civil War, private citizens aided military officers by taking measures to curb the spread of contagious diseases. Civilian volunteers also organized a system to collect and store medical supplies.

At the beginning of the war, people who had no choice but to stay on the home front found a way to help the Union cause. These private citizens put together care packages and sent them to military camps. After receiving many private donations in Cairo, Brinton wrote, "Women fitted up boxes containing every imaginable and unimaginable convenience and comfort for 'our boys.'"[17] Brinton appreciated having extra supplies, which he could dispense at his pleasure.

Soldiers looked forward to receiving the tempting boxes. In October 1861, William Onstat reported that the Twenty-seventh Illinois

16. Brinton, *Memoirs*, 103–4.
17. Ibid., 48.

had received a box containing hospital supplies. Patients at the regimental hospital enjoyed the contents very much. Onstat also mentioned a box of delicacies sent for his personal enjoyment, "Contents duly and fully appreciated. It reminds me that I am not neglected or forgotten by those I have left at Home."[18]

As more civilians embraced the idea of sending goods to soldiers, huge quantities of donated packages accumulated at train depots. Unfortunately, these care boxes usually contained a great many perishable items. Sitting unprotected in depots for long periods, the goodies frequently spoiled. All over the Union, freight cars and storerooms soon contained nasty, smelly messes. Seeking a remedy for the situation, Henry W. Bellows, minister to the affluent First Unitarian Church in New York City, started articulating a plan to combat the problem of valuable donations going to waste.

Bellows liked the idea of civilians cooperating with the army. On April 29, 1861, at the Cooper Union, he spoke to a group of women on that subject. Following the speech, the Women's Central Association of Relief organized with the intention of solving the problems surrounding donated supplies.[19] The WCA and Henry Bellows began working together, and that collaboration ultimately resulted in the formation of one of the most important civilian volunteer operations in American history.

After listening to reports on the overall health situation in Union army camps, Bellows and his associates decided that sanitary reforms based on the ideas of Florence Nightingale should be adopted in the United States. To implement the plan, four men—Henry Bellows, Dr. Elisha Harris, Dr. W. H. Van Buren, and Dr. Jacob Harsen—conceived the idea of a sanitary commission. The group envisioned civilians working with military medical personnel to create more efficient care in military hospitals. Once the organization appeared, important northern men held top positions. Landscape architect Frederick Law Olmstead and attorney George Templeton Strong assisted Bellows with the project.[20]

Unfortunately, the American military did not have a tradition of

18. William Onstat to Sister Lizzie, Oct. 12, 1861, William Onstat MSS.
19. Jeanie Attie, *Patriotic Toil: Northern Women and the American Civil War*, 57; William Quentin Maxwell, *Lincoln's Fifth Wheel: The Political History of the United States Sanitary Commission*, 2.
20. Judith Ann Giesberg, *Civil War Sisterhood: The U.S. Sanitary Commission and Women's Politics in Transition*, 28, 3, 48.

working with civilians and would not allow Bellows into the camps, a circumstance that threatened to thwart the entire project. Leading a nontraditional religious group had given Bellows determination and tenacity. He refused to give up. Help finally came to the men who had founded the Sanitary Commission in the form of a woman. Dorothea Dix had gotten permission from Simon Cameron to go into the military camps and hospitals. She took Bellows on some of her excursions to acquaint the minister with the needs of surgeons in the camps.[21]

During the visits to the camps, Bellows compiled information that he later presented to the army's medical director. When the military still resisted the idea of a sanitary commission, Bellows pursued another course. Armed with firsthand information concerning the conditions in the camps, Bellows met with President Lincoln. Although Lincoln had his doubts about the whole concept, Bellows persuaded him to sign an executive order authorizing the formation of the United States Sanitary Commission (USSC). The volunteer agency, based in Washington, D.C., would act as an advisory committee to the military.[22]

In the West, a comparable but entirely separate organization developed. Another Unitarian minister, the Rev. William Greenleaf Eliot, pastor of the Unitarian Church of the Messiah in St. Louis, doubted that the eastern organization would reach out to soldiers in the West. Thinking that distance and sensitivities might keep Bellows's volunteers far away from St. Louis, Eliot organized his own version, the Western Sanitary Commission.

In an audience with Eliot in August 1861, General and Mrs. Frémont embraced the idea. Frémont issued a draft of Eliot's plan as Special Order No. 159.[23] Acting quickly to aid a city already in conflict, Eliot sent a public plea on September 16, 1861, for funds and supplies to St. Louis and to Boston, his city of origin. The Western Sanitary Commission asked for contributions from St. Louis residents and "sent a few lines to the *Boston Transcript* requesting that New England women send 'knit woolen socks.'"[24] Every six months, the organization ran a similar notice.

21. Ibid., 3, 36.
22. Giesberg, *Civil War Sisterhood*, 8, 3, 6, 7.
23. Ibid., 68.
24. Eliot, "Western Sanitary Commission," 9.

Although Eliot alone conceived the idea of the western organization and proposed its formation to General Frémont, Bellows, Olmstead, and Strong believed that one of their former colleagues, Dorothea Dix, had proposed the western commission. Bellows and Dix had fallen out over her appointment as superintendent of nurses for the military. Throughout the history of the eastern organization a good deal of friction existed between men and women concerning questions of authority. Conversely, once the WSC started operations, the western commissioners viewed women as "an indispensable part of every good hospital."[25]

The USSC's animosity did not stop with Dix. Bellows's quarrel with the influential nurse led top officers of the eastern organization into an enmity with Eliot. Bellows, demonstrating total disregard for the principles of his faith, viewed the western commission as an affront to his own organization. So incensed was he at the perceived competition, he protested its existence to Lincoln.[26] Though Lincoln and Frémont had their differences, in this instance Lincoln deferred to the Pathfinder. After hearing Bellows's grievance, the president, always vigilant in regard to the West, stood firmly behind Frémont. Eliot and the WSC remained an independent entity under the authority of the army's medical director.

Two separate organizations addressing the same national problem might seem redundant, but William Greenleaf Eliot saw a need for a distinct sanitary society in the West. In the early months of the war, sanitary commissioners in the East struggled mainly with the issue of transporting supplies. But in the West, commissioners were already facing the task of assisting in the care of battle casualties; some of the first armed combat occurred in Missouri.[27] In addition, the problems associated with shipping supplies to the western camps from Washington precluded efficient distribution of necessary medical items.

Eliot sincerely believed that westerners could minister more efficiently to the medical and spiritual needs of soldiers in that theater, but he had another reason for creating his organization.[28] In St.

25. Ibid., 7.
26. Giesberg, *Civil War Sisterhood,* 48, 105.
27. Maxwell, *Lincoln's Fifth Wheel,* 7.
28. Earl K. Holt and William A. Deiss, *William Greenleaf Eliot: Conservative Radical,* 67.

Louis—a large metropolis located in a slave state—volunteers wishing to aid the Union had to tread carefully. Unionists still faced ferocious hostility from the many secessionists living in the city. Undoubtedly Grant agreed with Eliot's arguments concerning inefficient transport of supplies, and it is entirely likely that he concurred with Eliot on his other argument. As for Grant, having spent many years living in St. Louis, he could understand that a different situation in the West required a rather different sanitary organization. People familiar with settlements along the Mississippi River corridor between St. Louis and Cairo knew that if civilians from New York had come into St. Louis to care for Union casualties, Rebel sympathizers might have prevented them from functioning.

At first, both commissions worked to get whatever supplies the soldiers needed. The United States Sanitary Commission established ten subdepots around the country. These depots aided in the efficient movement of supplies. Chicago served as one of the hubs. A system developed whereby people donated goods, which volunteers then packaged and sent to either Louisville or Washington, D.C. From those main points, the USSC sent the goods to the designated regional depot.[29]

The Western Sanitary Commission operated mainly in St. Louis, where the volunteers outfitted fifteen general and post hospitals. When Brinton arrived at Cairo, soldiers battling illnesses were already being transferred to St. Louis due to the shortage of medical facilities at the southern Illinois base.[30] As the war escalated into bloody battles, the Western Sanitary Commission (WSC) followed Grant's troops wherever they were fighting in the field. Always looking for greater efficiency, Grant worked closely with the WSC to improve medical care for his troops throughout his western campaigns.

The presence of the regional commission in the West paved the way for acceptance of the national organization. Once workers for the USSC got into army camps, they realized the pressing need for better hygiene, as well as for competent medical personnel. The commissioners began writing guidelines for the implementation of proper sanitation in hospitals and camps, a subject little contemplated up to that time. Sanitary agents visited army camps regularly

29. Ibid., 154; Livermore, *My Story*, 134.
30. Brinton, *Memoirs*, 38.

to inspect the state of medical care and general sanitation and make recommendations if needed. The commission also dispatched trained nurses to military hospitals.[31]

One week after the formation of the USSC, the president of the organization visited Cairo. A report of the commission for October 1861 listed one "Post" (general) hospital in Cairo that held 90 patients. Inspectors found a total of 231 patients in the five regimental hospitals that existed in the town.[32]

Representatives from the USSC filed a negative report concerning Cairo's general sanitation. The commissioners noted that medical facilities, including an adequate medical staff, had existed at the base for several months, but sanitation still lagged.[33] The report covered the Eighth Illinois, Eighteenth Illinois, Twenty-ninth Illinois, Thirtieth Illinois, and Thirty-first Illinois regiments.

Addressing problems cited in the report, Grant ordered that a block of buildings in Mound City be used as a hospital for the Union military. Implementing a practice he had developed while marching the Twenty-first through Missouri, Grant targeted property owned by secessionists for the use of the Federal army. He calculated both a rental and a sale price and required the disloyal residents of Mound City to accept one or the other. After negotiations, the Union army rented the buildings, which became the Mound City general hospital.[34]

Shortly after arriving at Cairo, Dr. Brinton visited the Mound City hospital. At the time, the general hospital at that outpost could comfortably house between eight hundred and one thousand patients in a building three hundred feet wide and one hundred feet deep. By the time the Sisters of the Holy Cross began to work at Mound City, the general hospital consisted of twenty-four unfinished warehouses. Brinton had organized the buildings into twenty-six wards, using the letters of the alphabet as names.[35]

Mary Livermore assessed the Mound City general hospital as a well-run facility located in a block of brick buildings. Mother M. Angela of the order of the Sisters of the Holy Cross cited one service

31. Livermore, *My Story*, 131.
32. *Report of the United States Sanitary Commission* (Chicago Branch) Oct. 1861, no. 38, 38, 4.
33. Ibid.
34. Grant, *Papers*, 3:81; n. 82.
35. Brinton, *Memoirs*, 40, 55; Eleanore, *King's Highway*, 247.

that set the Mound City hospital apart from the rest. Mother Angela had installed a hospital kitchen that cooked special food for the patients so the indisposed men would not have to eat the greasy, unpalatable fare cooked in the mess. Serving healthy food to patients did much to aid their recovery. Contemplating the innovations implemented by the sisters, Mary Livermore stated that army medical officials considered the Mound City hospital to be one of the best military hospitals in the United States.[36]

On their first visit to Cairo, the sanitary commissioners concerned themselves with more than the general hospital. Mary Livermore guided them on an inspection of the regimentals. Time and additional surgeons had not improved the facilities. The commissioners found the regimentals still in a squalid state; crowded, dirty, and poorly supplied, even though the staff had access to supplies. Unlike the Bulletin, the regimentals commonly coped with poor lighting and inadequate ventilation. The commissioners found that these small hospitals lacked a supply of patient clothing and could not provide enough stoves to maintain patient comfort. Mary Livermore noted that no sign of a surgeon could be seen.[37]

Soldiers' letters support the image projected in the commissioners' report. Pvt. William Onstat, in a letter to his sister, discussed the regimental hospital of the Twenty-seventh. Stating that this facility needed many things, he described his stay there. He had eaten with his fingers because the staff could not even offer him a spoon. He had lain on the floor during the entire length of his stay since the hospital lacked sufficient cots. Patients did not enjoy the comfort of pillows and sheets; the hospital had none.[38]

Though the commissioners recorded very bad conditions at all of the regimentals in the district, John A. Logan's Thirty-first earned the dubious distinction of keeping the most unsanitary regimental hospital in Cairo. Logan had set up a medical establishment in one of the small hotels on the waterfront. Patients lay sick upon piles of straw thrown on the floor in crowded, filthy rooms. A "fetid odor" permeated the wards.[39] Again, a shortage of clean hospital clothing left patients in a dangerously unsanitary condition.[40] Logan's men

36. Ibid., 250; Livermore, *My Story*, 217.
37. USSC Report; Livermore, *My Story*, 203.
38. William H. Onstat to Sister Lizzie, Nov. 16, 1861, William H. Onstat MSS.
39. USSC Report, 4–5.
40. Ibid.

remained in their everyday clothes during their hospital stay, using their overcoats for pillows. Sanitary commissioners commented that the surgeons they did find in the facility appeared to be either ill-informed or grossly inefficient, while the officers showed indifference to the condition of the men.

At the time of the visit, five hundred soldiers in the Thirty-first had succumbed to the measles within days of each other.[41] The regimental hospital housed two hundred of these men. Joseph Skipworth, Logan's groom, reported to his wife, "James Arnold is in the hospital sick with the measles."[42] Two other friends had also suffered through the disease. Michael Stone was recuperating, and David Meyers had recovered sufficiently that he was able to walk to Skipworth's quarters for a visit. Skipworth informed his family that many men in the Thirty-first were still struggling to regain their health.

Displaying the valor that came to characterize Logan's men, Skipworth, undaunted by the specter of life-threatening illness, predicted that he and his comrades would be soldiers for life unless "the Secesh [sic] lay down their arms and return to the Union."[43] This sentiment, commonly expressed by soldiers in the West during the first months of the war, contradicts Barbara J. Fields's conclusion that preservation of the Union was too shallow a goal to be worth the sacrifice of a single life; therefore, the federal government had to add the objective of emancipation.[44] Primary sources reveal that, from the beginning of the conflict, soldiers in the western theater appeared quite willing to give their lives for the reunification of their country.

Concerning the measles epidemic in her husband's regiment, Mary Logan left a colorful account. When measles broke out in the Thirty-first, a dearth of supplies hindered efforts to care for Logan's ailing men. According to Mary's reminiscences, she and John could not procure the needed items at the commissary, and they decided that Mary would travel to Carbondale and Marion to gather supplies. Mary ended her story on a happy note, stating that friends and relatives of soldiers in the regiment donated everything Logan needed for the hospital: pillows, bed linens, jellies, marmalades,

41. Logan, *Reminiscences of a Soldier's Wife*, 109.
42. Joseph Skipworth MSS, Oct. 18, 1861.
43. Ibid.
44. McPherson, *Writing the Civil War*, 11.

fruits, and even wine.[45] Mary wrote that the homemade blankets, woven in brightly colored Roman stripes, gave rise to a nickname for Logan's hospital. The blankets that warmed many of the ailing soldiers attracted so much attention that people started referring to the regimental hospital as the Striped Hospital of the Thirty-first.

There may have been some grain of truth to Mary's tale, but official reports kept by the United States Sanitary Commission tell a different story. Encountering the deplorable condition of Logan's hospital, the sanitary representatives puzzled over the fact that this particular regiment should be in such an unsatisfactory state since it was encamped in its own region. Unlike the soldiers of several regiments at the Cairo camps, these men had resided in nearby communities. The officers' failure to collect supplies locally from relatives and friends confounded the commissioners.[46]

Combating hundreds of measles cases kept the entire medical establishment at the Cairo bases working around the clock. Smallpox posed an even greater challenge.[47] Periodically, several soldiers contracted the disease. In the fall of 1861, John Reese first told his wife, "all of the Boys from our Neighborhood are well."[48] But one month later he wrote to say, "We have several that are very sick. I think Lathrop is dying."[49]

Grant and his medical personnel could do little to alleviate the problem of contagious disease in the camps. To his credit, however, Grant recognized the value of the sanitary commissions and gave them wide latitude in remedying the terrible sanitation and supply shortages that had existed in the Cairo hospitals at the time he took command. By cleaning up the camps, the commissions did more than any other branch of the medical community to arrest the spread of these diseases.

By the time Grant left Cairo, the threat of smallpox had lessened somewhat. In April 1862, George S. Durfee wrote his uncle from Pittsburgh Landing, "One of our boys was taken with the smallpox yesterday. He was Clay's bedfellow, the boys don't pay any attention to it no more than if it was the measles."[50] Durfee explained why

45. Logan, *Reminiscences of the Civil War,* 48, 49, 51, 112.
46. USSC Report, 38, 4–5.
47. Edwin Loosley MSS, Sept. 18, 1862.
48. John Reese to Tissa Reese, Sept. 28, 1861, Sept. 10, 1862, John Reese MSS.
49. Ibid., Oct. 7, 1862.
50. George S. Durfee to H. B. Durfee, Apr. 26, 1862, George S. Durfee MSS.

the soldiers greeted the appearance of the deadly disease so nonchalantly: "The boys have been vaccinated as a general thing."[51]

Pursuing their 1861 inspection of the District of Southeast Missouri, the sanitary commissioners moved on. The outlying military hospitals impressed the commission inspectors more favorably than those in Cairo. Following their visit to Mound City, commissioners found five regimentals in Bird's Point run by the Eighth Illinois, the Eleventh Illinois, the Twenty-second Illinois, the Twenty-eighth Illinois, and the Seventh Iowa. The hospitals housed a total of 133 patients. The medical staffs at Mound City and Bird's Point kept their facilities in good sanitary condition.[52]

The entire post at Fort Holt impressed inspectors as a model operation. An excellent medical staff ran the hospitals. Dr. Brinton had organized the Army Medical and Surgical Society of Cairo in November 1861, when he was still working at the Cairo base. The society met weekly to discuss professional and official duties. Brinton started the organization at Cairo and then took it with him to Mound City and Paducah.[53]

The general hospital at Paducah could accommodate ninety-three patients. Eight regimental hospitals operated at Fort Holt in Paducah. The Seventh Illinois, the Ninth Illinois, the Twelfth Illinois, the Fortieth Illinois, the Forty-first Illinois, the Chicago Light Artillery, the Eighth Missouri, the Eleventh Indiana, and the Twenty-third Indiana ran these facilities. The hospitals housed 220 patients. Cairo, Paducah, Mound City, and Bird's Point received supplies from commission depots at Chicago and Cleveland.[54]

Eventually, the Chicago depot located a subdepot in Cairo as the need for hospital supplies at that base steadily increased. Not completely confined to St. Louis, the Western Sanitary Commission adapted to the needs of Grant's army as the soldiers hit the campaign trail. As soon as the WSC members got into the field, they introduced more satisfactory bathing methods and set up special diet kitchens. They gave instructions on appropriate beds and bedding for ailing men. Between the two commissions, a number of innovations in field medicine emerged. Eliot's own statement credited the Western Sanitary Commission, working alongside Grant, with fitting

51. Ibid.
52. USSC Report, 38, 4–5.
53. Ibid., 6–7; Brinton, *Memoirs*, 98.
54. USSC Report, 38, 4–5.

out almost all of the hospital steamers and supplying them during the first year of the war. Transporting patients by boat worked better in the West than moving them by wagon or train. The area had few satisfactory roads and many waterways.[55]

A French army surgeon, Dominique-Jean Larrey, had proven that transporting the wounded from the battlefield for further care preserved manpower. In mid-nineteenth-century America, the high value a democratic society placed on human life dictated follow-up care. In that same time period, the western commission directed all of the medical work on the western rivers. Eliot's organization supplied the gunboat flotilla on the Mississippi and kept stores of hospital supplies at every important point.[56] Naval transports and gunboats took fighting men from Cairo to southern battlefields. Hospital boats brought casualties back to Cairo for treatment and transfer.

Innovations made during the Civil War revolutionized medical technology in the nineteenth century. In the field of battle, the standards of medical care improved as the War Department and the sanitary commissions recruited trained staff and applied inventive solutions to the medical crisis. In Cairo, hospitals and medical personnel became crucial as Grant's army prepared to fight its way through the Mississippi Valley.

---

55. USSC Report, 154, 153; Livermore, *My Story*, 204; *Report of the Western Sanitary Commission*, 8; Duncan, *Medical Department*, 98.

56. Haller, *Farmcarts to Fords*, 13; Eliot, "Western Sanitary Commission," 6.

Grant in the field (portrait by Nast).

Placing the heavy ordnance in position at Cairo, Illinois.

Ohio levee at Cairo. Note the St. Charles Hotel on the left.

In Battery Company A, Chicago Light Artillery, Camp Smith, June 1861.

Occupation of Cairo, Illinois, by Federal troops, April 1861.

Graham-Halliday wharfboat on the left.

Demolition of the old distillery at Cairo, Illinois, to make room for Fort Defiance.

The confluence at Cairo: (left to right) Bird's Point, Cairo, Fort Holt.

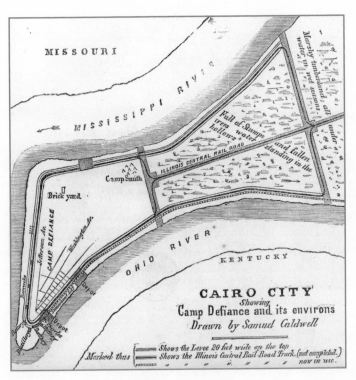

Map of Cairo area.

Eight

Night and Day and Sunday

The Navy

In the fall of 1861, Cairo seemed to be on everybody's mind. The town even came up in discussions at the White House. Lincoln had quickly realized the need for the army to secure the spot, and then–Attorney-General Edward Bates thought Cairo might serve very well as home to another branch of the military. In response to the Fort Sumter attack, the federal government had first devoted its attention to organizing the army. With that operation well under way, the War Department began studying possibilities for expanding naval power.

Hoping to gain momentum for his plan, Bates summoned engineer James B. Eads of St. Louis to Washington. Eads had also been thinking about Cairo. A loyal Missourian, Eads had forwarded a plan for a proposed blockade of the Mississippi River to Gideon Welles. The plan included a recommendation that a protected naval base be established at Cairo. Eads envisioned naval batteries mounted on the shore at the Mississippi/Ohio confluence. Eads further thought that if Kentucky remained in the Union, the Rebels' access to railroad depots at Louisville, Nashville, and Chattanooga could easily be barred.[1]

Impressed with the plan, Simon Cameron passed an account of it on to General McClellan. Cameron informed the general that the government in Washington liked the plan but wanted to consult him

---

1. Charles Brandon Boynton, *The History of the Navy during the Rebellion,* 498; 41; OR Navies, Simon Cameron to Gideon Welles, May 14, 1861, I:22, 277–78.

before making a decision. After the cabinet members and McClellan had perused the proposal, Gideon Welles ordered John Rodgers to go to McClellan's headquarters and get instructions for organizing a naval base at Cairo.[2]

Cameron promptly considered using iron-plated frigates in the East, but he showed little interest in fitting out gunboats for the western rivers. As usual, men in the West took the initiative and brought the government's attention to their concerns. Westerners had begun assessing their topography as soon as rebellion loomed large, and Eads, in particular, had concluded that in order for the navy to support the movements of the army, the western theater must be supplied with ironclad boats.[3] Once government officials and army generals conceded the need for combined operations between army and navy, support grew for Eads's plan.

Naval officers realized that existing riverboats, built for freight and passage, could not withstand Rebel artillery. Once the War Department decided to use ironclads in the West, a domino effect led to their appearance. Welles needed a design for boats that could operate on the interior rivers. He assigned Rodgers the responsibility of finding boats that might be adapted for defensive use on the Mississippi River. While Rodgers searched for boats to adapt, Eads gave Rodgers the idea for building special boats.[4]

The history of the woodclad steamers that Rodgers procured for adaptation to gunboats, the *A. O. Tyler, Lexington,* and *Conestoga,* is well documented. By June, Rodgers had reported to Welles that the little fleet was fitting out. The finished wooden flotilla would consist of three fortified vessels carrying sixteen cannon and sixteen gun carriages complete with gear, gunpowder, shot, shells, small arms, swords, pistols, and 198 seamen.[5]

Finding men from the West to serve as seamen in the Western Flotilla proved to be much more difficult than securing the vessels. Rodgers hoped to find western sailors who would already be familiar with the particular intricacies of navigating the muddy waters of the Mississippi River. Although problems in manning the western

2. OR Navies, Series I:22, 280; Gideon Welles to John Rodgers, May 16, 1861 I:22.
3. Boynton, *History of the Navy,* 500, 491.
4. Boynton, *History of the Navy,* 498; OR Navies, Gideon Welles to John Rodgers, May 16, 1861; I:22, 280.
5. Ibid., Series I:22, 283. John Rodgers to Gideon Welles, June 8, 1861.

navy persisted for many months, Rodgers continued working hard to bring the navy in the West up to speed. In July the overdue vessels started sailing downriver toward Cairo. They arrived two weeks behind schedule on August 12, 1861.[6]

On the arrival of the fortified wooden steamers at Cairo, the commander of the Department of the West voiced his concern about the fleet. From his headquarters in St. Louis, Frémont communicated first-hand information to President Lincoln regarding the enemy's gunboats. Ever instructing the president, Frémont pointed out that the Confederates had covered their boats with sheet iron and equipped them with cannon. The Rebel vessels appeared to be lighter and swifter than the three boats Rodgers had sent to Cairo. The fact that the Confederate gunboat officers were all veterans of the United States Navy while the Union's officers were inexperienced seamen rankled most of all. Frémont concluded that the fleet at Cairo needed heavy artillery immediately.[7]

Amply apprised of the situation in the West, the War Department had already opened bids to build ironclad gunboats for the western rivers. The War Department found a good man in Eads. The Missourian had worked with boats prior to the outbreak of the war and understood navigation on the western rivers. Predicting that ironclads would be needed in the West, Eads presented a design to the government and gained a contract to construct seven of the boats. Eads set up shop in Missouri, and, even though secessionist feelings still ran high in the area, many of the large machine shops and foundries in St. Louis contracted to work on the Union gunboats.[8]

Finding it necessary to establish an additional construction site, the federal government opened a naval yard at a site close to Cairo. Men at Mound City, Illinois, worked on three of the first seven ironclads while builders at the St. Louis suburb of Carondelet worked steadily to construct the other four.[9] Eads's design promised to produce vessels that could stand up to the Rebels' war craft.

By August, the War Department had made good progress getting the western gunboats in place but still had not appointed a com-

6. Ibid; Boynton, *History of the Navy*, 500–501; OR Navies, S. Ledyard Phelps to John Rodgers, Aug. 16, 1861, I:22, 299.

7. Joint Committee, 3: 121.

8. Boynton, *History of the Navy*, 502.

9. *Harpers's Weekly*, Oct. 5, 1861; Anderson, *By Sea*, 87.

mander for the fleet. Hoping to remedy the situation, Welles wrote Andrew Hull Foote, "Sir: You have been selected to take command of the naval operations upon the Western waters, now organizing under the direction of the War Department."[10] Welles finished the communication by stating that the western movement was of the greatest importance. Mystifyingly, Welles overlooked the hardworking Rodgers and instructed Foote to proceed to St. Louis, where he should report to Frémont.

On his arrival at Cairo in September, Foote learned that his fleet at Mound City currently consisted of the three woodclad gunboats, nine ironclad gunboats, and thirty-eight mortars still under construction. Foote wasted no time checking on the finished vessels. He sailed the *Lexington* to Mound City and, after conducting an inspection, found the three woodclads entirely satisfactory.[11]

When the ironclads had neared completion, Foote instructed one of his subordinates, "You will inform Mr. Hamilton, the superintendent of the construction of the gunboats now building at Mound City, Ill., that the following will be the names of the gunboats as they are launched, respectively: *Mound City, Cincinnati, Cairo*."[12] Capt. A. M. Pennock commanded operations at the Mound City naval yard, I. P. Sanford and O. H. Perry assisted him, and Capt. George D. Wise served as quartermaster. Romeo Friganza took the position of naval constructor.[13]

In October, the steamer *Conestoga* stood guard over the new gunboats at Mound City. Writing from Camp Cairo, William H. Onstat observed that most of the Union gunboats built in St. Louis had arrived at Mound City.[14] Concerning the fitting out of the gunboats, Foote cautioned his subordinate officers at Cairo, "When the guns arrive, you will be careful to have them placed in the boat and guarded, as already we find that evil-minded persons have made attempts to render them useless."[15]

10. OR Navies, Gideon Welles to Andrew Hull Foote, Aug. 30, 1861, I:22, 307.

11. Anderson, *By Sea*, 42; OR Navies, Andrew Hull Foote to Gideon Welles, Nov. 13, 1861, Oct. 9, 1861, I:22, 314.

12. Ibid., Andrew Hull Foote to Roger Perry, Oct. 29, 1861, 386–87, I:22.

13. David D. Porter, *The Naval History of the Civil War*, 135.

14. OR Navies, Andrew Hull Foote to Porter, Oct. 23, 1861, I:22, 377; William Onstat to Sister Lizzie, Dec. 6, 1861, William H. Onstat MSS.

15. OR Navies, Perry to Foote, Oct. 5, 1861, I:22.

As more and more vessels sailed out of the shipyard at Mound City and joined the western fleet, naval officers worked out a standard strategy for Union ships in times of nonengagement. Henry Walke, commanding the *Tyler,* and Roger N. Stembel, commanding the *Lexington,* patrolled the Mississippi River below Cairo, keeping an eye on the Rebel escalation at Columbus, Kentucky. The patrols frequently paid off. In one instance, Stembel, acting on an intelligence report, followed a Confederate steamer to the Ohio River and seized it at Paducah. In accordance with orders from the War Department, the Mississippi Flotilla made a priority of capturing or destroying every vessel that might be of use to the Confederacy or might be carrying munitions and supplies to Rebels in the South.[16] Naval officers turned the prize ships over to the army for adaptation or destruction. The practice of confiscating Confederate vessels made gaining control of the Cairo post a primary objective for the Rebels.

During the first two years of the war, Admiral Foote and General Grant wrote the War Department regularly, emphasizing the need to keep at least two gunboats anchored offshore at Cairo. This correspondence proved to be one of the few areas in which the two officers cooperated harmoniously during their early days at Cairo. Although some historians have concluded that Grant and Foote got along almost perfectly from the very beginning of their acquaintance, the two commanders actually experienced a bit of a rocky start.[17]

Having arrived in Cairo a few days before Foote, Grant immediately encountered problems with the naval officers at the site. Initially, Welles had decided that the navy in the western theater could operate most efficiently by placing the naval officers under the authority of the army, a command system that gave Grant supreme command of all forces at Cairo. Not until authority for the fleet passed to the navy in October 1862, did the Mississippi Flotilla become the Mississippi Squadron.[18]

Storage caused a conflict that illustrated the power struggle between army and navy. Throughout the war, part of Cairo's importance stemmed from the base's designation as a supply station. However, finding a practical means of storing the huge amounts of supplies that came into the post on a continuing basis proved prob-

16. Anderson, *By Sea*, 42.
17. Catton, *Grant Moves South*, 82.
18. Anderson, *By Sea*, 41; Milligan, *Gunboats*, xxv.

lematic. After wrangling with the navy over storage space for almost two months, Grant finally commandeered a big wharfboat that had a storage capacity of twenty-five hundred tons.[19] Unfortunately, Foote had earmarked the very same facility for use by the navy. Either unaware of, or unimpressed by, the navy's prior claim, Grant instructed Gen. Eleazer A. Paine to "Take possession of the wharf boats [sic] at the landing and make use of them for store houses."[20]

In early October, Foote instructed Roger Perry to take charge of ordnance, equipment, and supplies for the gunboat flotilla. Foote assured Perry, "You will have for this purpose, on application to General Grant, such a portion of the *Graham* wharf boat, lying at Cairo, as may be necessary."[21] By this time, however, the *Graham* already housed the army's commissary department. Had Foote been reading the newspaper, he might have noticed an article in the *Chicago Daily Tribune* that reported, "Graham, Halliday & Co.'s splendid wharfboat was to-day [sic] dropped to the levee landing, and occupied by Government for storage purposes."[22]

In the escalating crisis of the *Graham*, Grant persisted in his disinclination to accommodate Foote. Aside from the genuine problem of storage space, a personal friendship lay behind Grant's choice of that particular boat. N. W. Graham and William Parker Halliday had signed a contract with Grant for the army's use of the boat. The contract compensated the two Cairo businessmen one thousand dollars per month and showed no date of expiration. Only the Graham-Halliday wharfboat commanded this price at Cairo. It had been issued with the understanding that the army would pay the specified rate as long as the government used the boat. Grant justified the terms of the contract with the explanation that he anticipated using the boat for supply storage in the event that the army should move south from Cairo.[23] There may have been sound logic in the explanation, but Grant's decision to award such a high rate to that particular boat also emanated from his developing friendship with local entrepreneur George Washington Graham. Wash Graham bore a familial relationship to the boat's co-owner, N. W. Graham.

19. James Merrill, "Cairo: Civil War Port," 76: 242–54, 254; Catton, *Grant Moves South*, 54.
20. Grant, *Papers*, 2:199.
21. OR Navies I:22, 360. Andrew Hull Foote to Roger Perry, Oct. 5, 1861.
22. *Chicago Daily Tribune*, Oct. 8, 1861.
23. Joint Committee, 3:5.

Undeterred by the contract, Grant's personal associations, or even Grant's superiority over him, Foote decided to press the issue. He instructed Perry, "Say to General Grant . . . I hope that he will let us have the wharf boat *Graham,* as the commissary can be accommodated on shore better than we can be."[24] Matching Foote's determination with his own, Grant pulled rank and refused to yield his chosen facility. Perry replied to Foote, "General Grant states that he has all available storage and store occupied. [To] give us the wharf boat would oblige him to place all commissary stores on the wharf, unprotected from the weather."[25]

Finally, Foote decided to go over Grant's head. He referred the matter to Frémont. Foote stressed to the department commander that the navy must have its stores afloat. The steamer *Montgomery,* which Grant had selected for use as naval storage, Foote considered unsafe for that purpose.[26] After much wrangling, Grant grudgingly agreed to share the space, but by the end of October, Foote had finally conceded to Grant's original plan. In his capitulation letter, Foote explained to his department commander in St. Louis, "the commissary department has appropriated most of this boat to its use, and so much feeling has been manifested at our claiming it that I have relinquished our half of the boat."[27] Eventually, Foote learned to accept Grant's authority as senior officer, though he continued to chafe under it occasionally, and the two men learned to work well together.

The *Graham* incident holds some significance in demonstrating Grant's decisive exercise of authority as a commander. But more importantly, the situation is indicative of the jealousy that existed between the two branches of the military. A great deal of sensitivity existed between the army and the navy concerning boats on the western rivers.[28] The tussle over the *Graham* also demonstrates the difficulty experienced by northern generals early in the Civil War when trying to judge people from more southern societies.

The Western Flotilla included not only gunboats, but also chartered boats that transported supplies and men when the western troops traveled to battle sites. With the creation of the Western

---

24. OR Navies, Andrew Hull Foote to Roger Perry, Oct. 17, 1861, I:22, 370.
25. Ibid., Roger Perry to Andrew Hull Foote, Oct. 17, 1861, I:22, 370.
26. Ibid., Oct. 18, 1861, 370.
27. Ibid., Andrew Hull Foote to John C. Frémont, Oct. 31, 1861.
28. Ibid., Gideon Welles to John Rodgers, June 12, 1861, 284–85.

Flotilla, additional staff had arrived in Cairo for the purpose of purchasing supplies for the navy. Ample funds accompanied the naval supply officers. Competition for contracts to furnish these supplies gave rise to much speculation on the part of local men.

Wash Graham, one of the men vying for contracts, managed to strike up a warm friendship with Grant through other Cairo men. According to local sources, aside from the general's handpicked staff, Graham, nicknamed Wash, became the most influential man who served Grant at Cairo. In his position as a post sutler, Wash Graham necessarily enjoyed close contact with the district commander. Already comfortable from business enterprises in Cairo, Wash Graham supposedly spent a lot of money on Grant. Local historians concluded that the flattery and money Graham lavished on Grant accounted for Graham's high standing at headquarters.

Actually, Grant did not succumb so easily to sycophants. Quartermaster Hatch—a corrupt individual—had hired Graham after Grant instructed him to find a good seaman to take charge of all the Union boats.[29] Grant developed a friendship with the affable Graham during his first weeks at Cairo, when he was feeling his way in the treacherous local society. Some of the men in town viewed the Union general with suspicion, but Graham socialized with him easily and was soon smoothing Grant's interactions with the more subversive citizens of Cairo. The fine things Graham's money could buy may have held some charm for Grant, but more than anything, Grant valued Graham as a buffer against Cairo's unpredictable citizenry.

Grant's devotion to his official staff, particularly his personal assistant, John Rawlins, could not have been lightly displaced by little-known local men. Once he had assumed the position of commander, Grant tried to refrain from viewing the residents of Cairo as a subjugated people. Assisting Grant's assimilation, Graham drew him into the easy camaraderie of the local elite who frequented Bill Schuter's restaurant, allowing him to freely interact with the leading inhabitants of the town.[30] Realizing the importance of appearing friendly, Grant graciously accepted the hospitality of the locals.

Two of the men fraternizing with Grant through Wash Graham were William Parker Halliday and Charles Galigher. When Grant

29. Grant, *Papers*, 2:278.
30. Bradsby, *History of Cairo*, 60.

commandeered Halliday's wharfboat for the use of the Union Commissary Department, Halliday signed up to work as a commissary agent. Halliday's work with the commissary enabled him to forge a friendship with Grant that lasted a lifetime. Galigher, owner of flour mills at Cairo and Olive Branch, successfully negotiated contracts to supply the Union army. A loyal Union man with associations to the Democratic Party, the quiet, solitary Galigher found much to like in Grant. The friendship that sprang up between the two men over suppers at Schuter's lasted well beyond the war.[31]

The navy's practice of employing private citizens enabled some of these men, such as William Halliday, to socialize with Grant in Cairo and follow him into battle without actually enlisting. Ultimately, Wash Graham—who had enlisted—accompanied Grant on expeditions, serving as a member of the headquarters mess on Grant's boat.

It is perhaps ironic that Grant, an ardent opponent of secession and profiteering, was surrounded at his first district command with men of questionable loyalty and marked inclinations toward speculation. It seems likely that Grant discerned more about these people than anyone around him realized at the time. Undoubtedly, the company gave Grant both pleasure and information. Over time, experience taught northern officers the art of accurately assessing people they encountered in the South.

A month after the storage crisis, Foote reported to Welles that he had received applications for gunboats to cruise the Ohio River between Evansville and Cincinnati. Even though Foote stated, "I am using every means, working night and day and Sundays, to get our boats down to Cairo," there were only three available boats at the base.[32] According to Foote, Grant considered those boats essential for the protection of Cairo: "In fact, the general at Cairo says that he will keep them if the whole Navy direct them to move."[33]

Foote made no exaggeration concerning the difficulty of pulling together the Mississippi Fleet. The mere fact that he found it necessary to work on Sunday—a violation of his strong religious practices—attested to the immediacy of the work. On October 12, 1861, the Carondelet shipyard launched the first true ironclad in the West.

---

31. *Attractions of Cairo.*
32. OR Navies, Andrew Hull Foote to General M. C. Meigs, Nov. 1861, I:8.
33. Ibid., Andrew Hull Foote to Gideon Welles, Nov. 13, 1861, I:22, 393.

Christened the *St. Louis* by Foote, the boat preceded by ten days the *Carondelet, Cincinnati, Louisville, Mound City, Cairo,* and *Pittsburgh.*[34] The long-awaited vessels performed admirably in what the Joint Committee on the Conduct of the War later termed "our brilliant victories in the west."[35]

As the war progressed, Cairo stood out as the most important river port for western operations during the Civil War. Not only did the base supply and repair the fleet that participated in Grant's initial campaigns, but it also seasoned the western commanders. Those officers learned to make better decisions about organizing supply and ordnance for their gunboats than did the officers of the Confederacy.[36]

Ulysses S. Grant was one of the officers refined by his authority over both army and navy at Cairo. In the first weeks of the war, a time when the War Department had been struggling to frame an overall strategy, Grant himself had thought of the navy vessels only in terms of their potential as support for the army.[37] After leading his first engagement out of Cairo, Grant came to appreciate the gunboats as an intrinsically powerful offensive force. As a result, he developed a new vision that encompassed land and water forces working together.

34. Boynton, *History of the Navy*, 503.
35. Joint Committee, 3:6.
36. Merrill, *Port*, 254, 256.
37. Joseph Glatthaar, *Partners in Command: The Relationships Between Leaders in the Civil War*, 179.

Nine

A Brave Set of Men

In the first week of November 1861, the streets of Cairo fairly pulsed with people as soldiers' relatives and friends sought news of their men, gone to war with General Grant. Along the levees, people kept a quiet vigil, scanning the Mississippi River for some sign of the transports that would be carrying Union soldiers back from the battle that was raging in Belmont, Missouri.

The town of Belmont had worried Union officials since the first soldiers arrived in Cairo. After watching the Confederates' activities for a month, General Frémont ordered a force to occupy the site on August 28, 1861. Col. G. Waagner reported to General Frémont in St. Louis that, following orders, he had taken the steamer *Graham*, loaded with the Twelfth Illinois Regiment from Cairo, and headed toward Belmont at 5:00 in the morning. Waagner intended to destroy Rebel fortifications at that location.[1]

Before Waagner could complete his mission, Grant arrived in Cairo and learned that Polk had entrenched his Confederates in Columbus, Kentucky, just across the river. Following close on the heels of the message from Waagner, Frémont received Grant's first communication from his Cairo headquarters: "On the advice of Commander Rodgers I have ordered the withdrawal of troops from Belmont."[2]

---

1. OR Navies, Col. G. Waagner to John C. Fremont, Sept. 2, 1861, I:22, 311.
2. Ibid., Grant to Fremont, Sept. 4, 1861.

Grant decided to back off from Belmont until he could accurately assess the strength of the Rebels on the Missouri side of the river. By September 12, believing that gunboats and an army force moving in conjunction against Belmont would force the Rebels to evacuate Columbus, Grant had submitted a plan to Frémont for such a campaign.[3] He received no answer.

Throughout October, the area around Belmont remained lively. Regular reports of skirmishes between Union gunboats and Rebels at Columbus reached both Grant and Frémont.[4] The navy was keeping an eye on the situation, too. Allowing a little of his frustration with the chain of command to leak through, Foote wrote the commander of the gunboat *New Era* that he would gladly take the three gunboats himself, along with a military force, and go downriver to Columbus. Lacking the authority to do it, he lamented, "as it is, we must wait the action of the military."[5]

All of the commanders in the Department of the West looked covetously at Columbus. Most of them understood the problems involved in taking the Rebel fortress. Grant knew that the Confederate troops encamped near Cairo greatly outnumbered his forces. Still, he longed for a chance to face the enemy.[6] In his first few weeks at Cairo, however, he realized that the many troops in his command—divided among various posts—must remain scattered to keep the Rebels out of Union territory. Short of gathering those troops into one fighting unit, Grant could not contemplate a confrontation with Polk's force at Columbus.

Almost within hearing distance of enemy guns, Grant and his soldiers yearned for a fight, while in the East, a dearth of movement spurred Lincoln to start tutoring himself on military strategy.[7] Cooler fall weather seemed to heat up Rebel activity at Columbus, and the Confederates began seriously harassing Union troops at Bird's Point. Just when Grant was developing a deep concern over his men at that post, Lincoln felt confident enough to order that a simultaneous east/west movement be made on November 7.

---

3. Grant, *Papers*, 2:242.
4. OR Navies, Waagner to Grant, Sept. 8, 1861, I:22; Foote to Gideon Welles, Oct. 9, 1861, 360.
5. Ibid., Foote to Porter, Oct. 23, 1861, I:22, 378.
6. Grant, *Papers*, 3:63.
7. Ibid; Grant, *Memoirs*, 160.

In the West, a movement crystallized that very week. Acting on incorrect information, Frémont ordered Grant and Smith to make a demonstration against Columbus.[8] Believing that Polk was sending men to Gen. Sterling Price in western Missouri, Frémont had ordered the demonstration along with orders to push Jeff Thompson out of Missouri once and for all. Happy to be on the move, Grant sent Oglesby and Wallace overland after Thompson, while he took to the river. On November 5, he informed Smith that he was fitting out an expedition to menace Belmont. Grant asked Smith to feign a movement on Columbus.

The following day soldiers at the Cairo bases received marching orders. Shrieks of joy resounded through the camps. The waiting was over; Grant's troops were moving out.[9] Amid the bustle and excitement of preparing to depart, rumors circulated through the camps that Confederate General Pillow had surrounded part of the Union forces at Cairo. One soldier hurriedly scrawled, "All is confusion in camp now."[10] Joseph Skipworth prepared to march out with the rest of Logan's men, believing he would go into battle at Bird's Point.[11]

All of the volunteer soldiers in the Cairo camps readied themselves for their first blooding, taking time to write wills and jot down letters to loved ones at home. On November 6 soldiers fell into formation and boarded transports waiting to take them to meet the Rebels. The Twenty-second, Twenty-seventh, Thirtieth, and Thirty-first Illinois regiments, the Seventh Iowa, Taylor's Battery, and Delano's Cavalry boarded steamers at Cairo early that day. Under cover of night—as Grant had done at Paducah—the transports sailed downriver and waited to surprise the enemy at dawn.[12]

Heading for "a miserable little village, consisting of a very few houses" nearly opposite Columbus, Kentucky, Grant and his men moved toward an engagement that would confound Polk. The Confederate commander was looking for Grant's forces to challenge

---

8. Grant, *Papers,* 3:11, 3:114.
9. William Onstat to Sister Lizzie, Nov. 6, 1861, William Onstat MSS; Grant, *Memoirs,* 161.
10. John Reese MSS, Oct. 7, 1861.
11. Joseph Skipworth MSS, Nov. 6, 1861.
12. Logan, *Reminiscences of the Civil War,* 121, 122; Catton, *Grant Moves South,* 72.

him at his Columbus stronghold.[13] Smith hoped to maintain that impression as long as possible, while Grant's men floated expectantly toward Belmont. Sailing through the cool night air, Union soldiers prepared their minds for battle and consigned their fates to their officers. Riding with Grant, McClernand commanded the Cairo troops, Col. Henry Dougherty commanded the troops from Bird's Point, and Grant commanded the entire operation. The gunboats *Tyler* and *Lexington* would support the army's movements from the river.

A fleet of vessels carried part of the army on the river, while other troops marched overland to Belmont from Bird's Point. Traveling aboard the steamer *Montgomery*, William Onstat described his feelings: "Everything in nature seemed lovely and beautiful . . . I was engaged in a holy cause."[14] Expressing sentiments shared by many of his fellow soldiers, Onstat continued, "I had to fight for the cause of Constitutional liberty and everything that was dear to men against a treasonable horde."[15] In the early morning, "moving rapidly over the placid and beautiful [sic] Mississippi River," Onstat resolved to do his duty, though it might cost his life.[16]

Acting on his innate aggressiveness, Grant had chosen movement over inactivity. Lacking adequate numbers to assault Columbus, he found another way to hit the enemy by targeting the Rebel camp at Belmont. His strategy called for soldiers on the transports to attack from the front as the land force attacked from behind, thus trapping the enemy. Noting that native forests covered most of the country around the prospective battlefield, Grant landed his troops in front of a cornfield, near Lucas Bend, above Columbus.[17] The waterborne troops advanced first, following skirmishers Grant had sent out from the boats.

Once disembarked from the transports, the Union soldiers formed a line and marched forward through marshy ground covered with dense timber.[18] The men had not marched far before they were

13. *Harper's Weekly*, Dec. 7, 1861; Catton, *Grant Moves South*, 73; Harper's Weekly, Dec. 7, 1861; Bradsby, *History of Cairo*, 63; Catton, *Grant Moves South*, 72–73.
14. William Onstat to Sister Lizzie, Nov. 16, 1861.
15. Ibid.
16. Ibid.
17. Bradsby, *History of Cairo*, 63; Grant, *Memoirs*, 139.
18. Grant, *Memoirs*, 140.

engaging the enemy in earnest. Though Union soldiers were advancing only eighty yards in front of the Rebels, Confederate Col. John V. Wright noted, "the obstructions were so numerous that the enemy could not be seen."[19] Once in sight, the Federals engaged the forces of Gen. Gideon Pillow and Col. James Tappan at Belmont.[20]

By 9:30 in the morning, the battle was well under way. Fascinated with the spectacle, Dr. John Brinton succumbed to momentary exhilaration: "It was a grand and new sight to me to see how real war was to be carried on. I am afraid that at first I thought more of that than of my own particular department."[21] Disregarding his personal safety, Brinton rode up and down the line trying to absorb the scene.

Spirited fighting grew steadily more fierce, continuing for about four hours. Brush and timber impeded the Union advance somewhat, but Rebel infantry and artillery were firing too high. Many of their balls fell wide of the mark. Finally, the Confederates fell back, and Colonel Buford's regiment signaled a Federal victory by carrying the Union flag into the Rebels' camp.[22]

Around 11:30 a.m., W. L. Trask, commander of the Confederate steamer *Charm*, saw that the Federal forces had driven the Confederates from their camp and had planted batteries on the riverbank. Unchallenged by Confederate forces, Union soldiers were burning tents and destroying the Rebel camp. Trask attempted to land Confederate troops four hundred yards above the Union battery, but Rebels ran toward the boat shouting, "Don't land! Don't land! We are whipped!"[23]

From the Federal transport *Montgomery*, docked about two and a half miles upriver from Belmont, Acting Mate William Lonergan had heard the initial gunfire crackle through the air, followed by a sustained silence. After the lull, renewed shooting erupted from the direction of the battlefield. Peering in the direction of the firing, Lonergan saw two soldiers running toward the boat. One had suffered a wound to his arm.

The sailors learned that during the quiet interlude, Union soldiers had commenced a premature celebration of their victory, looting

19. OR Navies, Report of Colonel Wright, C.S.A., Nov. 8, 1861, I:22, 422.
20. Ibid., Report of Brigadier-General J. P. McCown, CSA, I:22, 420.
21. Brinton, *Memoirs*, 78.
22. Grant, *Memoirs*, 138; *Harper's Weekly*, Dec. 7, 1861.
23. OR Navies, Report of W. L. Trask, C.S.A., Feb. 14, 1862, I:22, 426.

and destroying the entire Confederate camp and garrison equipage.[24] At that time, Rebel soldiers crouching along the river would have surrendered had the Union men stayed organized and demanded it of them. If Grant's soldiers had retired after accomplishing the objective of the expedition, they could have left the battlefield with a decisive victory and very little loss. Instead, their lack of discipline gave the enemy time to cross over from Columbus in great force.[25] Exhilarated by initial success, the Federal men lost all cohesion as they cavorted around the captured camp. Noting that many officers behaved little better than privates, Grant described the scene: "They [the officers] galloped about from one cluster of men to another and at every halt delivered a short eulogy upon the Union cause and the achievements of the command."[26]

McClernand participated in the revelry at the Rebel camp. He stopped fighting to lead cheers for his soldiers' victory. Amidst the chaos, Grant struggled to restore order while Polk started sending reinforcements to support his beleaguered troops.[27] Finally, Grant set fire to the camp in order to gain the soldiers' attention. The noise of the Rebels' surround alarm and enemy gunfire got the attention of Grant's officers.

Sobered by their commander and the advancing enemy, the novice troops refocused their attention on the Confederates, who, by this time, had rallied and were lining up along the river between the Union troops and their transports.[28] The flush of victory quickly changed to panic. Soldiers who had riotously celebrated a victory moments before now clamored for surrender. Grant took charge, announcing "we had cut our way in and could cut our way out just as well."[29]

Back at the *Montgomery,* retreating soldiers told Lonergan that the Rebels had crossed over from Columbus and were "cutting our men all to pieces."[30] The Confederates had indeed launched a counterattack, initially hitting the Thirtieth Illinois. John Logan's Thirty-first

24. Bradsby, *History of Cairo,* 64; OR Navies, Grant to Brigadier-General Seth Williams, Nov. 17, 1861, I:22.

25. Catton, *Grant Moves South,* 75; OR Navies, Foote to Gideon Welles, Nov. 9, 1861, I:22, 399.

26. Grant, *Memoirs,* 141.

27. Kiper, *McClernand* 45; Catton, *Grant Moves South,* 75.

28. Grant, *Memoirs,* 141; Anderson, *By Sea,* 89.

29. Grant, *Memoirs,* 141.

30. Bradsby, *History of Cairo,* 65.

came to the aid of the Thirtieth. In retreat, the Federal soldiers maintained a running fight all the way back to the transports. Confusion reigned as the men pressed to get on board. Loaded transports pushed off toward Cairo with Rebel soldiers shooting at them from the banks.[31] Working their way out to midstream, the *Tyler* and *Lexington* started firing on the Rebels with grape, canister, and shells, inflicting considerable damage.

Late in the evening on November 7, people keeping a vigil on the levees at Cairo finally saw transports full of subdued Federals rounding the bend. More transports, loaded with butternut prisoners, followed close behind. Union spoils included captured Rebel artillery and enemy transportation. Grant had left Cairo intending to chase Rebel reinforcements away from Sterling Price and ended up routing a Confederate camp.[32]

Although Grant scholars and military historians have only recently given attention to the battle of Belmont, it was in this first real battle that Grant was already displaying the great force of will identified by T. Harry Williams as one of the characteristics that made him a successful general.[33] Sustained by sheer willpower when his soldiers lost control, Grant had remained calm and focused. His cool head kept green troops from unraveling into defeat.

Grant's earlier experiences in Missouri may have accounted for his reaction at Belmont. While in command of the Twenty-first Illinois, Grant was ordered to move against Col. Thomas Harris, who was encamped at the town of Florida, Missouri. His previous battle experience many years behind him, Grant felt again the trepidation of the uninitiated. Ironically, when he reached the Rebel camp, he found that Harris had fled. At that moment he realized that the Confederate colonel had been equally intimidated. Possessing the valuable ability to learn from experience, Grant never forgot that lesson.[34]

The Confederate trap at Belmont also allowed Grant to test another of his valued maxims: when in a draw with both sides weakened, the side that takes the initiative will prevail. Grant guessed accurately that the Rebels were just as frightened and tired as his own troops. He took a gamble and ordered his men to attack. They

31. *Harper's Weekly*, Dec. 7, 1861; Bradsby, *History of Cairo*, 65.
32. OR Navies, Grant to Seth Williams, Nov. 17, 1861, I:22; Livermore, *My Story*, 173.
33. Donald, *Why the North Won the Civil War*, 25.
34. Grant, *Memoirs*, 148.

quickly put panic aside, rallied and fought through what looked like a lost cause. Later in life Grant remembered that the Rebel soldiers at Belmont were weakened and didn't put up much resistance.[35]

Shock compounded fatigue when the Confederate soldiers moved in to round up their captives and saw the Federals shooting their way out of the trap. The circumstances of superior enemy numbers that turned Grant toward Belmont brought forth another of his valuable qualities: great resourcefulness. Outnumbered by an enemy force, but wishing to inflict some destruction on them nevertheless, Grant figured out a way to strike. Although Belmont did not give Grant the exact results he had envisioned, Union forces realized enough success to claim a victory.

The Confederates did likewise. Polk congratulated his troops, but attributed most of the credit to God for the "glorious victory achieved by them at Belmont on the 7th instant."[36] Albert Sidney Johnston also complimented the Rebel troops, "This was no ordinary shock of arms. It was a long and trying contest."[37] Boasting of a Federal rout, and even reporting the death of General Grant, the Confederates believed they had been victorious.[38]

But the consensus among historians is that Grant's soldiers simply outfought the Rebels on that autumn afternoon. Soldiers returning to Cairo after the battle testified that Union men had driven the Rebels back to their camp in a brilliant and determined charge. Grant bypassed God and credited the Union volunteers when he commended his men for their success at Belmont, saying that he had never seen any more gallant fighting, including the action he had witnessed in the Mexican War.[39]

The feisty little general commanding an army of frontier soldiers concluded that Belmont had served as a seasoning experience for his men: "the confidence inspired in our troops in the engagement will be of incalculable benefit to us in the future."[40] For his part, William Onstat viewed the outcome of the battle of Belmont with

35. Ibid., 164.
36. OR Navies, General Orders No. 20, General Leonidas Polk, I:22, 428.
37. Ibid., General Orders No. 5, General A. S. Johnston 424.
38. Ibid., Leonidas Polk to Jefferson Davis, Nov. 8, 1861, 406; Catton, *Grant Moves South*, 84.
39. OR Navies, Leonidas Polk to Jefferson Davis, Nov. 8, 1861, 406; Catton, *Grant Moves South*, 84; *Cairo City Weekly Gazette*, Nov. 21, 1861; OR Navies, Grant to his Troops, Nov. 8, 1861, I:22, 389.
40. Ibid.

satisfaction. He stated that he had been neither discouraged nor depressed, as the *Chicago Tribune* reported the Union forces to be after the fight. Onstat declared, "I have certainly recovered for I felt like fighting any living Secesh."[41]

Grant also praised the performance of the gunboats, acknowledging that they had made a valuable contribution to the overall campaign. The first real engagement for the Cairo troops had demonstrated the need for cooperation between army and navy. In retrospect, some of Foote's officers concluded that animosity developed between Grant and Foote after the battle of Belmont because, they claimed, Grant kept the movement a secret.[42]

Flag Officer Foote decried Grant's failure to telegraph him in St. Louis and notify him of the imminent movement on Belmont.[43] Foote interpreted Grant's behavior as an effort to exclude him from the campaign. In truth, Grant did not know himself where his feint toward Columbus would lead, and he simply expected that all officers under his authority would follow him and trust his judgment.

Inevitably, detractors appeared after the battle, trying to discredit Grant and the Union forces. Secessionists in Cairo chose to view the battle as a failure, stating that Grant had led the men into a trap that the surviving soldiers had barely escaped. Critics of the Union, bent on finding fault in any case, cast the Federal retreat as an ignominious flight. These critics emphasized the Union losses in dead, wounded, and captured, painting a depressing picture for civilians.[44]

Perhaps the most stinging criticism sprang from among the ranks of the officers who had participated in the battle. As the transports wound their way back to Cairo from the battlefield at Belmont, soldiers overheard John A. Logan criticizing Grant. Logan denounced the general, stating that Grant had deserted Union soldiers, leaving them behind to die.[45] Logan's statement shifted blame for the retreat from the men who had lost control to the general who had first led them to victory and finally rallied them to an ordered departure.

Logan's inflammatory statements aboard the transport did not diminish Grant's victory. Many of the men within earshot knew the fallacy of Logan's remarks. When the Federals had reengaged

---

41. William H. Onstat MSS, Nov. 16, 1861.
42. Henry Walke, "Operations of the Western Flotilla," 29:426.
43. OR Navies, Foote to Gideon Welles, Nov. 9, 1861, I:22, 399.
44. Bradsby, *History of Cairo*, 63; Cole, *Civil War*, 266.
45. Bradsby, *History of Cairo*, 65.

the Rebels, they left the wounded in farmhouses near the battlefield. Before the transports departed for Cairo, Grant rode to the different farmhouses and had as many of the casualties as possible carried to the boats.[46] Loyal soldiers in Logan's presence ignored his erroneous remarks and quietly acknowledged Grant's valor. Those who shared Logan's sentiments retained their devotion to him. Joseph Skipworth stated that soldiers of the Thirty-first liked Logan very much and would follow their colonel to whatever battlefield he led them, "or our bones must bleach upon her hills."[47]

Recovered from the elation and trauma of actual engagement, the Cairo soldiers came to regard Belmont as a great victory. For several months after the battle, if an officer wanted to motivate his troops, he gave the command "Belmont charge."[48] With a wild cheer, the men moved forward in line at the double-quick. Grant's superiors in the West and his civilian supporters also saw the Missouri engagement as a victory, but among leaders in Washington, only Washburne truly appreciated Grant's abilities.[49]

Grant himself considered the engagement at Belmont a valuable and necessary victory. He believed that Col. Richard Oglesby and his three thousand men would have been captured or destroyed at Bird's Point had he not driven the Rebels out. Moreover, in Grant's opinion, the first fray involving the soldiers at Cairo accomplished two objectives: the enemy gave up all idea of detaching troops from Columbus, and the Federal troops gained a confidence in themselves that did not diminish throughout the remainder of the war.[50]

The battle of Belmont also demonstrated unequivocally the value of the Union policy against plundering and looting. In the early years of the war, the federal government believed in the necessity of protecting private property. People in areas of questionable sentiment needed to see that the government intended to protect loyal citizens and their property. Grant's initial clash with the enemy proved that the policy also helped officers to maintain discipline. Officers had seen firsthand that once troops broke ranks to plunder it was nearly impossible to get them regrouped.[51]

46. Catton, *Grant Moves South*, 77.
47. Joseph Skipworth MSS.
48. Morris, *History Thirty-first Illinois Regiment Volunteers*, 26.
49. Hattaway, *How the North Won*, 53.
50. Grant, *Memoirs*, 144, 143.
51. Catton, *Grant Moves South*, 83.

Soldiers at Cairo had braved "the murderous Confederate fire at Belmont."[52] They could feel confident about their fighting ability and feel secure in the leadership of their commander. The western gunboats had also proven their worth in the initial action, and Grant had witnessed the potential of gunboats for supporting troops on land.[53] For Foote, perhaps the fact that the gunboats performed admirably despite his absence made his exclusion the more bitter.

Days after the battle, people were still getting conflicting reports. George Durfee wrote home from Camp Lyon in Missouri that a messenger brought news to them of the battle of Belmont. The early report claimed that Union troops had been all cut up and Bird's Point was still threatened. After returning to Cairo, Durfee got more accurate information and passed it along to the people at home, "things bad enough but not as bad as represented there is a good many wounded men this morning in camp, some have their heads bound up some their armes [sic] some are limping on crutches, but all in good spirits."[54]

Joseph Skipworth numbered among the battle veterans with bound heads. Skipworth had sustained a head injury from flying tree splinters. Before he made his way back to the transports, Rebels bayoneted one of his arms and shot him in the back of the head. Proving the hardiness of Logan's men, he went to the hospital and recovered to fight again.[55]

As much joy as Grant's soldiers took in their victory, the celebration did not overshadow a deep sorrow for the accompanying loss of life. In the Confederacy, the tough fighting ability of Grant's army was evidenced in the great number of dead and wounded that Rebel officials sent to Memphis, Tennessee, for care and burial. Grief cast a shadow over that entire town. Soldiers at the Cairo base, after their first clash with the enemy, understood the true consequences of southern secession: their friends had died in battle. Statistics for the Union showed 250 casualties and 130 prisoners taken.[56]

Sorrow visited the household of Senator Orville Hickman Browning in Quincy, Illinois. On the evening of November 8, Adam Smith

52. Cole, *Civil War*, 288.
53. OR Navies, Perry to Foote, Nov. 7, 1861, I:22, 398; Anderson, *By Sea*, 91.
54. George Durfee to H. B. Durfee, Esq., Nov. 13, 1861, George S. Durfee MSS.
55. Joseph Skipworth MSS, Nov. 10, 1861.
56. Grant, *Papers*, 3:192; Victor Hicken, *Illinois in the Civil War*, 24; Grant, *Papers*, 133.

called on the Brownings with a message. Smith's son, William, was stationed at Cairo. The younger Smith had told his father of a terrible battle near Cairo. The name of Lt. William Shipley, the Brownings' foster son, appeared among the list of missing.[57]

The following day, just after breakfast, another dispatch arrived from William Smith. Under a flag of truce, Union soldiers had exchanged Lieutenant Shipley. Mortally wounded at Belmont, the young soldier died among friends at Cairo. General Prentiss, Capt. William Smith, and a military escort brought Shipley's body back to Quincy. At three o'clock on the afternoon of November 13, the Brownings held a funeral in their home for their fallen son. Senator Browning took some comfort from the fact that "an immense concourse of people" attended the solemn occasion.[58]

The seasoning of the soldiers at Cairo began at Belmont. The campaign readied them for more demanding work. In the eastern theater Federal forces occupied Hilton Head Island and took Port Royal on the day that Grant led his troops into the Battle of Belmont. The armies in the West and the forces patrolling the Atlantic coast carried Lincoln's objectives forward. The Army of the Potomac was not yet sharing in the glory.

Following Belmont, volunteer soldiers in the West pushed on courageously toward the next campaign with Grant. Summing up the first conflict in his theater of the war, John Brinton reflected, "Then when our exodus or retreat was ordered, I watched our people rallying in line, and I thought that even if they had scattered a little to pillage the enemy's camp, they were still a brave set of men."[59]

57. Browning, *Diary*, 509.
58. Ibid.
59. Brinton, *Memoirs*, 79.

Ten

Nothing of Importance

In his *Memoirs*, Grant consistently summarized the periods between his early military campaigns at Cairo as times when nothing of importance occurred in his command. He characterized the time after Belmont as one of these uneventful periods, but in reality so many serious matters required his attention that he had no time to correspond with family members. The day after the battle, Grant wrote one personal letter and directed his clerk to send it out to all his relatives. The victor must claim some spoils, and when the townspeople in Cairo competed for the privilege of entertaining Grant and his officers, he occasionally enjoyed a social evening. Officials of the Illinois Central Railroad hosted one especially pleasant dinner party.[1]

Socializing, however, claimed only a minute percentage of Grant's time between battles. Clashes with the enemy honed the general's strategic thinking, but during the lulls between battles, Grant's organizational and administrative skills evolved. At these times Grant dealt with a range of situations, some of which threatened the fragile lives of soldiers and Unionists who could only find help at Cairo. Some problems threatened to destroy Grant's entire command.

The Rebels were equally busy after Belmont, reinforcing Columbus in expectation of another Federal attack. But in Cairo, Grant spent time improving the systems, which he had organized prior to his first engagement. Accustomed to dealing with people of every

1. Grant, *Papers*, 3:136, 3:96.

ilk who were facing various problems, Grant immediately tackled the biggest problem associated with the aftermath of battle. Before he had even taken time to ponder the results of his first fight, Grant went to his headquarters office and sent for Wash Graham. He instructed Graham to take a force back to the battlefield to bury the dead and collect the remaining wounded.[2]

Acting on the compassion that was an integral part of his nature, Grant put aside his rejection of the legitimacy of the Confederate states long enough to petition Polk on behalf of the wounded. The day after the fighting at Belmont, Grant notified the Rebel commander that he wished to remove the wounded from the battlefield and return sixty-four prisoners to Polk on unconditional release. Motivated by his religious training, Polk decided to support the humanitarian endeavor. He agreed to Grant's requests but pointedly mentioned Grant's refusal to recognize the Confederate government.[3]

Grant's actions at this juncture belied John A. Logan's accusations of callousness. Far from leaving men to die, Grant acted on the same day of his communication with Polk. He sent a force under Lieutenant Colonel Hart of the Twenty-second Illinois to the battle site, where many wounded men still lay unattended. A burial detail took care of the dead; Hart's men transported the others to Cairo for medical care.[4]

When all of the casualties were returned to the base, the post hospital in Cairo was filled to capacity. Mother Bickerdyke oversaw the work of the nurses at the Bulletin, but Mary Livermore wrote in her reminiscences that Mary Jane Safford had preceded everyone else to the battlefield at Belmont. Tying a white handkerchief to a stick to indicate noncombatant status, she busied herself immediately. After binding what wounds she could in the field, she saw many of the soldiers safely back to Cairo.[5]

In the regimentals, surgeons struggled to provide adequate care for their patients. Burke and Brinton were kept busy for days attending to the wounded. Lack of experience on the part of surgeons serving under Brinton required that he perform many operations by himself. While he operated, Brinton instructed his staff on surgical procedures. The sanitary commissions sent women nurses, who

2. Ibid., 3:130.
3. Ibid., 3:131, 132.
4. Ibid., 3:132.
5. Livermore, *My Story*, 215.

helped wherever they could, but inexperienced surgeons sacrificed limbs that could have been saved.[6] The incoming wounded overflowed into Mound City, where members of the sanitary committee, the Sisters of the Holy Cross, and Dr. Brinton cared for them.

The best construction techniques and medical supplies available had not totally eliminated discomforts from the military hospitals in Mound City and Cairo. One nurse at the Mound City facility noted that after battles blood leaked down from upper floors, sprinkling operating surgeons and nurses below. At the general hospital in Cairo nurses experienced similar problems. The women frequently awakened in the night to find blood dripping from the wards above them onto their beds in the dormitory. In the middle of November, Grant ordered Quartermaster Hatch to build an additional hospital.[7]

The strain of caring for casualties from the battle of Belmont caused Mother Bickerdyke to break down physically. The devoted nurse returned home to Galesburg to recuperate. Possessed of some of the same iron will one might observe in a great general, she returned to Cairo before the start of the next campaign.[8] As unpleasant as caring for battle casualties proved to be, dedicated female nurses stayed on the job throughout the war. Many other women spent brief periods of time on particular battlefields or in certain camps trying to comfort and care for their men.

Despite the sincere efforts of Union officers to round up their men and see them back to the transports, a number of the Federal soldiers had failed to make their way through the Confederate line at Belmont. For one Union soldier, Pvt. Lemuel Adams, facing down the Rebels proved disastrous. As Adams stood in line preparing to strike out for the transports, a Confederate bullet tore into his left forearm. The shot severed a radial artery.[9]

Adams found help close by. Dan Sheely, Adams's friend and fellow soldier, dropped out of line to administer first aid. Sheely quickly made a tourniquet from a handkerchief. The improvised remedy stemmed the bleeding. Sheely's quick thinking kept Adams from bleeding to death, but the two men fell behind the rest of their regiment in the push to reach the river. Seeing Adams's predicament,

6. Brinton, *Memoirs*, 89; Livermore, *My Story*, 480; Hicken, *Illinois*, 23; Logan, *Reminiscences of the Civil War*, 55.

7. Eleanore, *King's Highway*; Grant, *Papers*, 3:174.

8. Frank Moore, *Women of the War*, 90.

9. Adams, "Memoirs."

one of McClernand's aides came to the rescue and put the wounded soldier on a horse. But Adams, weakened by the loss of blood, slid out of the saddle before reaching safety.

Sheely stayed with him, trying to help him catch up to their regiment on foot. As fate would have it, instead of finding their own men, the pair ran headlong into a Rebel cavalry unit. This time there was no alternative; the two men surrendered.[10] The Confederate captors took Lemuel Adams and Dan Sheely back to the Rebel fort on the Kentucky side. Adams traveled on a hospital barge to Columbus and then the Confederates transferred him to a post hospital they had set up in an old hotel. Suffering intensely from his own wound, Adams learned that Colonel Dougherty was lodged in the same facility. The knowledge did little to comfort Adams, who was quickly realizing that the Confederate doctors at Columbus faced a medical situation similar to, if not more deficient than, that confronting the doctors at Cairo.

All through the night, Adams heard the grinding, shrieking sounds of primitive amputations in progress. The next morning, the view outside his window showed a large pile of human limbs thrown carelessly into the yard. Consistent with practices in the Cairo hospitals, Confederate doctors had too hastily amputated damaged appendages. Looking at the sickening heap, Adams forced himself to believe that the dismembered parts had been severed mainly from Confederates. Later he learned that one of the legs lying in the pile had belonged to Henry Dougherty.[11]

More fortunate than Dougherty, Adams slowly gained strength despite the poor caliber of care in the Confederate hospital. After a few days, his captors allowed him to leave the infirmary and walk into the town of Columbus. Since uniforms had not yet been standardized, the townspeople mistook Adams for a Confederate. Still desperate for information about the recent battle, people plied Adams with questions. Being careful not to reveal his true allegiance, Adams answered, all the while taking in the comments of his audience. He soon realized that the Southerners believed the Confederacy had carried the day at Belmont.

Adams personally benefited from Grant's compassion toward patients. The Confederates freed space in their hospital by sending

10. Ibid.
11. Ibid.

captives back to Grant. One of those exchanged, Lemuel Adams returned to Cairo and was admitted to the general hospital. His initial recovery at Columbus devolved into a relapse. At the Bulletin, doctors concluded that an abcess was responsible for Adams's worsening condition.

Lingering between life and death, Adams received the capable ministrations of Mother Bickerdyke and the tender attention of Mary Jane Safford. He left no impressions of the older nurse but recorded that Safford made a habit of sitting by sick soldiers all night to watch over them. Under Mary Jane Safford's watchful care, Adams defeated the Cairo surgeons' diagnosis of doom. He survived his illness as well as the war.[12] Adams noted how much Safford's kind demeanor uplifted her patients. She provided reading material for Lemuel Adams when he felt strong enough to look at the newspapers.

Safford's nursing skills sated more than the hunger of the mind and the spirit. She knew the way to a man's heart. During one of her bedside visits with Adams, Safford asked what food he liked best. Unhesitatingly, he named chicken pie as his favorite. The next morning, the young nurse appeared in Adams's ward carrying a savory chicken pie. To his delight, she made her way to his bed, offering it to him. He declared it the best he had ever eaten. During the early campaigns that departed from the Cairo base, Mary Jane earned a reputation for efficiency in caring for the sick and wounded that followed her throughout the war.

An incident in Cairo pertaining to the medical needs of the Belmont veterans sheds light on another aspect of Grant's generalship: his ability to assess the competence of the men under his command. Grant scholars have concluded that he demonstrated the strength of delegating well to his subordinates.[13] By the time Grant left the West, he did possess this ability. In the interim between Belmont and Donelson, Grant took the measure of three junior officers who would all become leaders in the West.

Two days before the campaign on Belmont, Grant had considered sending Logan and Michael K. Lawler on a reconnaissance trip up the St. Francois River. Grant assessed the two southern Illinoisans as officers with leadership potential. Grant also perceived McClernand as competent and felt confident leaving him in command of the

12. Ibid.
13. Williams, *Lincoln and His Generals*, 312.

district occasionally. Further experience in battle reinforced Grant's instincts about Logan and Lawler but led him to relieve McClernand.

In the weeks following Belmont, Logan nearly went the way of McClernand. John A. Logan experienced such a drastic transformation between 1860 and 1863—going from known secessionist to one of the ablest of all the Union generals—that his life has invited interpretation from many Civil War historians. Almost without exception Logan's early treachery has been glossed over in light of his later contributions to the Federal cause. In explaining Logan's distinguished service record, historians have overwhelmingly concluded that his patriotism never really wavered and he never seriously intended to betray the Union.

But the evidence concerning Logan demands further clarification. A deeper examination of the documents suggests that Logan was, indeed, a traitor at the beginning of the war. A more plausible explanation for his change from Rebel to patriot can be traced to his exposure to Grant. In a discussion of the Battle of Belmont one of Logan's apologists concluded that Grant "embraced" Logan during the campaign because of Logan's popularity in southern Illinois and the fact that Logan was a ready fighter and excellent horseman.[14] Grant and Logan did share a love of horses. And certainly Grant would have preferred to keep a known secessionist in his circle under his watchful eye rather than antagonize him and risk sabotage.

However, in Grant's official written description of the battle at Belmont, he praised McClernand, Lagow, Hatch, and Graham for their performances.[15] He did not mention John A. Logan. Perhaps Grant had heard rumors of Logan's critical remarks made on the trip back to Cairo, or possibly, Grant shared Sherman's opinion of Logan as an opportunist. It is also possible that having so recently changed his allegiance, Logan did not have his heart in this first fight and did nothing to attract Grant's attention.

Whatever the case, following Belmont, Logan enmeshed himself in further intrigues that could only have strengthened Grant's reservations about the paradoxical colonel. In the midst of the turmoil of caring for the wounded, Logan and McClernand created a crisis over authority. A week after the campaign, Grant received a complaint from McClernand on behalf of his subordinate, John A. Logan.

14. Battle of Belmont, 19.
15. Grant, *Papers*, 3:141–42.

As soon as McClernand's force had arrived at Cairo following the battle, McClernand issued an order to all Union officers to deliver Logan's soldiers to their own regimental hospital.

When it came to Grant's attention that McClernand's order had been ignored, instead of enforcing it, Grant countermanded the order. Familiar with the quality of McClernand's medical judgments and aware of the sanitary conditions in Logan's regimental hospital, he believed that Brinton could best judge the care of the wounded. Grant stated that Logan had no authority over the wounded and that medical decisions rested entirely with the medical director. Consequently, Brinton placed many of Logan's seriously wounded in the general hospital at Mound City.[16]

Informed of Brinton's actions, both Logan and McClernand protested the surgeon's decision and continued pressing to have the men moved. Some of the men had sustained potentially fatal wounds—one man having been shot through the lungs—but, nevertheless, Logan insisted on taking them to the regimental.

Facing Brinton in person, Logan expressed his objections by calling Brinton a brute. To Grant, McClernand argued that he had issued the order before Logan's soldiers were placed in the general hospital; so, the men should now be moved in compliance with Logan's wishes. Then, without waiting for Grant to revise the orders, McClernand authorized Logan to march to Mound City and remove his men. He authorized Logan to use force of arms against the medical personnel, if necessary.[17]

Worked nearly into exhaustion over the many dangerous issues threatening his district, Grant still took time to review the situation. He thought perhaps McClernand had some justification after all. On the second pass, Grant noticed that he had signed McClernand's original order but with a qualification: Logan was authorized to take his men to his regimental hospital if he judged their condition to be stable enough that they could recover with nothing more than the minimum care offered at that facility.

Problems started when Logan, acting on the order, abandoned good judgment regarding the condition of his men. Well aware of Logan's treacherous nature, and beginning to reassess McClernand, Grant wrote a diplomatic answer to the post commander's com-

16. Ibid., 3:162, 171, 172.
17. Ibid., 3:171.

plaint. Assuring McClernand that he had no interest in interfering in the administration of his official duties, Grant made clear that McClernand should be fulfilling his duties by tutoring Logan on military protocol: Logan should stop characterizing other officers in derogatory terms unless he wished to defend the charges in a court-martial.[18]

Grant's willingness to back down somewhat from the disgruntled duo no doubt stemmed from the fact that he sincerely believed, on review, that McClernand's complaint had some validity. He also suspected that, even after leading two successful campaigns from Cairo, his position as commander of the crucially important district might not be totally secure. A short time after the hospital debacle, Logan and McClernand's actions validated Grant's suspicions.

In late November, Grant wrote Washburne pitching the plan he had formed on his arrival at Cairo. Grant believed that Cairo should be made headquarters of a new department whose force would delve into the South from the West. In his petition, Grant was magnanimous enough to credit McClernand with helping to outline this strategy.[19] Perhaps Grant believed that McClernand's political ties would prompt the War Department to accept the plan.

Unlike Logan and McClernand, Grant asked nothing for himself; he simply enumerated the reasons why he thought the federal government should focus on Cairo: the necessary supplies were closer to Cairo than to other points in the West, and those supplies could be transported and purchased inexpensively; Illinois was a loyal state that deserved the benefits of the presence of a departmental base. Grant had no trouble convincing Washburne of the merits of the idea, and Washburne began working to create the new department.[20]

The identity of the new commander posed the question of the hour. Grant's foes at Cairo moved ever closer to each other as officials in Washington worked out the details of the new district. A month after the battle of Belmont, Logan's Thirty-first entertained a group of ladies visiting from Carbondale. The admiring women presented the regiment with a splendid flag and listened to speeches delivered by Logan and McClernand. The post commander complimented the Thirty-first's gallant behavior on the battleground.[21]

18. Ibid.
19. Grant, *Papers*, 3:204.
20. Ibid., 3:204–5.
21. *Cairo City Weekly*, Dec. 12, 1861.

Logan's soldiers declared their willingness to follow McClernand, not Grant, unquestioningly. The episode symbolized the new relationship that had developed between two Democratic generals, men who were, perhaps, still smarting from the defeat of their party and hoping to gain political advantage through military service.

Calling in all of his political cards in the power struggle with Grant, McClernand maintained a correspondence with Lincoln and relied on support from Logan. In spite of the fact that Lincoln was agonizing over McClellan's inactivity in the East, the president took time to write McClernand and praise the Cairo troops, "You have had a battle, and without being able to judge as to the precise measure of its value, I think it is safe to say that you, and all with you have done honor to yourselves and the flag, and service to the country."[22]

McClernand interpreted Lincoln's letter as an acknowledgment of his claim that credit for the victory at Belmont belonged solely to him.[23] Actually, the letter showed a tone of reprimand. In the letter, McClernand had demanded that Lincoln supply superior arms for his men. The president, aware of the true circumstances in the western theater, denied the request. Lincoln went on to extend his most grateful thanks to all the men who had fought at the battle of Belmont, reminding McClernand that in his present position he was charged with caring for the entire nation. Hoping it would not be interpreted as an injustice if he indulged a little "home pride," Lincoln assuaged McClernand by saying, "Illinois does not disappoint us."[24]

Not one to relinquish his ambitions easily, McClernand kept writing the president. While Grant was appealing to Washburne for a new department at Cairo, McClernand plied Lincoln with the same request but in a more self-serving tone. McClernand suggested that Cairo should be the headquarters of a new department and a "new, energetic, enterprising and judicious commander" should be appointed to the command.[25] Lincoln hardly need read between the lines to discern McClernand's agenda. Playing politics, McClernand

22. Roy P. Basler, *The Collected Works*, Abraham Lincoln to John McClernand, Nov. 10, 1861, 20.

23. Kiper, *McClernand*, 49.

24. Ibid.

25. Grant, *Papers*, 3:206.

coupled his request with a grievance against Grant. Attempting to paint Grant as a commander of poor judgment, McClernand expressed dissatisfaction with Grant's candidate for post commissary. Showing poor judgment once again, he advised Lincoln against approving the recommendation.[26]

Meanwhile, Logan had managed to get leave from his duties at Cairo that he might meet with Lincoln. He spent his time with the president pressing the idea of the new department and pushing for McClernand's promotion. Satisfied with the interview, Logan wrote McClernand and assured him that, if a separate department were created at Cairo, McClernand would be appointed commander over Grant.[27]

After Grant had expressed his ideas to Washburne, he put doubt and insecurity aside and forged ahead with the many duties that required his time and attention. By mid-December, a political issue of another nature was claiming his attention. A bountiful harvest of prisoners in the district spurred the construction of two additional guardhouses, one for political prisoners and one for prisoners of war.

The old guardhouse reverted to its original purpose: housing soldiers under arrest. Unfortunately, the Cairo camps produced no dearth of candidates for incarceration. Two locals commonly seen around the town had been soaking up information about the Union army and delivering it to the Confederates at Columbus. With the pair in custody, Grant thought that B. F. Lowe of Williamson County and his partner in crime should be tried at Cairo. Halleck thought differently. He ordered Grant to appoint eight officers from Cairo, send them to St. Louis with the prisoners, and try the two men at that location.[28]

Disciplinary breaches were by no means confined to the town of Cairo. Two of Oglesby's men at Bird's Point claimed Grant's attention by committing a crime that Grant found particularly repugnant. The Bird's Point soldiers had entered the home of a civilian family in Sister Island, Missouri, and raped the daughter of the house. Unsatiated in their lawless spree, the miscreants left the scene of the rape only to steal private property from other citizens of the town.[29]

26. Ibid., 3:206 n.
27. Ibid., 3:207 n.
28. Ibid., 3:297, 234.
29. Ibid.

Grant ordered that the two men be arrested and put in irons. He informed Oglesby that the rule of military discipline required that the offenders be shot. In the future, if soldiers were caught in the act of rape or theft they should be shot on the spot.[30] These quick, definite methods of discipline, though seemingly harsh, tended to focus the soldiers in Grant's command on their military duties and render them battle-ready.

Troops at Bird's Point required further discipline for problems with property. Grant reinforced his antilooting policy when he learned that Oglesby's men possessed plunder from Belmont. He ordered Oglesby to "cause an immediate investigation...of the property now illegally held by officers and soldiers of your command."[31]

Reprimanding the soldiers for "bartering away horses and other property captured at Battle of Belmont," Grant reminded them that captured property belonged to the federal government and should be turned over to the post quartermaster.[32] All officers found in possession of captured property taken at the Belmont battlefield would be arrested; soldiers would be put in confinement.

The lure of battle plunder ensnared other men besides the testy Bird's Point troops. In Mound City, Michael Lawler received similar orders. Grant ordered the wild Irishman to return "accoutrements obtained by your Regiment without requisitions duly signed."[33] Perhaps the accoutrements included a length of rope. Always a firebrand, Lawler went from thievery to committing one of the worst breaches of discipline that occurred during Grant's tenure in the West. In the process, he provided a spectacle that everyone in Cairo followed with interest.

The vigilante tendencies of southern Illinois society in general, and of Cairo in particular, may have contributed to the course of action taken by Lawler and his men, or perhaps it can be attributed merely to the colonel's insular arrogance. On June 27, 1861, the *Chicago Daily Tribune* had announced the arrival of Col. Michael Kelley Lawler's Eighteenth Illinois Volunteer Regiment in Cairo. Six months

30. Ibid., 3:235.
31. *The War of the Rebellion: A Compilation of the Official Records of the Union and Confederate Armies* (hereinafter, OR Armies), Grant to Richard Oglesby, Nov. 20, 1861, I:8.
32. Grant, *Papers*, 3;169.
33. Ibid., 3:314.

later, the same paper reported that a court-martial and military commission would convene at Camp Defiance (Cairo) the following day.[34]

During the intervening months, Lawler had incited what the journalist referred to as a Cairo Frolic. Lawler's acts, however, exceeded the bounds of the local vigilante tradition, which generally involved a dunking. Referring to the mores of western society that embraced lynching, John Brinton gave an eyewitness account of the incident in his memoirs.[35] Although Brinton actually witnessed the incident and participated in the trial, his account of it was written retrospectively.

The *Chicago Daily Tribune* covered the story on the spot. Reporting that, "Citizens of Mound City and soldiers of the 18th Regiment had a 'grand frolic,'" the Chicago journalist spun the tale.[36] Lawler's regiment had been preparing to go on the march when Robert Dickerman shot a fellow soldier, William Evans, in cold blood. Lawler decided he didn't have time to wait on a general court-martial or a civil process, even though McClernand "positively instructed [Lawler] to hand Dickerman over to the civil authorities of Pulaski County for trial."[37] Giving no more respect to McClernand's order than he gave any other military protocol, Lawler purposely absented himself from Mound City while his regiment chose a jury of soldiers and citizens and a judge. The chosen few then held court.

The kangaroo court called on John Brinton to give testimony during the trial. Brinton attested to the fact that the victim had died of a gunshot wound. The "judge" then pronounced Dickerman guilty, and the "jury" sentenced him to be hanged. At eight o'clock the following morning, Lawler's men took Dickerman to a strip of woods and executed him. The deceased's former comrades in arms dug a grave under his body and dropped him into it. Reporters noted that everyone around Mound City approved of the hanging, and one local clergyman even refused to pray over the convicted man.[38] The next day, Lawler returned to Mound City from Cairo and feigned

34. *Chicago Daily Tribune*, Dec. 19, 1861.
35. Brinton, *Memoirs*, 45.
36. *Chicago Daily Tribune*, Oct. 9, 1861.
37. Brinton, *Memoirs*, 46; *Chicago Daily Tribune*, Oct. 9, 1861; Grant, *Papers*, 3:267 n.
38. Brinton, *Memoirs*, 46–47; *Chicago Daily Tribune*, Oct. 9, 1861.

surprise. Lawler's superiors at Cairo recognized his protestations for the ruse they were.

After allowing an unauthorized court to convict one of his own soldiers, Lawler came under indictment himself. Grant drew up a list of officers who could serve at the court-martial of Lawler and named one man to act as judge advocate. In Cairo, W. H. L. Wallace presided over the court-martial proceedings. Lawler faced five charges, including the hanging of Robert Dickerman. Although Lawler felt that he had been unjustly assailed by the press, the military court found him guilty and dismissed him from the service.[39]

Lawler began to see his rash actions in a less exciting light when he heard the verdict. Searching for a sympathetic ear he sent a report to McClernand claiming that he had acted out of military necessity for the good of his regiment. He told McClernand that the court in Pulaski County had refused to take Dickerman because they feared they wouldn't be able to try him for several months. The claim was as false as the justice Lawler had given Dickerman.

Always looking for opportunities to trump Grant, McClernand took up Lawler's petition. He sent a personal testimonial on Lawler's behalf to General Halleck in St. Louis. Halleck, newly appointed to the West, reviewed Lawler's case and decided the charges against him had accumulated over too long a time. The departmental commander, who had replaced Frémont in St. Louis two days after Belmont, reasoned that Lawler should have been tried promptly or not at all, so he dismissed the charges. Lawler resumed his command. He remained impervious to orders from his own superiors to the extent that his brash actions threatened the success of Grant's move on the rear of the fortress at Vicksburg.[40]

In the weeks between Belmont and Donelson, if Grant's own troops did not cause him enough extra work and anxiety, the Rebels happily supplied the deficit. Already faced with more administrative work concerning his army than time could accommodate, Grant soon found it necessary to carve out a slot for civilians from neighboring states. Before Grant ever reached Cairo, great numbers of

39. Grant, *Papers*, 3:267 n.; Brinton, *Memoirs*, 47; Jane Wallace Chrichton, "Michael Kelly Lawler: A Southern Illinois Mexican War Captain and Civil War General," 68; Grant, *Papers*, 3:267 n.
40. Michael Kelly Lawler to John McClernand, Jan. 1, 1862, John McClernand MSS; Chrichton, "Michael Kelly Lawler," 71.

loyal people had fled St. Louis and other parts of Missouri, escaping Rebel terrorists.

In Border States where Southerners challenged Union control in heated battles, armed secessionists organized into guerrilla bands and turned to marauding. These terrifying raiders gave Unionists no quarter. On the march in Missouri, Grant had reported to Julia that these desperadoes committed every imaginable outrage against loyal citizens. They seized property and literally drove Unionists from the state. Hundreds of families had been chased off of their land, leaving crops, stock, homes, and all personal belongings to the Rebels. Ulysses and Julia Grant followed events in Missouri with a particular interest since Julia had spent her entire childhood on a plantation not far from the city. She and Grant still counted many Missourians as friends.

Small bands of armed guerrillas tracked the Union army in Missouri. Once they were certain that the soldiers had passed through a town, the secessionists turned on that town and destroyed the homes of suspected Unionists. They threatened not only property, but lives as well. Grant stated that the notorious Jeff Thompson murdered loyal Missourians and brutally butchered their bodies. As a warning to others, Thompson and his men left the mutilated remains to rot in public places.[41]

After Grant's successful campaign at Belmont—an intrusion into Missouri—Rebel guerrillas retaliated ferociously. In the Cape Girardeau area people whom Grant termed "rabid secessionists" were murdering some Unionists and forcing others to stay on their farms and provide crops for the Confederacy. Missourians learned to fear Rebel outlaws, but the Confederate army preyed on Unionists as well. Rebel soldiers killed stock, stole horses, burned crops, destroyed household goods, and actually stole clothing off the backs of women and children. Violating the code of chivalrous warfare, these ruffian soldiers kidnapped young girls from their parents' homes and kept them captive at their camps.[42]

Union refugees from Missouri and Kentucky had been crossing the rivers and pouring into Cairo since the nation split. Loyalists from divided states saw that they must fight fire with fire. They sought

41. Grant, *Papers*, 3:106, 2:244.
42. OR Navies I:22, 300–301. John Rodgers to Richard Oglesby, Aug. 18, 1861.

protection from harassment by large, armed groups. Loyalists sought sanctuary in any location where they could find the Union army in force. Desperate to get out of disputed territory, refugees arrived at Union posts with little or nothing to sustain them.[43]

At the Cairo post, Grant enforced policies he had created while still in Missouri with the Twenty-first. Although one of Grant's first biographers concluded that Grant merely followed Halleck's lead in dealing with the white refugees, some of Grant's policies pre-dated Halleck's command of the Department of the West.[44] In the summer of 1861, at Jefferson City, Missouri, Grant had impressed teams that belonged to secessionists when the army had need of them. To these people, Grant paid nothing. In order to assist belea-guered white refugees in the same city, Grant hired their teams for a fair price.[45]

In St. Louis, Halleck added quartering to the already established practice of commandeering the property of Rebels. Secessionist cit-izens had to provide housing for the white refugees by offering quarters in their own homes. Those who refused to cooperate saw their property seized and sold. In Cairo, Grant implemented quar-tering as well as the collection of "contributions" from secessionist residents. Halleck employed contributions in St. Louis, but Grant added his own twist: he required secessionists of northern birth to pay 50 percent more than those of southern extraction.[46] At the Illi-nois post, the proceeds of Grant's particular policy augmented the collections greatly.

A shortage of cavalry at Cairo initially hindered Grant's desire to drive the Rebel marauders from his district. On receiving permis-sion from department headquarters in St. Louis to move against the terrorists at Cape Girardeau, Grant organized an expedition to that location. The Cairo commander's persistent pursuit of Thomp-son allowed many loyal Missourians to refugee across the Missis-sippi River into Cairo.[47] The Mississippi Flotilla also played an important role in rescue operations. In one of many incidents the *Lexington* sailed to Commerce, Missouri, following reports of seces-

43. Grant, *Papers*, 2:26, 72, 149; Grant, *Memoirs*, 154.
44. Catton, *Grant Moves South*, 128.
45. Grant, *Memoirs*, 154; Catton, *Grant Moves South*, 21.
46. Catton, *Grant Moves South*, 127, 128.
47. Grant, *Papers*, 3:182, 183.

sionist outrages in that town. The crew found loyal Missourians clustered along the riverbanks looking for transportation to Illinois.

Both the army and the navy went to the aid of Unionists in Crittenden County, Kentucky. Col. Isham N. Haynie reported to Grant that Unionists in Crittenden County—just across the Ohio River from Cave-In-Rock, Illinois—needed assistance from Federal troops. The majority of residents in the Kentucky county supported the Union, but a group of violent secessionists at Hopkinsville were taking it upon themselves to purge the entire county of loyal citizens. The loyal Kentuckians begged Grant for Federal boats to help them refugee over to the Illinois side of the Ohio.[48]

Many of the refugees arriving in Cairo had been forced out of their homes by disparate bands of outlaw marauders, but longtime residents of southern Illinois began to recognize the tactics associated with a group of proslavery terrorists who had organized in the 1850s. Originally created by George W. L. Bickley for the purpose of extending slavery into Mexico and Central America, the Knights of the Golden Circle turned their attention to persecuting Unionists once the war started.[49]

Historian Frank L. Klement concluded that the Knights were merely a myth created by the Republican Party to win elections, but military officers and public officials documented dealings with the lawless group early in the war. Two weeks before the battle of Belmont, Lieutenant Phelps led a naval expedition to Shawneetown, Illinois, for the purpose of capturing seventy Knights of the Golden Circle. Learning of the presence of the organization in the district, Phelps had planted a spy in their midst. When his informant failed to return after a reasonable period of time, Phelps set out after the offenders himself.[50]

Grant reported Phelps's expedition to Yates, informing the governor of the presence of the Knights near Cairo. Stating that both he and McClernand knew of the group, Grant referred to them as "southern sympathizers that molest Union men in the North."[51] Both generals signed the report to emphasize their concern over

48. Ibid., 3:185; Grant, *Memoirs*, 154.
49. Bruce Tap, *Over Lincoln's Shoulder: The Committee on the Conduct of the War*, 21.
50. Grant, *Papers*, 3:120 n., 120.
51. Ibid., 3:118.

the guerrillas. Fully informed of the activities of the Knights of the Golden Circle, Yates cautioned Grant to make no arrests without concrete evidence, but he closed by adding that traitors and secessionists should leave Illinois because the state government would not hesitate to punish treason.[52]

Such overwhelming problems arose concerning Union refugees fleeing Rebel terrorism that army officers in the western theater finally despaired of being able to deal with it adequately. To address the problem, the Western Sanitary Commission ventured forth from its St. Louis stronghold to assist the army. In the second year of the war, Generals Halleck and Schofield decided that the question of refugees fit the mission of that medical organization.[53]

During Grant's tenure at Cairo, he dealt successfully with the problem in his district. In the fall of 1862, the War Department designated Cairo as the center for handling white refugees in the West. To alleviate space and supply problems, the white Southerners were sent on to northern states, where they assumed jobs vacated by men who had enlisted. If white refugees refused to work, they were placed under military surveillance.[54]

Performing essential labor in a different society brought new life to many poor southern whites. Freed from the domination of tyrannical planters, these humble people saw for the first time in their lives that they reaped benefits from hard work. The existence of public schools in the North allowed them to educate their children. With the money they earned from their jobs, they could acquire items that had seemed unattainable to them in the South. Drawn by the higher standard of living, many refugees became permanent residents of northern states.[55]

Through all of Grant's administrative duties, some part of his mind continued to dwell on the status of his command at Cairo. Relying on intuition, by December 18, Grant had confided to his sister that he believed he would keep his district.[56] Lincoln and

52. Ibid., 3:119 n., 119.
53. Eliot, "Western Sanitary Commission," (Apr. 1864):7.
54. John Eaton, *Grant, Lincoln, and the Freedmen: Reminiscences of the Civil War, with Special Reference to the Work for the Contrabands and Freedmen of the Mississippi Valley*, 37.
55. Ibid., 38.
56. Grant, *Papers*, 3:331.

Washburne shared the same instinct. When the new commander of the Department of the West arrived at St. Louis he also looked favorably on Grant.

Halleck sent a board of officers to make a general inspection of the camps at Cairo. Based on the results of the report he received, he created the District of Cairo through General Order No. 22. The order retained Grant as district commander and added new territory to what had been the District of Southeast Missouri. Grant's sphere of command now included the area of Kentucky west of the Cumberland River and the counties of Missouri south of Cape Girardeau. The change came three days before Christmas.[57] General Order No. 22 left a void on McClernand's Christmas wish list, but it did not cancel his rivalry with Grant. For anyone paying attention, Grant's promotion over McClernand forecast the direction of the future chain of command.

Logan, an experienced politician, started gravitating toward the winner. Grant's elevation after Belmont may have been the beginning of Logan's true transformation from traitor to patriot. As with many Civil War leaders, Grant and Logan both dove into the war as Democrats and surfaced on the other side as Republicans. Grant's practice of focusing discipline and drill instruction on company officers instead of soldiers undoubtedly taught Logan valuable lessons and put him in touch with his natural military instincts.

By December 1861, Grant's Order No. 5, banning the usual vices from the town, had done its work. A quieter, more orderly atmosphere prevailed in Cairo, but some townspeople thought the generals should keep the saloons open and confine the soldiers to camp. People argued that the blockade had ruined all the other businesses in town, and if they stopped selling liquor, Cairo would wither away completely.[58] No such dire fate befell the town, but one editor remarked on the quietest Christmas in Cairo's history under General Order No. 5.

The editor had observed only three intoxicated persons all day. One was a man who had bought a plate of oysters just to drink the alcohol left in the chafing dish. The editor concluded that the residue didn't produce a sufficient effect to do justice to the day. Other reports evidenced that for the first time in the history of the

57. Grant, *Memoirs*, 169; Catton, *Grant Moves South*, 97; Grant, *Papers*, 3:331.
58. *Cairo City Weekly Gazette*, Oct. 10, 1861.

town, no fights and no criminal activity marked the holiday season in Cairo; general good feeling radiated toward all.[59]

Grant's retention as district commander removed one worry from his mind. The days since the success at Belmont had been marked by exhilaration even in the midst of settling the troops back into camp. The commission of an enlarged command made his success in the field even sweeter. But with the greatest threat to his career resolved, Grant learned that the sweet often mixed with the bitter. The duties of command in the District of Cairo would involve sacrifice, hard work, and an enemy who never rested.

59. Ibid., Dec. 26, 1861.

Eleven

The Cairo Ring

During the first stages of the war, editors in southern Illinois had worried more about the loss of business than about the possible loss of human life. The editor of the *Jonesboro Gazette* announced that the war had entirely ruined trade in the country, and business of all kinds had seriously declined. The article echoed a story run by *Harper's Weekly* the previous spring.[1] But as soon as soldiers started filing into army posts, many businessmen made fortunes furnishing supplies for the troops.

As in all wars, corruption quickly infused supply contracts. In Cairo, after only four months of war, an aura of dishonesty in trade and contracts hung over the post like a pall. In those early months one resident wrote, "Treason [exists] in all corners, corruption up to the smallest employees of the machine of the state. Waste and spoiling by negligence ... this is how it looks at home."[2]

Corruption had preceded Grant to Cairo, and, inevitably, he inherited the problems generated by it. After nearly losing his command at the hands of one corrupt cabal, Grant concluded that the patriotism of speculators could be measured in dollars and cents. These ambitious men cared only for profit; the fate of the country meant nothing to them.[3] In his district, Grant pursued perpetrators

1. *Harper's Weekly*, May 4, 1861; *Jonesboro Weekly Gazette*, June 29, 1861.
2. Kircher, *German*, 20.
3. Catton, *Grant Moves South*, 349.

of fraud and corruption as courageously as he fought the enemy in the field.

In both theaters of the war, soldiers frequently suffered from lack of needed supplies, especially during the first year. Greater distance from the nerve center in Washington translated into greater need. In the early months at the Cairo post tempers had erupted over food. Reportedly, rations were insufficient, and what food the soldiers did get was of an inferior quality.[4] In June 1861, journalists reported that two or three hundred soldiers at Camp Defiance broke into the commissary department and took food. Colonel Cook's regiment had instigated the raid.

Family and friends tried to make up the deficiency by sending goods from home. Unfortunately, the express service that delivered personal packages to the Cairo camps charged such exorbitant rates that soldiers who did not receive regular pay could ill afford the price of retrieving the incoming goods. One soldier instructed his sister to stop sending supplies unless she could ascertain that the charges would be reasonable.[5]

Soldiers had little more success finding reasonably priced goods in town. After the occupation of Cairo, army camps brought tens of thousands of people into the tiny town. The *Jonesboro Weekly Gazette* reported the presence of a large number of "unlicensed interlopers" on the Ohio levee who were engaged in the business of gouging and swindling soldiers. These sutlers existed at every military base and followed the soldiers when they were marching in campaigns. Dr. Brinton wrote that he could never quite bring himself to like these people, "who infested the levee, and its neighborhood."[6] A Belleville, Illinois, soldier made another observation on the subject: "of course everything that an officer is obliged to buy or have, is hell and damnation heigh [sic]. The darn sutlers must all be rich by this time, or else spent their money as fast as they make it."[7]

Local journalists decided that sutlers should be chastised for cheating soldiers. One correspondent predicted that "they [the sutlers] will soon be 'spotted.'"[8] *Spotting* referred to a vigilante system practiced by locals that consisted of targeting, or "spotting," particular

4. *Jonesboro Weekly Gazette*, June 22, 1861.
5. William H. Onstat to Sister, Oct. 20, 1861, William H. Onstat MSS.
6. Brinton, *Memoirs*, 68.
7. Kircher, *German*, 17.
8. *Jonesboro Weekly Gazette*, June 29, 1861.

people for harassment. The victims would frequently be reported to Union authorities as suspicious individuals who should be arrested and placed in the guardhouse. In another tactic, spotters sometimes attempted to destroy a public figure by falsely accusing the man of misbehavior or treasonous sentiment.[9]

In a move that marked his administrative efficiency, Grant brought the sutlers at Cairo under military control. He implemented a system that required sutlers to apply for permits. In order to be licensed, the sutlers had to show certificates from the proper officers to prove that they had obtained permission to trade with the army in Cairo. The men had to swear an oath that they would not sell to anyone but the Union army.[10] The required permits cut down on inflated prices in the District of Cairo.

Although time did not permit ferreting out every instance of dishonest trading, Grant did eliminate some large-scale schemes that had been designed to cheat not only the soldiers but also the federal government. In this pursuit he made a mortal enemy of a Bloomington lawyer who had ridden the Eighth Judicial Circuit with Abraham Lincoln. Leonard Swett showed up at the Cairo base in 1861. Known as Cameron's mouthpiece, Swett engaged in activities at Cairo that showed him to be of the same moral caliber as his benefactor in Washington.[11]

Fortune having thus far eluded him, Swett pursued a number of questionable schemes during the war. The would-be entrepreneur, whom C. H. Ray assessed as a brilliant, competent attorney, lacked luster in the area of business. After insinuating himself into shady dealings with local contractors and speculators in Cairo, Swett attempted to promote his corrupt transactions by circumventing Grant's authority. As a result, Grant came to view Swett as one of his most bitter enemies.[12]

Relying on his connections with Lincoln, Swett devised a plan to establish an official post sutler position at Cairo. The appointee would answer directly to him. His undoing came when he proceeded to instruct Grant concerning the appointment of such an official. Grant, demonstrating that his judgment of men could be astute,

9. Ibid.

10. Joint Committee, 3:573.

11. Mark E. Neely, *The Abraham Lincoln Encyclopedia*, 299.

12. Monoghan, *The Man Who Elected Lincoln*, 81; Grant, *Letters*, Grant to Washburne, Nov. 7, 1862.

immediately mistrusted Swett. Unintimidated by Swett's political connections, the district commander enlightened the lawyer on the law. In strictly legal terms, no such appointment existed.

Determined to replicate the fortunes he saw accumulating around him, Swett countered that he had already made such an appointment and expected Grant to honor his action. But Grant dismissed the appointment and declared that if Swett's appointee appeared at the base, he would be required to trade on an equal footing with all the other merchants. Grant explained that no particular sutler could expect to gain a monopoly of trade at Cairo. In spite of Grant's explanation, Swett pursued the appointment so persistently that Grant finally told him that any authorization to distribute funds to a post sutler would be refused. Swett, seeing that Grant had rendered his plan worthless, finally abandoned the project.[13]

Swett's unsavory behavior added to Grant's stress, but the debacle produced some positive results. Showing that he could be roused to appropriate anger when necessary, the mild-mannered Grant came down hard on Swett. Venting unusual wrath over the lawyer's vicious meddling in military affairs at Cairo, Grant first threatened to seize the Illinois Central Railroad, a commodity in which Swett had invested heavily, then Grant ordered Swett out of his district, stating that he would shoot him if he ever came back to Cairo.[14]

Drawing on his political ties, Swett appealed to the president to intervene; however, Lincoln demonstrated that his penchant for unprincipled men was tempered by keen judgment. He supported Grant's decision and warned Swett against defying the general's instructions. Lincoln already perceived Grant as a fighting man. He thought it possible that Grant might make good his threat. Left with no other choice, Swett left Cairo. But, furious over losing his chance for quick riches, he waited until he had traveled a safe distance away from the Cairo District and then wrote Grant a number of offensive letters. Perceiving Swett's unpredictable character, Grant kept the letters locked in "Mr. Safford's safe" in case he should ever need concrete evidence[15]

The problem of sutlers siphoned valuable time away from Grant's strategic campaign planning, but another group of profiteers rivaled

13. Monoghan, *Man Who Elected Lincoln,* 81; Grant, *Letters,* Grant to Washburne, Nov. 7, 1862.
14. Catton, *Grant Moves South,* 94.
15. Ibid., 21.

the Confederate army in challenging Grant's command capabilities. The wealth harvested by sutlers became no more than petty cash when compared to the lucrative sums realized by those men who succeeded in gaining contracts to supply an entire army with a particular commodity. The abuse of contracts on the part of unconscionable profiteers eventually degenerated into scandals that covered the front pages of newspapers across the nation. No department of the army went untouched by the activities of corrupt contractors, and no post lay beyond their reach.

Harper's Weekly told the sordid story of the first contract awarded for supplying cattle to the army at Washington. A politician secured the contract, sold it to a speculator, and made thirty-two thousand dollars from the deal. The speculators who supplied the cattle made twenty-six thousand beyond the politician's profit. By July 1861 so much graft and corruption had come to be associated with war contracts in Washington, D.C., the government appointed Col. Joseph W. Webb to serve as inspector of subsistence of the troops in that location.[16]

In the West, the *Chicago Tribune* ran a particularly inflammatory report concerning army contracts. Referring to contractors as "scalpers trying to clothe the troops in rags and feed them sour flour and stinking meat," the journalist outlined what he considered to be a just punishment for these treacherous traders: if apprehended, fraudulent contractors should suffer the same military discipline as deserters. They should be brought up to the drumheads and shot outside the lines. The reporter did not doubt that some forms of speculation were tantamount to treason.[17]

Once sordid stories of speculation circulated to the public, pressure mounted for Simon Cameron to retire as Secretary of War. A reputation for fraudulent business practices had preceded Cameron to Washington, and government officials as well as the public held him personally responsible for the contract problems. Lyman Trumbull, one of the triumvirate of Radical Republicans in Congress, thought Cameron should be turned out of office immediately for incompetence and jobbing.[18] Trumbull concluded that the replacement of Cameron would "be equal to the gaining of a battle to the

16. *Harper's Weekly*, Feb. 1, 1861; *Cairo City Weekly Gazette*, July 4, 1861.
17. *Chicago Daily Tribune*, June 21, 1862.
18. Tap, *Over Lincoln's Shoulder*, 19.

Government."[19] Although John Hay questioned Trumbull's opinions overall, in this assessment, Trumbull was very likely correct.

Regarding another key figure in the scandals, Trumbull's judgment proved less sagacious. Frémont, in attempting to protect areas already under attack and shoulder sole responsibility for supplying his forces, committed many infractions. His handling of these important duties created so many scandals that his reputation in the West began to rival that of Simon Cameron in the East. Finally, public frustration with Union disasters in the field pushed the Radical Republicans to seek investigations of military matters. Preoccupied with military ineptitude and political preferment, Congress had allowed the issue of contracts corruption to languish.[20] But public outrage had forced Cameron to step down from his cabinet post, and that act had alleviated the corruption in the East somewhat. The Radicals then turned their attention to Frémont.

In the western theater, Lincoln's dismissal of Frémont from his department command led to investigations of military ineptitude and contracts corruption. In the president's opinion, the Pathfinder lacked military acumen. Resistant to executive authority, the Radicals would not accept the dismissal of one of their favorite sons from such an important command without a serious effort at redemption. Once an inquiry got under way, investigators in the West focused on supply transactions in St. Louis and Cairo.

On December 2, 1861, Senator James Grimes of Iowa proposed the creation of a committee of investigation. That body would look into every military reversal suffered by the Union forces with an eye to identifying problems in the chain of command. At the suggestion of Senator John Sherman of Ohio, brother to Gen. William T. Sherman, the scope of the committee was expanded to include investigation of every aspect of the war. Thus, the Joint Committee on the Conduct of the War came into being.[21] Another investigative body— the House Committee on Government Contracts—had questions of its own concerning supply transactions. The reports of both committees told tales of carelessness, deception, and outright illegalities.

In St. Louis, M. C. Meigs ran the Quartermaster's Department with impeccable honesty. Unfortunately, some of the men around him

19. Trumbull, "Papers," Aug. 31, 1861.
20. Tap, *Over Lincoln's Shoulder*, 25.
21. Ibid., 36.

failed to profit from his example. At department headquarters in St. Louis, Meigs attempted to comply with Frémont. The quartermaster-general did everything he could to see that the western armies received supplies under the most reasonable terms. He requested $500,000 for the Quartermaster's Department in the West. He instructed Maj. Robert Allen to use careful discretion in settling accounts for supplies. When dealing with "legal and advertised contracts," Meigs thought it best to check local prices and reduce the contractors' demands if the terms seemed unfair or inequitable.[22]

Meigs could not, however, regulate the contracts personally negotiated by Frémont, who routinely circumvented proper procedures in order to award contracts to dishonest men. Under Frémont's administration, great latitude had been taken in verbal orders. Frémont supported a system whereby accounts concerning hundreds of thousands of dollars had been presented to the quartermaster of the Department of the West in an informal, irregular, and unauthorized manner. In addition, Frémont had awarded contracts by verbal agreement without advertising for bids as required by law, granted only on his personal approval.[23]

Testimony revealed that corruption in a particular commodity at St. Louis tended to correspond with corruption in that same commodity in Cairo. In one particular instance, a certain Capt. Edward M. Davis had received a contract to supply blankets by verbal order of General Frémont. A board of army officers examined the blankets and found them to be rotten. In spite of the unacceptable quality of the merchandise, Frémont insisted on purchasing the goods. In Cairo, nurses discovered that army blankets used in the military hospitals left black dye on the skin of the sick and wounded.[24]

Attempting to address problems with another of Frémont's contracts, M. C. Meigs had discussed with Cameron Frémont's system for procuring clothes for the troops. Unaware that he was seeking answers to corruption in the West from the maestro of corruption in the East, Meigs explained that Frémont had delegated the powers and duties of contracting and providing clothes for the soldiers to a Union Defense Committee in Chicago. Meigs thought it unwise to place government funds under the control of private citizens since

22. OR Armies, M. C. Meigs to Robert Allen, Sept. 3, 1861, I:8.
23. Joint Committee, 3:18, 10.
24. Eleanore, *King's Highway*, 249.

the "Practice of going outside the legal agents of the Quartermaster's Department to make contracts and disbursements is liable to great abuse."[25]

In Cairo, the quartermaster and his assistants practiced outright thievery in conjunction with local entrepreneurs. Abuse on the part of private contractors, more interested in profit than in victory, may have been predictable. But even Meigs failed to foresee that the legal agents of the Quartermaster's Department might also abuse the system in their individual departments. Such a situation arose at Cairo. Not only did the staff in the quartermaster's office behave dishonestly, but also some of the regular army personnel in Cairo engaged in corrupt transactions.

The abuse of contracts for clothing in Cairo made it difficult and costly to furnish uniforms to the soldiers at that post. A Cairo editor documented one incident involving an officer from the Quartermaster's Department who ordered fifty uniforms from a local merchant. When the merchant delivered the uniforms at two dollars and fifty cents each, the officer in question forced the merchant to write a bill showing the cost as twenty-five dollars per uniform. The officer then proceeded to pay the merchant the original price, pocketing the surplus.[26]

Corrupt contractors infuriated officers and private citizens alike. Soldiers bore the brunt of fraudulent trading either through deprivation of desperately needed items or injuries caused by inferior matériel. Writing from Cairo in May 1861, George Durfee told his uncle that "we have not got our uniforms yet and the Capt [sic] says he thinks it is doubtful if we get them at all as the man that had the contract failed to fulfill it."[27]

Grant had quickly identified problems with local contractors in his district. The local newspapers in Cairo reported that businessmen in the community were enjoying much greater success than they had in peacetime. Local editors failed to publicize the source of the wealth: excessive profits from army contracts. By December 1861, local speculators had already invested large sums of money in housing, new businesses, and real estate.[28] The unprecedented

25. Joint Committee, 3:18, 10.
26. Bradsby, *History of Cairo*, 66.
27. George Durfee to Uncle, May 21, 1861, George S. Durfee MSS.
28. *Cairo City Weekly Gazette*, Dec. 26, 1861.

profits at Cairo had originated with the Commissary and Quartermaster departments.

The quartermaster at Cairo had been practicing Frémont's system of awarding contracts, a system that resulted in much abuse.
Methods of the Commissary Department allowed further corruption
to creep into contract awards. Grant found evidence that a group
of persons in the town, whom he referred to as "a combination
of wealthy and influential citizens" had gained a near-monopoly
on army contracts.[29] The men had been in business together since
the beginning of the war. Just as Frémont had organized a system
to award contracts locally, Thomas J. Ragsdale, a Cairo man working with the army's Commissary Department, dealt as closely as
possible with local men. Grant nicknamed the group the Cairo
Ring.[30]

Compounding the problems at Cairo, an unidentified man from
Washington—possibly Leonard Swett—had come to town for the
purpose of handling contracts. Under a system that he instituted,
this man would "put out the word" that a contract was going to be
offered an hour before the bidding.[31] Potential contractors gave
bids at the commissary's office, which at that time was housed in the
Halliday/Graham wharfboat. In the absence of a post commissary
officer, the state commissary officer took the bids orally. Each bidder
could hear the other bids offered, a system that facilitated corruption. Even worse, commissary officers frequently gave contracts
without even opening them to bids. The ring of contract monopolists
in Cairo pursued a system of bid-rigging, keeping contracts in their
circle by bidding just under the highest bid offered from any outside person and then pulling out all lower bids.

The greedy group of speculators claimed to have enough influence
to remove any general from the District of Cairo who displeased
them, and Grant put the claim to a test over forage contracts.[32]
Prior to Grant's arrival, some contracts for forage had been awarded
on bids that ran higher than 30 percent above the average costs.
Recognizing the contracts for the scam they were, Grant annulled
them. When the ring learned what Grant had done, they sought to

29. Grant, *Letters*, 21.
30. Catton, *Grant Moves South*, 55; *Cairo City Weekly Gazette*, May 16, 1861.
31. House Select Committee, Cairo, Oct. 31, 1861, 12.
32. Grant, *Letters*, Grant to Washburne, Nov. 7, 19, 20, 21, 1862.

counter the general's action by appealing in person to Robert Allen at St. Louis.

Confronted by men attempting to cheat the federal government, Grant's fighting instincts came to the fore. He wired Allen with details of the transactions. When Allen learned that the unethical suppliers were inflating bids, he supported Grant and turned against the contractors. Allen refused to take vouchers from the quartermaster in Cairo without the approval of the district commander. Grant won the first round by refusing to approve the vouchers, leaving the contractors with no choice but to abandon the contracts and sell the forage for its true value.[33]

Efforts by members of the Cairo Ring to "spot" Grant prompted the general to send Captain Baxter, quartermaster for the District of Cairo, to Washington to plead his case. Grant sent a message along with the loyal officer, "Captain Baxter can tell you of the great abuses in this Department here and the efforts I have put forth to correct them, and consequently the number of secret enemies necessarily made."[34]

After Baxter had delivered Grant's message in Washington, the Joint Committee decided to conduct an investigation into military matters in Cairo. During the committee's initial investigation into the conduct of the war in the western theater, none of the committee members had actually visited the West. Then, as a result of Grant's letters and Baxter's visit, the House of Representatives sent commissioners to hold inquiries at Cairo.[35]

During Grant's tenure of command at Cairo, members of both committees took testimony from his officers concerning military movements in the West and contract awards to local men. Grant himself gave testimony in regard to contract bidding and supplies. Armed with information from colleagues, committee members paid special attention to the Quartermaster's Department at Cairo. Continuing their investigation, the commissioners saw indications that

33. Ibid.
34. Ibid., 3.
35. OR Armies, Memo, War Department, Feb. 28, 1862, III:1:122; *Reports of Committees Made During the Second Session of the Thirty-Seventh Congress, 1861–1862*. Report No. 2, House Select Committee on Government Contracts, I, 36; OR Armies, Memo, War Department, Feb. 28, 1862, III:1:122; House Select Committee I:36.

the large dealings in coal for steam and gunboat service had been frequently tainted with fraud.[36]

As early as December 1861, George Wise, assistant quartermaster in St. Louis, had written to Foote in Cairo to suggest that Mr. Candee—brother-in-law to A. B. Safford—should be granted a pay raise of one hundred dollars. Wise noted that Candee worked as a quartermaster's clerk and concluded, "as his duties are arduous and responsible" the raise would be wise.[37] Perhaps Wise intended the raise to serve as a safeguard against the temptation of dishonest profits in a department where corruption flourished.

Once representatives of the House committee arrived at the base, they looked into the transactions conducted under the charge of Quartermaster R. B. Hatch. In the interim between battles, Grant had read an article in the *Chicago Tribune* accusing the quartermaster at Cairo of running a scandal in lumber. Chicago lumber dealers told correspondents that Hatch and his agent had been buying lumber at one price and then telling the dealers to write invoices for a higher price.[38]

Determined to ferret out the truth, Grant sent Hillyer to Chicago to investigate. Hillyer found enough evidence to support Grant's conclusion that Henry Wilcox, Hatch's confidential clerk, should be arrested. After looking into the matter more closely, Hillyer discovered that Hatch himself had dealt dishonestly with the federal government. In an attempt to save his position, Hatch wrote Grant, perhaps believing that his personal association with the general might lead to clemency.

Hatch denied any wrongdoing and claimed that his clerks were responsible for the fraud. Unconvinced, Grant supported the investigators from Washington. They concluded that Hatch had planned the deception and carried out the scheme in collusion. Subsequent evidence showing that Hatch had contracted to supply the Confederacy with wagons put him beyond even the help of his brother, Illinois Secretary of State Ozias Hatch.[39] Continued testimony revealed that Hatch's corruption ran deeper than lumber and wagons.

36. Ibid., LI.
37. OR Navies, George D. Wise to Andrew Hull Foote, Dec. 11, 1861, 460, I:22.
38. Grant, *Papers*, 3:289–90.
39. Ibid., 3:324 n., 326 n.

Gross inefficiency characterized transactions for another commodity at Cairo, one that had also been tainted with corruption at St.
Louis. With the many horses housed at army bases, contracts to supply hay drew large profits. Before the investigators, Cairo grocer
John W. Trover testified that he had been supplying the military on
the authority of Hatch and Rutherford—the state commissary officer—ever since Union troops first came to town. Trover furnished
nails, tar, tallow, rosin, commissary supplies, and hospital supplies
on requisition from the quartermaster, without advertised contracts.
When pressed, Trover stated further that Hatch had illicitly contracted for hay and lumber with men in Cairo. However, Trover
could remember neither the names of the men nor the price of the
supplies.[40]

Grant's testimony addressed both cattle and hay. Under oath,
Grant also had difficulty remembering names, stating that he did
not know the names of the men who held contracts to supply his
army with beef. No collusion attended Grant's misremembrance.
The contracts had been awarded before his arrival at Cairo.[41] After
stating that the quality of the beef provided by unnamed contractors had recently declined, Grant turned to the quality of hay coming into Cairo, which was also very poor.

Under Frémont, Major McKinstry had given orders to Hatch to
draw all supplies for Cairo from St. Louis. The arrangement had
come under suspicion when Senator Browning visited the western
theater. Browning accompanied Samuel Holmes, Speaker of the
House in the Illinois legislature, to the Quartermaster's Department
in St. Louis. Holmes had wished to gain a contract to furnish oats,
corn, and hay for the armies of the West. Holmes planned to provide the grain at the market price in St. Louis at the time of delivery.
McKinstry refused to deal with Holmes, informing him that the Quartermaster's Department of the West wished to contract only with
local men. Holmes left without closing a deal. Eventually, Browning suggested that the Quartermaster's Department at Cairo be
watched. Grant freed Cairo from the questionable practices going
on in St. Louis. Faced with the prospect of being forced by McKinstry
to pay shipping costs to bring hay from St. Louis to Cairo, Grant
decided that he could buy local hay for less.[42]

40. Joint Committee, 10; House Select Committee, 11.
41. Ibid., 2–3.
42. Browning, *Diary*, 499; House Select Committee, 2–3; 4.

The committee then turned to investigating who was providing the horses and mules that consumed the hay. Another lucrative commodity open to private contractors, the supply of horses generated serious scandals at both St. Louis and Cairo. In truth, irregularities in the procurement of horses plagued the West. Meigs had discovered that contracts for supplying the army at St. Louis with horses were being sold to unscrupulous speculators. Legal contractors in Chicago charged the army $95 for a horse, while in St. Louis, a comparable horse sold for $130.

The dishonesty reached beyond price. The committee learned that in Chicago in 1861, Quartermaster W. A. Webb had issued contracts for horses without advertising for bids. A quartermaster's clerk in the Eighth Illinois Cavalry Regiment testified that the firm of Sanger, Wallace, and Mix had furnished twelve hundred horses for that regiment without advertising.[43] Wishing to deprive dishonest contractors of high profits, Meigs had given Allen instructions to pay speculators last.[44]

A similar, if not more corrupt, system existed at Cairo. Hatch, of course, had been involved. Early in the hearings, sufficient evidence existed to suspend Hatch from his office. Hatch's successor enjoyed no more confidence from Illinois officials than had Hatch himself. After his visit to the base, Browning had asked Meigs to watch Quartermaster James Dunlap, formerly brigade quartermaster for McClernand. Based on reports from friends in the community, Browning suspected Dunlap of having stolen supplies.[45] The reports proved true.

The testimony of U.S. Marshall David L. Phillips revealed corruption in horse-trading at the Cairo post. G. B. Dunton, a quartermaster's clerk, had been buying horses and mules at the base without the benefit of advertisements or contracts. Dunton had perpetrated a scam against local providers who attemped to sell stock. After instructing other quartermaster clerks to tell potential sellers that the government was not buying stock, Dunton would require sellers to see him when they arrived at the Quartermaster's Department. He would then convince the livestock owners that, rather than drive their animals all the way back home, he could take the beasts off their hands for rock-bottom prices. After bilking

43. House Select Committee.
44. Ibid.
45. Grant, *Papers*, 3:178; Browning, *Diary*, 522.

the farmers, Dunton billed the government for the full cost of the animals.[46]

The corruption of the Quartermaster's Department concerning horses and mules ensnared many officers who had been under Hatch's authority. Marshall Phillips testified that one Captain Taylor irregularly disposed of contraband horses and mules seized in Missouri and Kentucky. In one complicated transaction, Taylor took charge of contraband property entailing sixty to seventy horses. He first traded five mares for mules, then sold all the mules, and traded off the rest of the horses except for eleven that he shipped to Hatch's farm in Griggsville, Illinois. Taylor turned over the money made from this deal to Hatch and Dunton, but they refused to give him a receipt. For undisclosed reasons, in October 1861, Hatch dismissed Taylor from the military.[47]

Hatch's illicit dealings involved more than culling prime livestock for his personal farms. A quartermaster's clerk stated that at one time Hatch drew up a contract to supply the army with two hundred mules. He awarded the contract to himself under a fictitious name. Hatch then sent a Frederick White and an H. Dallas to purchase the mules. Preliminary investigations resulted in the arrest of Hatch and suspended payment of all contracts at Cairo.

As the committee continued probing into military business transactions at the Cairo base, Swett's sutler scheme came to their attention. Investigators uncovered an organized system of "plunder and corruption practiced against army sutlers."[48] The report assigned responsibility for the corruption to an army general who had been charging all sutlers a monthly tax of one hundred dollars. The conspirators planned to establish a division sutlership and force sutlers to pay the tax to that person. Grant's banishment of Swett had put an end to the scheme.

Under Grant's command of the Cairo District the activities of the Cairo Ring decreased significantly. From that time on, all vouchers for contract payments in the Cairo District would require Grant's signature. When Grant discerned that a contractor was charging an inflated price, he simply refused to sign the voucher. Considering the great power he had over other men's opportunities as com-

46. House Select Committee, 19.
47. Ibid., 17.
48. Ibid.

mander of first a district, later a department, and finally all of the
Union armies, Grant demonstrated exceptional integrity and honesty throughout the war. He adopted the policy of distancing himself from the entire process of contracts awards. When his own father
asked for assistance in securing a contract to supply harness to the
armies in the West, Grant patiently explained that he could not be
involved in securing contracts.[49]

Doing the right thing toward the federal government came at a
price in the District of Cairo. Grant's intervention in the profiteering
of the Cairo speculators bore long-range, potentially disastrous consequences. During this treacherous time, Grant's personal assistant,
John Rawlins, recognized that dangers surrounded the general at
the Cairo base.[50] Rawlins knew that Grant possessed an amiable dis-
position. The general tended to get attached to easygoing men and
extend them undeserved generosity. Surgeon Brinton recalled, "Bad
men were ever approaching him, seeking to further their own plans
and interests; some wanted promotion; some, place; and others, contracts, or the equivalent, recommendations, by which they could
covertly grasp money."[51]

One Cairo editor concluded that Grant loved all jolly, liberal men.
That assessment is perhaps too general, but for various reasons,
some strategic and some personal, Grant had befriended a number
of local men who, like himself, harbored some hope of improving
their financial status during the war. However, a great chasm separated Grant from the profiteers. Grant thought of economic benefit
from the war as purely ancillary to his duty to the federal government. In his case, the eventual financial rewards that resulted from
his military service could not possibly have surpassed or even adequately compensated him for the contributions he made to the
preservation of the Union. Profiteers, on the other hand, came away
from the war with unjustified profits after frequently endangering
the federal government's strategic goals.

Grant's judgment of the men in his social circle at Cairo and of the
officers on his staff matured progressively so that before he undertook his most taxing campaigns, he had relieved the pernicious
hangers-on of their positions in the army. It must be concluded that

49. Catton, *Grant Moves South*, 94; Grant, *Papers*, 3:227.
50. Brinton, *Memoirs*, 137.
51. Ibid; Bradsby, *History of Cairo*, 60.

a man so honest as to refuse to assist his own father's hopes of profit would not assist the money-grubbing schemes of questionable men who surrounded him at Cairo or any other post. Grant undeniably socialized with local men who were later shown to be corrupt, but their corruption was unknown to him until its public exposure.

In the final analysis, corruption could not be entirely stamped out at either Cairo or any other Union post. In the stressful atmosphere of readying and supplying raw recruits to go into battle, Grant could expend only a limited amount of time and energy toward fighting dishonest trade. However, the strategies Grant implemented toward shoddy speculators and unconscionable profiteers at Cairo decreased the corruption in that district. As Grant moved closer to the enemy in fiercer campaigns, he drew on his administrative experiences at Cairo when dealing with increasingly avaricious speculators.

In the Department of the West, a high level of efficiency in supplying the Union armies finally came in the person of Col. Lewis B. Parsons, a man who followed many of the methods already employed by Grant. Parsons had befriended George McClellan in 1860, when both men worked for the Mississippi and Ohio Railroad. When the war broke out, Parsons first served on McClellan's staff in the East. Then in October of that year, Lincoln personally recommended him for the Quartermaster's Department in St. Louis.[52]

When Parsons arrived at St. Louis, he joined a commission with Phil Sheridan, Henry M. Hoyt, and Samuel R. Curtis to assess claims turned in under Frémont's administration. Parsons, who had graduated from Harvard Law School in 1844, possessed knowledge and abilities that qualified him very well for the task Lincoln had given him.[53] The inclination to perform well as a military officer came to him naturally. He developed an interest in transportation in the West when he helped build the Mississippi and Ohio Railroad, a line reaching from St. Louis to Cincinnati. He had served, at different times, as treasurer, director, and president of that line.

Parsons's good character further qualified him to work with a system that held enormous potential for corruption. Commissioners from the House Select Committee on Government Contracts inter-

---

52. Harry Pratt, "Lewis B.Parsons: Mover of Armies" (Winter 1951) 44:4, 351.
53. Ibid., 351, 352.

viewed Parsons in St. Louis and assessed him as being "one of the most efficient and upright gentlemen connected with the quartermaster's department."[54] He uncovered a scheme that profiteers had developed in the East for shipping beef circuitously to designated camps so the railroads could charge local rates, which, in the East, were higher than long-distance rates. Simon Cameron had originated the scheme, but Parsons abolished it.

In St. Louis, Parsons served with Chief Quartermaster Robert Allen, drafting contracts, auditing accounts, and investigating claims. In 1862, He joined Halleck's staff and drafted new sets of regulations for all systems of transportation. He reinstituted competition for the railroads and negotiated new rates. He negotiated a rate with the railroads of one to one and a half cents per mile on lines east of the Mississippi River and one and a half to two cents a mile on lines west of the Mississippi. The western rates had risen to a higher level due to the unstable situation in Missouri, which resulted in the destruction of railroad property.[55]

Parsons's accomplishments with the railroads improved the movement of troops and supplies immeasurably, but his achievements in river transportation represented another very important dimension of his work in the West. From the time Grant arrived in Cairo, Federal officers had faced a difficult situation in trying to deal with riverboat pilots in regard to the cost of securing river transports. Grant improved the system by confiscating vessels belonging to secessionists and denying them the outrageous rental rates they had been demanding.

When Grant found it necessary to commandeer private property of loyal persons he offered a fair price; he rewarded traitors by paying them nothing at all. In regard to the many transports needed on the western rivers, the War Department had developed a charter system whereby the government paid a lump sum to Unionist pilots for each day that the army used their boats. That system, which was subject to abuse, placed a great financial burden on the federal government. Parsons first brought many additional boats and barges to the western rivers, and then he broke the charter system.[56] He

54. House Select Committee, XVIII, XX.
55. Nancy Hunt, "Biographical Sketch of Lewis B. Parsons," n. p., Lewis B. Parsons MSS; House Select Committee, XVIII.
56. Grant, *Papers*, 3:17; Hunt.

instituted the contract system, which required the government to pay by the piece or by every one hundred pounds carried. Consequently, contracted boats carried twice as much cargo for the same price as they had under the charter system.

In 1863, Parsons was promoted to the position of chief quartermaster of western river transportation. In this new position, he supervised all steamboat transportation and oversaw all quartermasters on western rivers. At this time he was sending supplies, troops, horses, cattle, and mules to Pittsburgh, Cincinnati, Louisville, Cairo, Memphis, and New Orleans.[57]

Extant documentation leaves no doubt that profoundly illicit operations existed in the Department of the West and in the District of Cairo. As in the case of other treasonous activities, many details will never be known since a large percentage of business conducted with the armies took place without benefit of any documentation and some of the transactions were purposefully covered up. In an attempt to remedy much of the corruption, Congress adopted the False Claims Act on March 2, 1863. The act allowed the federal government to recover twice the value of any amount of damages caused by corrupt contracts plus two thousand dollars.[58]

Acknowledging that war had come quickly to the West while supplies came slowly, some historians have concluded that haste, necessary in recruiting troops, combined with neglect on the part of the federal government led to some of the problems in supplying the military. As Mary Logan noted, "The West was so far from the [main] seat of the war that they were the last to receive consideration."[59] Members of the Sanitary Commission writing immediately after the war took this benevolent view of the supply problems in the western theater. They were the only contemporaneous chroniclers who did.

It cannot be refuted that some portion of the supply problems in the West did indeed emanate from just such factors. From that perspective some measure of waste concerning supplies did not upset westerners in the early months of the conflict. Many politicians and private citizens were willing to overlook waste if it accommodated

57. Ibid., Pratt, 350.
58. United States Reports 16:305, Oct. Term, 1975.
59. Logan, *Reminiscences of the Civil War,* 49.

victory; however, historians must concede, in light of investigative reports, that bona fide corruption also existed alongside the inevitable waste.[60]

Grant and Parsons made great strides in controlling the rampant dishonesty associated with legitimate supply contracts in the West, but entrepreneurs all over the country still managed to accumulate great fortunes through means of illicit trade. From the inception of the conflict, a form of trading even more sinister than fraudulent contracts appeared in the western theater. The best efforts of honest officials could not crush the lively smuggling trade that sent war matériel and other desperately needed supplies down the Mississippi River to the Confederate army.

60. Tap, *Over Lincoln's Shoulder*, 83–84.

Twelve

Necessary Goods

Late in the war Adm. David D. Porter reminisced about the spread of illicit trade in both theaters of the war. Naming federal treasury agents as the culprits most responsible for the proliferation, Porter wrote, "a greater pack of knaves never went unhung."[1] In his first district command, Grant not only kept the enemy from invading the Union through southern Illinois, but also fought traitors who were attempting to smuggle goods into the Confederacy through the District of Cairo.

In a letter to General Curtis in St. Louis, Grant called Cairo one of the "most exposed" posts in the entire theater of war.[2] By the time Grant had assumed command of the District of Southeast Missouri, smuggling had become voluminous. The trade was supported by a combination of divided loyalties and close proximity to the Mississippi River.

Just as blockade running in the East brought many goods to the Rebels from the high seas, smuggling in the western theater steadily supplied the needs of the Confederate army via interior waterways. In the first year of the war, prize ships that had been turned in to the court of customs at the port of Cairo already lined the docks on the waterfront, their runs for wealth and glory ended. The more immediate threat to Grant's district occurred in inland smuggling.

1. Porter, *Incidents and Anecdotes of the Civil War,* 251.
2. Grant, *Papers,* 3:177.

The trade ran along north/south routes and took place mainly on railroads and along the Mississippi River and its tributaries.[3]

Within days of the Cairo Expedition, soldiers from Chicago had seized a steamer owned by Adams Express. After the secessionist crew deserted the ship, Federal troops inspected the cargo at their leisure. Bales marked "Charleston," and boxes marked "New Orleans" yielded rifles, Colt revolvers, bell metal, and woolen shirts.[4] In addition, the men found costly instruments intended for Confederate officers. Beautiful red, blue, and gray military caps had also been traveling south. The day after the raid—glorying in their blow against the Confederacy—Cairo soldiers paraded through the camps accompanied by a Rebel drum, sporting "Secession caps" and waving a captured Rebel flag. Witnessing the revelry, one Chicago correspondent teased, "If they will only keep on sending us supplies this way, it will be a great relief to the Quartermaster's Department."[5]

The success rate of Federal raids being somewhat hit-and-miss, Secretary of the Treasury Salmon P. Chase officially forbade the shipping of goods to insurrectionary ports one month after Union soldiers entered Cairo.[6] However, in the Western Department mail delivery for Unionists and soldiers campaigning in the South continued. That system posed some problems for the commander of Cairo.

Lincoln and Chase then made the situation even more challenging. Although the federal government prohibited trade with citizens of the South, it was decided that liberated Southerners should be able to trade with the Union for necessary goods.[7] Secretary Chase designated Paducah as a point of exchange, a place where Tennessee Unionists could trade cotton, tobacco, and turpentine for staple products produced in the western theater. Chase put General Smith in charge of supervising the exchanges, which "must be guarded with the utmost vigilance."[8]

The Rebels quickly availed themselves of the opportunities presented by the Paducah exchange site and the federal mail packets,

3. Anderson, *By Sea*, 25; Catton, *Grant Moves South*, 55; Grant, *Papers*, 2:217; Anderson, *By Sea*, 253.
4. *Chicago Daily Tribune*, Apr. 27, 1861.
5. Ibid., Apr. 29, 1861.
6. *Report of the Adjutant General*, 9.
7. Anderson, *By Sea*, 251.
8. Joint Committee, 3:575.

which passed through Cairo and then down the Mississippi and Ohio rivers. The men who had been piloting packets knew the western rivers very well, as they had been following those routes for a year prior to the war.[9]

Blockade running and inland smuggling both involved transshipment. In the West, Cairo's location made it a prime destination for the transfer of illicit goods going south. Accustomed to treachery in Missouri, Grant realized immediately that the Rebels were shipping goods through his district. But smugglers in the Cairo quadrangle—Cairo, Fort Holt, Cape Girardeau, and Bird's Point—met with an obstacle in the person of Grant. Whether by boat, rail, or wagon, illicit goods entering the environs of Cairo ran the great risk of having to bypass Ulysses S. Grant.

Years of living in the St. Louis area may have given Grant a particular sensitivity toward the secessionist mind. Additionally, a network of spies augmented insight, and Grant learned to detect Rebel sympathizers. Although he struck out at every possible means of conveyance for smuggled goods, he believed that packet boats carried the bulk of the illegal trade moving into the South. Greed alone did not motivate the runners. Grant remembered that many men piloting boats for the federal government in the West had formerly been employed by what he termed "the so called Confederacy."[10]

He suspected that many of the packet boat pilots harbored secessionist sentiments. Grant alerted J. C. Kelton at St. Louis to the existence of this system: "I have frequently reported to the Western Department that the line of steamers plying between Saint Louis and Cairo, by landing at points on the Missouri shore, were enabled to afford aid and comfort to the enemy."[11] The pilots would simply leave cargo off along the way, and the Rebels would retrieve it.[12]

To curb the transport of illicit goods by boat, Grant's antismuggling policy stated that all boats suspected of being illegitimate would be hailed and brought to. Papers and cargo could be examined, "Every thing must be done to prevent the enemy receiving supplies."[13] Traffic on the Mississippi felt the brunt of Grant's vigilance first. A few days after occupying Paducah, Cairo soldiers

9. Anderson, *By Sea*, 16.
10. OR Navies I:8. Grant to J. C. Kelton, Nov. 22, 1861.
11. Ibid.
12. Grant, *Papers*, 3:4.
13. Ibid., 2:243.

enjoyed another successful raid. On September 11, 1861, Union troops confiscated three boats manned by secessionists. The cargoes contained a "fine lot of horses, cattle and mules."[14] The Federal troops involved in the raid felt satisfaction at having robbed the Confederates.

Three weeks later, Grant followed the progress of the *J. H. Dickey*. The boat docked between Bird's Point and Commerce, Missouri. As it turned out, the place had been aptly named. One of Grant's spies, Noah C. Johnson, informed the general that, at Commerce, businessmen were selling supplies to anyone who had the money to pay for them, regardless of political allegiance. The same situation existed at Benton, Missouri, and Thebes, Illinois. As soon as the boat docked, the *Dickey*'s crew unloaded seven boxes marked for Charleston, Missouri. Shortly thereafter, twenty men showed up with a wagon and loaded the boxes for transport to the Confederate army. But the boxes never reached their destination. Grant sent a regiment to confiscate the supplies. From his camp in Cairo, William Onstat wrote his sister lamenting that he had been too ill to participate in these raids. Price's Landing, located halfway between Cairo and Cape Girardeau on the Mississippi, also surfaced as a hot spot for the transfer of goods to the Rebels.[15]

On the Ohio, another route beckoned to smugglers. Stating that entirely too much smuggling was occurring between Evansville, Indiana, and Paducah, Kentucky, Lieutenant Phelps bemoaned the regular delivery of mail from Cairo to towns on the Kentucky shore. Phelps described to Admiral Foote the problem of illicit supplies entering Kentucky through Cairo: "Goods are brought down by wagons from the central railroads of both Indiana and Illinois, and carried across the Ohio thence to rebel camps."[16] Phelps believed the contact not only supplied the Rebels with matériel, but also afforded a means of communication and information to the Confederates camped at Bowling Green.

Grant responded to the problem of illicit traffic on the Ohio and Mississippi rivers by requiring that soldiers and sailors traveling from Fort Holt to Cairo have written passes. Eventually, military personnel traveling to any of the posts in the district—Cairo, Bird's

14. James McIlrath to Jane McIlrath, Sept. 11, 1861, James McIlrath MSS.

15. Grant, *Papers*, 3:119 n; Onstat to Sister Lizzie, Oct. 17, 1861, William Onstat MSS; Grant, *Papers*, 3:55 n.

16. OR Navies I:22. Phelps to Foote, Dec. 30, 1861.

Point, Cape Girardeau, or Fort Holt—had to have such a pass. Even commissary officers traveling from Fort Holt and Bird's Point had to show a pass to enter Cairo.

Under Grant's command, Union soldiers halted many boats that had departed from St. Louis. After several raids had yielded a wealth of military supplies intended for the Rebels, Grant further amended his earlier belief that most Missourians wanted the restoration of the Union. In a moment of frustration he stated that there was not enough Union sentiment left in southeast Missouri to save Sodom. Finally, he recommended that government boats charging uniform rates carry all cargo passing between Cairo and St. Louis. He buttressed that policy with a requirement that only his handwritten authorization would allow anyone to travel or trade on the Mississippi River.[17]

Grant's policies prevented many cargoes from resupplying the Rebels, but for enterprising Americans, the lure of fantastic profits fueled daring creativity. As the gray gloom that is December in southern Illinois settled over the Cairo post, Grant concluded that heavy smuggling continued to occur; goods landed at ports north of Bird's Point and were carried south by wagon.[18] Illegitimate goods traveling on land came under Grant's scrutiny as well.

If secessionists thought they would have better luck getting secret cargoes past Grant on the rails, they were mistaken. Grant had secrets of his own. He learned that shipments of quinine were leaving St. Louis by way of two Illinois railroads that unloaded at Du Quoin, Illinois. At that location, a government agent picked up the medicine, took it down the Mississippi River and then into the South. Doubtful of the agent's loyalty, Grant sent one of his detectives to investigate. The detective recovered one hundred ounces of quinine along with evidence that it had been en route to Rebels in Memphis. The Confederacy had been supporting the movements of the agent.[19]

Illicit activities on river and rail increased the burden of Grant's duties in the District of Cairo, but smuggling in conjunction with Rebel marauding in communities close to his district added unease to exertion. The town of Jonesboro in Union County, Illinois, had

17. Grant, *Papers*, 3:55 n, 56, 287, n.
18. OR Series I:8. Grant to Oglesby, Dec. 21, 1861.
19. Grant, *Papers*, 3:296.

provided a haven for Rebel sympathizers since the split in the Union. Early in the conflict, in a very public demonstration of their sentiments, secessionists had torn down the United States' flag flying in the public square at Jonesboro and taken it to the nearby village of Anna.[20] Unionists had later retrieved the flag and restored it to its proper place, but the incident demonstrated an absence of love for the Union in the town of Jonesboro.

Grant indulged his intuition concerning Jonesboro. He maintained surveillance of movements in and around the village. If his hunch proved correct, he might be able to close one port of entry to local smugglers and stop citizens of Jonesboro from aiding and abetting the enemy. As Grant had expected, an organized group of armed desperadoes in Jonesboro, Illinois, was operating a center of illegal trade with the Rebels. According to the intelligence, the goods passed from Jonesboro to the Mississippi River and then into Missouri. The report accused an armed band of men, headquartered in Jonesboro, of intimidating Unionists in order to protect the supplies until they left the Illinois shore. On December 21, Grant sent McClernand, along with Capt. Warren Stewart's company, to Neely's Creek at Jonesboro to track down the desperadoes and disperse the criminal ring.[21]

On the other side of Cairo, an even more dangerous situation for Unionists had developed on the Ohio River. At Shawneetown, a village within easy range of the Rebels, marauding enemy troops staged regular raids, riding away with ample goods to supply their camps. Grant brought the problems at Shawneetown to the attention of Governor Yates, who authorized the organization of two regiments that would go in and clean up the place. Under Grant's authority, the "Shawneetown force," comprising one cavalry regiment and one infantry regiment, patrolled the shoreline at the village. Naval officers at Cairo believed that the special force would stop all smuggling and marauding from Shawneetown to the Cumberland.[22]

The allure presented to smugglers by southern Illinois towns such as Jonesboro and Shawneetown prompted Grant to implement even more stringent measures. Gunboats started patrolling

20. *Jonesboro Weekly Gazette*, June 22, 1861.
21. Catton, *Grant Moves South*, 101; Grant, *Papers*, 3:324–25, 328, 329; Catton, *Grant Moves South*, 101.
22. Grant, *Papers*, 3:252–53; OR Navies, Phelps to Foote, Dec. 30, 1861, I:22.

the Ohio and White rivers in addition to guarding the Mississippi. Union forces on this patrol apprehended many Confederate guerrillas, ending their violent raids. Captured steamers yielded much cargo destined for the Confederacy.[23]

Until Grant reached Cairo, the confiscation of illicit cargoes represented only half of the problem. Union soldiers at the Cairo posts did manage to prevent much contraband from reaching the Confederacy, but the confiscated supplies did not necessarily augment the stores of the Union army. While Grant scrambled between campaigns, trying to keep up with his many duties, he came face to face with the man who was responsible for the problem—a man who believed that Grant's district command should have been his.

The transgressions of Benjamin Prentiss unfolded in the Congressional investigation of corruption at Cairo. During hearings, investigators turned their attention to the issue of confiscated goods. Under oath, Prentiss had difficulty remembering details. When questioned concerning confiscated goods taken from the steamer *Daniel Hillman*, Prentiss claimed to have mislaid the schedule. In truth, he had never turned it over to the United States marshal, even though Marshal Phillips requested that he do so. The goods in question had simply disappeared from the base.[24]

In the case of the *Daniel Hillman*, a boat that had loaded at St. Louis and headed for Nashville, Tennessee, Prentiss sent all the confiscated lead to Springfield to be turned into weapons, but he could account for none of the other varied and valuable items. Fine furniture, Enfield rifles, and high-quality pistols, removed from the Rebel boat by Cairo troops, had simply disappeared.[25] Dr. Daniel Arter, surveyor of the port at Cairo, appeared confused concerning procedures for contraband articles. He professed ignorance of the fact that the possession of such items had to be reported to the federal government and could only be disposed of legally through civil proceedings. Before Grant came to town, Arter and other military authorities at Cairo under Prentiss's command had made a practice of arbitrarily taking and using contraband boats and other confiscated goods.[26]

Although smuggling started in 1861 and tested Grant sorely at

23. Merrill, "Port," 256.
24. House Select Committee on Contracts, 14.
25. Ibid.
26. Ibid., 18.

Cairo, the practice did not reach voluminous proportions through-out the country until later in the war.[27] Despite the best efforts of dedicated Federal forces, inland smuggling continued as traitors designated specific regions of the South to serve as receiving cen-ters for illicit goods. As late as 1864, Michael Lawler cited Bayou Barburne in Livingston Parish, Louisiana, as such a place.[28] By the time Lawler recorded this information, he and Grant had left the West to fight many Rebel soldiers who had undoubtedly been armed with guns smuggled down the western rivers.

In Cairo during December 1861 and January 1862, grim holidays passed under the steely skies of winter. Military rule—and occa-sionally freezing weather—prevented the usual fistfights on the Ohio levee that ordinarily entertained the locals through long win-ter months. But in early February, a faint hum of activity started echoing through the town. When the hum rose to a buzz, Chicago correspondents saw the unmistakable signs of an impending move-ment in the District of Cairo.

The *Chicago Daily Tribune* reported 35,000 to 40,000 men being readied to move out, gunboats prepared to sail, and a noticeable military buildup occurring at Smithland, Kentucky. William Onstat wrote his sister Lizzie of the very lively atmosphere at Camp Cairo. Troops were arriving constantly, mostly being sent on to Smithland at the mouth of the Cumberland River, where, Onstat stated, the Union was forming a large and important camp. He observed that gunboats and mortar boats soon would be ready for a campaign.[29]

Mary Logan saw great quantities of munitions and commissary stores concentrating in Cairo, and Julia Grant decided to stay in her austere lodgings at district headquarters. This time, she wanted more than the prophetic visions that had come to her in Galena during Grant's Belmont campaign. When the time came for Grant to lead the Cairo troops into their first concerted movement, Julia would stay in town, as near to him as possible. Grant's unpopular Order No. 5 may have eliminated the traditional melees on the levee, but in a matter of days, the aggressive instincts of this western gen-eral would draw the people of Cairo into a fight of another kind.

27. OR Navies, 22:8.
28. Michael Lawler MSS, Sept. 25, 1864.
29. *Chicago Daily Tribune,* Feb. 6, 1862; William Onstat to Sister Lizzie, Feb. 1, 1862, William Onstat MSS.

Thirteen

Gone up the River

By the winter of 1862, the American Civil War had become a tourist attraction. Europeans, not yet sated by the sanguinity of warfare on their own continent, traveled across the ocean to view the American conflict firsthand. In February of that year, celebrated British author Anthony Trollope visited Cairo. He recorded that one of his traveling companions "entertained the idea that Cairo was the nucleus or pivot of all really strategic movements in this terrible national struggle."[1]

Trollope stated that, at the very point where the Mississippi and Ohio rivers met, a town had been built. Mud seemed to be the one thing that really caught Trollope's attention, even though the Civil War was bringing wealth and culture to Cairo: "Every street was absolutely impassable from mud."[2] He recommended visitors use the wooden sidewalks because on those walkways the mud came only to one's ankles. Trollope expressed disappointment over many of the things he found in Cairo, but his greatest disappointment concerned that which was missing from the town: "all the generals were gone up the Ohio river [sic] and up the Tennessee in an expedition with gun-boats, which turned out to be successful."[3] Trollope referred, of course, to Grant's Tennessee River campaign.

1. Anthony Trollope, *North America* II:150–65, 402, 403.
2. Ibid., 404.
3. Ibid., 407.

By the middle of the war, secrecy concerning his movements characterized Grant's campaigns. But regarding the Tennessee River campaign, Halleck instructed Grant to keep the community of Cairo, still rife with secessionists, and the press in the dark. Even so, almost everyone in Cairo recognized that certain activities signaled a coming campaign. Sharing their commander's instinct to strike at the enemy rather than take a blow, soldiers in Cairo had quickly learned that a review of the troops generally heralded an imminent campaign. Grant, astride his white-maned sorrel named Jack, first rode up and down the columns of men. Then he positioned Jack near the ambulance and watched the troops as they passed by.[4]

Reporters and townspeople alike saw supplies of every description pouring into Cairo and realized something was afoot. Perhaps most telling of all, activities of the U.S. Sanitary Commission and military hospitals accelerated. Doctors transferred recovering patients to free beds, prepared new hospitals, and inventoried huge quantities of medical supplies.[5] The doctors and nurses could not foresee that their most conscientious preparations would prove unequal to the task of caring for the great number of wounded who would be returned to Cairo.

Early in 1862, several months after the last significant action in the West, naval officer Ledyard Phelps discovered a Confederate buildup at Fort Henry, Tennessee. Phelps's reconnaissance along the Confederate line of defense in the western theater revealed the outfitting of three ironclad steamers at the Rebel fort. Phelps reported his intelligence to Foote at Paducah, stating that he had examined Fort Henry and found the works to be formidable. Located at an angle that prevented full reconnaissance, Fort Donelson eluded Phelps's complete evaluation. Union officers, ill-informed about Donelson, concluded that, of the two forts, greater fortifications protected Fort Henry. Confederate officers also inspected Fort Henry. At the time, they found no sign of a Federal presence in the vicinity.[6]

Some confusion remains as to how the Tennessee River campaign originated. One thing is clear: Lincoln promoted such a campaign

4. Catton, *Grant Moves South*, 138; Grant, *Memoirs*, 94.
5. Livermore, *My Story*, 219.
6. Catton, *Grant Moves South*, 133; OR Navies, Phelps to Foote, Jan. 7, 1862, I:22:486; Catton, *Grant Moves South*, 142; OR Navies, Lloyd Tighlman to S. Cooper, Feb. 12, 1862, I:22:553.

early on, and Grant saw merit in the plan from the beginning. Grant himself wrote in his memoirs that the plan for the campaign could not be attributed to any one individual. Forts Henry and Donelson represented weak links in the Confederate line that Lincoln wanted his generals to break. Sharing the president's strategic thought of waging an offensive movement all along the perimeters of the Confederacy to keep the Rebels from transferring troops from one threatened area to another, Grant had pressed for this movement. In any case, before Grant actually received orders from Halleck to move out, Foote, Porter, and Don Carlos Buell had all recommended to the departmental commander in St. Louis that the Union forces should make an attack on the two forts. Finally, the president, who had become impatient with Halleck's hesitancy, took the initiative and ordered an advance against the Rebel line in the West.[7]

In Cairo, excitement and anticipation filled the air. High spirits overtook Grant, who trusted that the campaign would be a huge success. Foote preceded the army with the gunboats. *Cincinnati* served as flagship, and the new armored gunboats, *Carondelet, St. Louis, Essex,* and *Conestoga,* were followed by the two woodclads, *Tyler* and *Lexington.* Twelve thousand soldiers followed Grant out of the Cairo camps, as Smith moved out of Paducah with a force numbering six thousand.[8]

The movement of the Union forces up the Mississippi escaped the notice of Gen. Lloyd Tighlman, who had left his post at Fort Henry to conduct an inspection of Fort Donelson. Sometime on February 4, Tighlman heard firing coming from the direction of Fort Henry. He immediately left Donelson with an escort of Tennessee cavalry. Edwin Halliday, William Parker Halliday's younger brother, numbered among those cavalrymen. By February 5, Tighlman had discerned an imminent attack on Fort Henry and taken what measures he could to defend the Rebel fortifications.[9]

Tighlman transferred the Forty-eighth and Fifty-first Tennessee from Danville and the Sandy River to Fort Henry. He then moved the Twenty-seventh Alabama and the Fifteenth Arkansas from Fort Heiman to Fort Henry. By that time, he could plainly see Federal

7. Catton, *Grant Moves South,* 28–29; Anderson, *By Sea,* 92; Cole, *Civil War,* 285.
8. Catton, *Grant Moves South,* 138; Anderson, *By Sea,* 93; OR Navies, Report of Lloyd Tighlman, Feb. 12, 1862, I:22:557.
9. OR Navies, Tighlman to S. Cooper, Feb. 12, 1862, I:22:555.

forces at Bailey's Ferry, three miles below Fort Henry. As he watched the enemy, he could see more Union boats arriving every hour. In the evening, several large transports joined the Union forces.[10]

Drenching rain fell throughout the night of February 5. To keep morale high, Union soldiers read symbolism into the unpleasant weather. They interpreted the storm as a prophecy of impending wrath against the Rebels. On February 6, Foote's gunboats fulfilled the prophecy. Although McClernand's troops had come ashore and were working their way to the east side of the river, the gunboats had little difficulty reducing the fort.[11]

From inside the fort, Tighlman assessed the situation after two hours of steady firing. The Confederate commander saw that the Union turtles were breaking Fort Henry right in front of the Rebel guns. After consulting with his officers, Tighlman decided on surrender. Further firing could only lead to terrible, unjustifiable loss of life; so, the scant Rebel force sent up a flag of truce, but smoke hanging over the fort was so thick, the flag was initially hidden from view.[12]

Finally, around two o'clock in the afternoon, before the bulk of Grant's troops had arrived, Tighlman boarded Foote's flagship and surrendered. Union officers described Tighlman as a "soldierly-looking man, a little above medium height, with piercing black eyes and a resolute, intelligent expression of countenance."[13] Captain Stembel, commanding the *Cincinnati,* acted on behalf of Foote and took Tighlman's petition. The terms of surrender Tighlman requested carried only minimal conditions: Rebel officers would retain their sidearms; officers and soldiers alike would be treated with the highest consideration due prisoners of war.[14]

Serving in the position of Tighlman's chief of commissary, Edwin Halliday supervised supplies. Halliday left Fort Henry with Nathan Bedford Forrest's cavalry. In his haste to escape to Fort Donelson, he left behind guns, tents, ordnance stores, and commissary supplies. As Halliday fled Fort Henry with the rest of Tighlman's force, brother William was transporting Union soldiers to the scene.[15]

10. Ibid., 556.
11. Boynton, *History of the Navy,* 517–18; Catton, *Grant Moves South,* 141.
12. Walke, "Operations of the Western Flotilla," 29:430.
13. Ibid.
14. OR, Navies, Report of Lloyd Tighlman, Feb. 7, 1862 I:22: 559.
15. Ibid., Feb. 12, 1862, I:22:559; Catton, *Grant Moves South,* 144.

Citing muddy roads as the deterrent, Foote reported to Welles that the army had not participated in the assault against Fort Henry. Still, Grant had the satisfaction of knowing that men under his command had caught Tighlman at Fort Henry after the Kentuckian had eluded him at Paducah. After the surrender, Walke took possession of Fort Henry until Grant arrived. Inside the fort, the captain and his men observed, "On every side the blood of the dead and wounded was intermingled with the earth and their instruments of war."[16] Col. Michael Lawler's Eighteenth Illinois, part of McClernand's command, led the army's entry into the evacuated fort.[17]

Grant landed fifteen thousand soldiers four miles below Fort Henry, planning for them to attack from the rear while the gunboats shelled from the river. Moving in the advance, McClernand was to have cut off the road leading from Fort Henry to Fort Donelson so the Rebels could not escape. The plan went awry when the storm left the ground so muddy that McClernand and his men could not get through to block the road. The exposed path allowed two thousand Confederates to escape to Fort Donelson.[18]

George Durfee confirmed the presence of debilitating mud at Fort Henry, "The Tenn river is out of its banks and it is very mudy [sic] here and hard getting around."[19] Durfee's regiment remained at the evacuated fort while, Durfee stated, Grant kept busy organizing the troops as they came in from Cairo. Durfee anticipated that the Union forces would move out in a few days "as we want fort Donalson [sic] as soon as convenient."[20]

Grant sent Tighlman to Fort Warren near Boston Harbor. Six months later, the Confederate government exchanged Gen. J. F. Reynolds for Tighlman. Still thoroughly secessionist in sentiment, the Rebel general proceeded to Jackson, Mississippi, to organize new recruits. He eventually led those men against Union forces at Coffeeville. Several years after the general's death, Jefferson Davis, speaking at a Confederate Society meeting in Mississippi City, Mississippi, compared Tighlman to ancient Greek and Roman warriors,

16. Ibid., 431.
17. McPherson, *Ordeal*, 223; OR Navies, Foote to Welles, Nov. 13, 1862, I:22: 314; OR Armies, I:7, McClernand's Report.
18. Ibid., 141.
19. George S. Durfee to H. B. Durfee, Feb. 10, 1862.
20. Ibid.

whom Davis thought had not served their countries better than Lloyd Tighlman had served his at Fort Henry.[21]

Union supporters all over the country welcomed the news of the victory at Fort Henry, though they did not yet appreciate the movement's whole significance. The campaign did make clear, however, to the public and to Grant, the worth of Eads's gunboats. The wounded turtles carried the visible sign of victory to Cairo: returning on February 7, the lead ship flew the United States' flag over that of the Confederacy to indicate a victory.[22]

Julia Dent Grant stood on the Ohio levee with other spectators as her husband's troops swung out into the Mississippi River on transports brightly decorated with an array of military flags.[23] Grant himself had remained in the field, moving steadily toward the next objective. A festive atmosphere prevailed at the Cairo base as friends and relatives waved the troops off toward Fort Donelson on the Cumberland River. Having vanquished one stronghold on the Confederate line, Union soldiers sailed confidently toward what they believed would be another easy victory.

Dissenting from the common opinion concerning Donelson, Gen. George Cullum—Halleck's chief of staff—attempted to bring to Halleck's attention the true situation, "I understand, though not from reliable authority, that there are 40,000 rebels concentrated above Dover, and that Fort Donelson is a much stronger work than Fort Henry."[24] Cullum commanded the Cairo post in Grant's absence, seeing that recruits and supplies found their way to Donelson. A promising general from Ohio, William T. Sherman, took command at Paducah.[25] Cullum's assessment had no bearing on Grant's movements because land forces that had missed the action at Fort Henry were already marching twelve miles across country as the gunboats ascended the Cumberland River to Fort Donelson.[26] Finally in the field, closing in on his desired objectives, Grant was prepared to proceed in any case.

21. Neuman, *Paducahans in History*, 41, 43.
22. Catton, *Grant Moves South*, 150.
23. Julia Dent Grant, *Memoirs*, 97.
24. Catton, *Grant Moves South*, 146; George Cullum to Henry Halleck, Feb. 9, 1861, George Cullum MSS.
25. Catton, *Grant Moves South*, 149.
26. Morrison, *Ninth Regiment*, 22.

Acting once again without specific orders, Grant called his subordinate officers to a meeting aboard his headquarters ship, the *Tigress*, on February 11. Henry Walke described the group: Grant, quiet and conscientious, took in everything going on around him; C. F. Smith, a superb physical specimen, absorbed the discussion with the insight of one who knew army regulations by heart; and John Rawlins, a slender, earnest man with large black eyes listened with the intensity of one devoted to Grant and to the Union cause. At the time, Walke thought John McClernand appeared industrious and clever.[27]

Out of this gathering came the decision to send Walke to Fort Donelson with the *Carondelet* on February 12. Walke's boat would serve as a signal ship. Grant left for Donelson that day with the force that would become the Army of the Tennessee. Although Grant did not have specific orders regarding Donelson, he had informed Halleck of his impending movements, and Halleck had not objected. On the twelfth, McClernand and Smith's forces ran down Rebel skirmishers and then camped close to the Confederate lines.[28]

George Durfee's regiment had left Fort Henry on the eleventh. The morning of the thirteenth, Durfee and his comrades came in full view of the Confederate battery. Shot and shell whizzed overhead, and the soldiers spent the day dodging Rebel sharpshooters. Just as Durfee began rationing out supplies, a shell burst within four rods of him and scattered his men. That night, a snowstorm descended on exposed Union troops. Soldiers in the Ninth Illinois remembered experiencing a very unpleasant night. At midnight on the thirteenth, the regiment reported to John McClernand and took a position in his division. Soldiers were still moving around at midnight when Foote arrived from Cairo with ironclads *St. Louis*, *Louisville*, and *Pittsburgh*, holding the wooden boats in reserve. Grant had been unwilling to start the assault without the gunboats, but he was now ready to move.[29]

In camp at Cairo, William Onstat wrote his sister Lizzie, "the Gun Boats have as yet not been so successful as at Fort Henry leaving the principal [*sic*] part of the Fighting to be done by the Infantry."[30]

27. Glatthaar, *Partners in Command*, 139; Wallace, 29:289.
28. Catton, *Grant Moves South*, 152, 146, 153.
29. George Durfee to Uncle, Feb. 17, 1862; Catton, *Grant Moves South*, 143, 155.
30. William H. Onstat to Sister Lizzie, Feb. 17, 1862, William H. Onstat MSS; OR Navies, Pillow to Derrick, 18 Feb. 1862, I:22:559.

Indeed, the victory would be won on foot. With the gunboats out of commission, Grant sent Lew Wallace to strengthen the middle of the Union line.[31] McClernand moved further to the right, but Rebels managed to break this thinly stretched line.

The morning of the fifteenth, Rebels had quite unexpectedly attacked McClernand's extreme right. Meeting in conference on Foote's boat to accommodate the injured flag officer, Grant knew nothing of this assault. As soon as he heard of it, he personally organized McClernand's troops in a counterattack. Falling back on the lesson he had learned at Belmont and relying on his logical mind and good moral sensibility, Grant held together in the crisis. His first fray had taught him that when a battle reaches its pitch, both armies are exhausted; the one that takes the initiative and attacks will be victorious. Now Grant gave greater expression to that maxim. As the Union troops had done at Belmont, the Rebels rejoiced in their success and fell back to regroup. Grant rallied the Federal troops. He hoped to discourage the Confederates by showing a determined aggression.[32]

Smith led the countercharge. Following his lead, foot soldiers marched behind the sharpshooters and skirmishers, route step, colors flying, after their respective colonels.[33] McClernand's troops fought a closely contested battle with the Confederates for several hours. At the height of the fighting, men from McClernand's division poured into a field hospital. Providing a refuge for the living as well as the dead, the field facility offered protection for hundreds of soldiers who rushed into it to escape a volley of enemy musket fire. Army doctors recorded, "the slightly wounded, the mangled, the dying, and the dead presented a scene which baffles description."[34]

The skies over Fort Donelson finally cleared on the night of February 15. Moonlight shone down on stretcher-bearers carrying casualties to the many hospitals organized in nearby farmhouses. Ambulance corps and field hospitals appeared first in the western theater in support of Grant's Tennessee River campaign.[35] Surgeon

---

31. Catton, *Grant Moves South*, 162.
32. Morrison, *Ninth Regiment*, 22; Donald, *Why the North Won*, 25; George Durfee to Uncle, Feb. 17, 1862; Catton, *Grant Moves South*, 169.
33. Catton, *Grant Moves South*, 169.
34. OR Armies, Report of Thomas Fry and H. S. Hewitt, Surgeons, I:7.
35. Catton, *Grant Moves South*, 172; Duncan, *Medical Department*, 98.

H. S. Hewitt, Grant's medical director, established four field hospitals at Fort Donelson and created an ambulance train on the same battlefield. In the East, the regular army still used regimental hospitals and had not embraced the idea of the ambulance train.

Demoralized after the Union's countercharge, John Floyd, Simon Bolivar Buckner, Nathan Bedford Forrest, and Gideon Pillow conferred inside the Rebel fort. Finding the idea of surrendering to the Federals too frightening, Floyd and Pillow sneaked away in the night. Forrest would not contemplate surrendering his men, and he took them and left. In the early morning hours of February 16, Buckner sent a flag of truce to Smith, requesting negotiations for surrender. At Smith's suggestion, Grant demanded unconditional and immediate surrender. Poised to attack should Buckner refuse, Grant left the Confederate general with no choice but acquiescence. Buckner, the second Confederate to have escaped Grant at Paducah, surrendered the works at Fort Donelson.

Grant gained a new nickname after the victory at Fort Donelson. Buckner found capitulation to "Unconditional Surrender" Grant the more bitter since at one time the two men had been sufficiently close that Buckner had extended Grant a loan.[36] But Grant's luck was changing, and the new appellation seemed to fit the scrappy general who had now tucked two victories and a draw under his belt. In the East, McClellan continued to hesitate, waiting for more men, more supplies, and ideal weather, but in the West, Grant had pursued the enemy in the face of miserable weather using what resources he had on hand.[37]

The Ninth Illinois and the Second Iowa were the first regiments to enter the Rebels' outer works after the surrender. The report Grant sent to St. Louis boasted of an unconditional surrender at Fort Donelson that delivered into the hands of the Federals 12,000 to 15,000 prisoners, forty pieces of artillery, and much property.[38] As George Durfee observed, "There is an immense amount of property in our possession."[39] Then, showing that Grant's chastisement for confiscating enemy property still had not taken full effect with the

36. Grant, *Memoirs*, 184.
37. Hattaway, *How the North Won*, 64–45.
38. OR Armies, Grant to Cullum, Feb. 16, 1862, I:7:595.
39. George Durfee to Uncle, Feb. 17, 1862.

Cairo soldiers, Durfee wrote, "The only trophy I have is a horse that I took yesterday."[40]

In Cairo, anxious relatives of the campaigning soldiers once more inundated the town. Cut off from communication with the military, they could only hear the cannon roaring in the distance as hour after hour passed with no sign of returning troops. Finally, after two days, people on the levee spotted the lights of the Mississippi Flotilla.[41] William Onstat noted that the gunboat *Carondelet* had just arrived in Cairo with the news that Fort Donelson had fallen to the Union: "everybody is wild with excitement."[42]

Transports loaded with blue and butternut soldiers choked the river. As the boats docked at the Ohio levee, shrieks of joy skipped across the water to greet the victors of Donelson. Those soldiers who had come through the battle in good physical condition walked down the gangway and marched to their camps to collapse inside the tents. A happy clamor went up from the waiting crowd whenever an onlooker spotted a loved one in the mass of weary men. The absence of a soldier in the marching formation produced wails of agony.

Even if the loved one had only been wounded, a stint in a military hospital could easily translate into a death sentence. Fear enveloped wives and mothers whose men could not be found among the returning soldiers. Cloaked in dread, the women scoured lists of dead and wounded published by the *Cairo Telegraph*. In Carbondale, Mary Logan saw her husband's name listed in the local newspaper among those killed in action.[43] After traveling to Cairo, however, Mary learned that Logan was only wounded.

As soon as George Durfee settled into camp at Cairo, he wrote his uncle, "I am here safe and sound but the 8th has suffered severely in killed and wounded."[44] Capt. Daniel Arter of Cairo commanded the hospital transports that carried the dead, wounded, and dying soldiers back to their point of departure. As the steamers continued to unload at Cairo, the additional hospital buildings set up by army

40. Ibid.
41. Logan, *Reminiscences of a Soldier's Wife*, 115, 116.
42. William Onstat to Sister Lizzie, Feb. 17, 1862, William Onstat MSS.
43. Logan, *Reminiscences of the Civil War*, 61.
44. George Durfee to Uncle, Feb. 17, 1862.

surgeons and the Sanitary Commission overflowed with patients. To make matters worse, the rain and sleet that had complicated battle operations on the Cumberland had fallen on Cairo as well. Arter and the medical personnel struggled to get the wounded into the limited medical facilities at the half-flooded base.[45] Once hospitals in the District of Cairo filled, casualties went to St. Louis. William Onstat commented on the scene: "The wounded from Fort Donelson have been passing here enroute [sic] or St. Louis. I went down on the *City of Memphis,* which had about 200 aboard. It was no pleasant sight."[46]

The United States Sanitary Commission's *City of Memphis* hospital ship had departed from Cairo to follow the military to Fort Donelson and provide what relief it could. Many fallen soldiers, left without the benefit of such a boat, lay on the open decks of transports or packed into cabins where they received little or no medical attention. Male nurses loaded aboard men who had suffered such grievous wounds and then endured so many hours of exposure and exhaustion that they appeared mangled almost beyond human recognition. In the field, medical personnel appropriated convenient sheds, barns, houses, or churches for use as hospitals. In these makeshift infirmaries, wounded soldiers lay unattended on bare floors. Many died before medical staff could get to them.[47]

The Chicago Board of Trade raised three thousand dollars for supplies. The Chicago Sanitary Commission had been sending supplies to the Cairo depot for several weeks before the Tennessee River campaign got under way. In the aftermath of Fort Donelson, doctors and nurses used these items liberally. Sister Eleanore recorded that at one point the hospital at Mound City held fourteen hundred sick and wounded men. The sisters slept on the floor because there were no available beds. Moving among terribly wounded men in the hospitals at Cairo, Mary Livermore grieved for soldiers whose wounds were claiming their lives. In battle, roaring cannon, cheering officers, and blaring bugles drove men to action, mindless of the consequences. Maddened by a desire for victory, soldiers welcomed a

45. Livermore, *My Story,* 201; Logan, *Reminiscences of a Soldier's Wife,* 124, 116.
46. Ibid., 180; William Onstat to Sister Lizzie, Feb. 25, 1862, William Onstat MSS.
47. USSC Report, 38, 163; Livermore, *My Story,* 483; Logan, *Reminiscences of a Soldier's Wife,* 116; Livermore, *My Story,* 180.

glorious death.[48] But a slow, lingering death in an army hospital fell far short of the mens' visions of glory.

While battle casualties either died or recovered in hospitals, the many Rebel soldiers captured at Donelson passed continually through Cairo. Marched through the streets of the business district on the Ohio levee, the prisoners appeared ragged and forlorn. By the time the battle ended, the Rebels had been buried in trenches for five days. The state of their clothing and their demeanor testified to their recent miserable confinement.[49] One Union soldier commented on the parade of Confederate prisoners: "I wish the secesh in the north could see them. They are a pitiful sight. I think they were never [away] from home before. they think we are taking them almost out of the world when we take them to Chicago."[50] Union officials marched the prisoners past the St. Charles Hotel on the waterfront into incarceration camps outside of town. The captured Confederates remained in Cairo until they could be sent north to prison camps.[51]

Victory sparked the return of the festive atmosphere that had pervaded Cairo at the departure of the troops. The town erupted in wild celebration. All business transactions ceased as church bells rang, crowds cheered, and the cannon at Fort Defiance boomed. Public buildings and private dwellings flew Union flags. Indeed, the first resounding Union victory sparked celebrations all over the North. In Washington, D.C., unrestrained joy overtook the city. Senators, in session at the time, cheered and hurrahed the Union troops. Loyal citizens all over the Union hailed Grant as a deliverer. Lincoln began to see him as the only general with an inclination to fight. In fact, Lincoln gained sufficient faith in Grant to promote him. After Donelson, the Illinois general outranked everyone in the West except Halleck.[52]

Grant's victory on the Cumberland River fueled optimism all over the Union. Morale soared in the North and plunged in the South, and with the first decisive victory in a fiercely fought battle falling to the North, foreign nations thought twice about aiding the southern

48. Livermore, *My Story*, 180; Eleanore, *King's Highway*, 235; Livermore, *My Story*, 325.

49. Bradsby, *History of Cairo*, 66.

50. J. B. Paisley to Cousin Jane, Feb. 23, 1862, William McLean MSS.

51. Lansden, *History of Cairo*, 137.

52. Catton, *Grant Moves South*, 180, 188.

cause. Outnumbered when they launched the assault, Grant's troops had dispelled the myth that one Southerner could equal three Yankees in a fight. Officials in Washington saw that—under the proper leadership—Union soldiers could outfight the Rebels.[53]

As a commander, Grant learned much from Donelson. The battle reinforced his faith in the moral value of being on the offensive. Grant did allow himself a moment of pride in a letter to his good friend Elihu Washburne. To Washburne—whom he had promised good conduct in appreciation for his appointment—Grant reported that his soldiers had fought a battle on the thirteenth, fourteenth, and fifteenth that would compare favorably with many of the battles fought in Europe.[54] In the official Orders of Congratulations to his troops, he testified further to his belief that he had achieved a great victory. He stated that Fort Donelson would be "marked in capitals on the maps of our united country and the men who fought in the battle will live in the memory of a grateful people."[55]

In these remarks, Grant showed that he could objectively assess his campaigns and appreciate his successes. He could even take pride in his victories without sharing McClellan's fatal flaw of assuming that he had won the entire war with one successful campaign. Never becoming complacent, Grant finished one victorious campaign impatient to move on to the next battle. Feeling his way through the assault against Donelson, Grant framed the personal strategy that stayed with him throughout the war: find the enemy, strike at the enemy as hard as possible, and keep moving forward.[56]

Grant's soldiers, meanwhile, had been deeply impressed by the Rebels' fierce fighting at Donelson. On the sixteenth George Durfee walked over the battleground, still littered with dead and wounded. He stated that the Confederates had annihilated some Illinois regiments. Rumors had reached Cairo that the Rebels had "entirely cut up" the Eighteenth Illinois, killing Col. Michael Lawler and most of his officers. William Onstat informed his sister of the disturbing news, suggesting that the loss of the Eighteenth demonstrated the ferocity of the battle, "the eighteenth is principaly [sic] composed of the desperate characters of Southern Illinois who know how to

---

53. Catton, *Grant Moves South*, 179; McPherson, *Ordeal*, 225, 226.
54. Williams, *Lincoln and His Generals*, 312; Grant, *Letters*, Feb. 21, 1862.
55. Catton, *Grant Moves South*, 183.
56. Donald, *Why the North Won*, 43.

Fight."[57] Lawler actually survived the battle, along with some of his men, but the Eighteenth Illinois had to be rebuilt before the next campaign. The Eleventh Illinois had also suffered devastating losses. Durfee stated that the aftermath of the battle was *awful*, a sight he did not want to see again anytime soon.[58]

Cairo native Isham Haynie bragged that, more so than any other Illinois regiment, his regiment participated in the hardest fighting over the longest period of time. The press, however, made heroes of Logan and McClernand. While Grant and Logan found a greater appreciation for each other, Grant's doubts about McClernand deepened. A short time after the campaign on Donelson, a group of Grant's staff officers presented him with a ceremonial sword. McClernand did not number among the officers present. John Brinton vaguely recalled being aboard Grant's flagship after the battle when John Logan, Richard Oglesby, and Michael Lawler surrounded Grant. The group also included Wash Graham, C. R. Lagow, C. C. Marsh, and John Cook.[59]

At this time, Gen. James McPherson complained to Halleck about some of the men who made up Grant's personal circle. McPherson assessed them as disreputable characters. Time proved McPherson's opinion to be fairly accurate: Lagow drank heavily and irresponsibly; Cook eventually faced charges for stealing food and other supplies at Fort Donelson; and Graham's efforts to try to tempt Grant with liquor ultimately came to light.[60]

In the joy of conquest, people in the North, as well as the soldiers in the West, fell prey to McClellan's Achilles' heel. Unionists thought that Grant had crushed the Rebels' center. The Chicago newspaper correspondent at Cairo reported that the backbone of the rebellion was broken. In that belief the public was overly optimistic. But in another firmly held idea, Grant's enthusiasts may have been prophetic. They believed this victory assured the success of the Union and the defeat of the Confederacy.[61] Perhaps that conclusion carried

57. William H. Onstat to Sister Lizzie, Feb. 17, 1862.

58. Livermore, *My Story*, 224; George Durfee to Uncle, Feb. 17, 1862.

59. Isham Haynie to Pa, Mar. 22, 1862, Isham N. Haynie MSS; Catton, *Grant Moves South*, 208; Brinton, *Memoirs*, 148.

60. Catton, *Grant Moves South*, 209.

61. Ibid., 179; Morrison, *Ninth Regiment*, 26; William Onstat to Sister Lizzie, Feb. 17, 1862, William Onstat MSS.

some merit. For the duration of the war, Grant continued to harass the Rebels until he finally achieved unprecedented success.

For Grant's soldiers, buoyed by the euphoria of victory, even witnessing the horrible aftermath of battle did not cause them to shrink from marching into enemy fire when duty called.[62] George Durfee recovered from the trauma of witnessing the dead and wounded and couldn't help boasting: "General McClernand complimented us very highly and said that we were in as hot a fire as ever American troops stood under."[63] Affirming the rivalry felt between the soldiers in the eastern and western theaters of the Civil War, Durfee summed up the importance of the battle to the men who had fought in it when he said that "it was no bull run."[64]

At the conclusion of the Tennessee River campaign, Julia Dent Grant left Cairo and returned to her home in Galena, Illinois, via St. Louis. The Union gunboats departed from Cairo for Grant's next battle, but the general, now commander of the Department of the Tennessee, was already leading his men on the southern march that would ultimately culminate in the realization of his and Lincoln's strategy to sever the Confederacy and push the Rebels out of the West. At the Cairo post, military personnel busily fulfilled their duties in the many operations that Grant had organized, but from now on, the general would see little of Cairo.

62. George Durfee to Uncle, Feb. 17, 1862, Durfee MSS.
63. Ibid.
64. Ibid.

Fourteen

Burden of War

After Donelson, soldiers who had started at Cairo passed through the terror of Shiloh and pushed on toward Vicksburg. In May 1863, on the Big Black River in Mississippi, a dying campfire cast eerie shadows across the face of a weary soldier. Pvt. Edwin Loosley finished his cooking duties for the day, and straining to see paper and pen in the light of the embers, leaned forward and carefully recorded the events of the past month. Fighting off sleep, Loosley recorded the movement that had taken the Eighty-first Illinois from their base at Lake Providence, Louisiana, to Port Gibson, Mississippi.[1]

The beauty of Mississippi in the spring did not escape the notice of northern men who had never been in the South, "The soil yields her burden of grain and fruit with scarcely any labor...vegetation is most dense and abundant and it does seem that this is the very paradise of flowers, especially roses which grow wild in endless profusion."[2] But soldiers marching through Tennessee and Mississippi had observed more than lush vegetation. Fruit and flowers might have sprouted without the assistance of human hands, but cotton had not, and volunteer soldiers acknowledged the more sinister side of the Old South as well.

Slave cottages contrasted noticeably with plantation manor houses, the cottages "being built in the most loose manner and inside are the very picture of abject poverty and degraded slavery."[3] Southern

1. Edwin Loosley to Mrs. Loosley, May 6, 1863, Edwin Loosley MSS.
2. Ibid.
3. Ibid.

Illinoisan John Reese offered a wry comment on his impression of the South's peculiar institution. He noted "two great objections to slavery... in the south, that is tracking them and Mixing with them."[4] Reese stated that people in the North could talk about equality with the Negro if they wanted to, "But the south can beat the North in that Respect, on every farm you can see a large percent of the slaves are Mulattoes."[5] Reese concluded from viewing the slaves in Mississippi that "there is plenty of living witnesses here to testify that some person at some time did put themselves on a Equality with Niggers."[6]

Edwin Loosley concluded that Southerners had built their society on the wrong foundation, a foundation that could only lead to war.[7] Following the same campaign trail, John Preston Mann of Liberty, Illinois, wrote, "The negroes grinned with delight as we passed the plantations."[8] He then observed the phenomenon that brought runaway slaves under the aegis of Union army commanders, "Many of them left the farms and came away with us."[9]

With Shiloh and Corinth behind him, Grant remained in the field. Supplies and soldiers still departed from Cairo to follow Grant, whose headquarters had moved to Tennessee. Consistently overlooked as a candidate for an eastern command, Grant continued pursuing the Confederates down the Mississippi River. Grant's strategy took him far from the District of Cairo, but, as long as he remained in the West, his administrative decisions continued to impact the town.

Moving steadily toward the seemingly impregnable Confederate stronghold at Vicksburg, Mississippi, Grant's army marched past numerous plantations. Rebel planters refugeed south to escape the Union army, but, whenever possible, their slaves ran to the blue-coated soldiers. Often, groups of freedmen large enough to populate a city approached the army together. No government plan existed to deal with this spontaneous exodus.[10] Despite the federal govern-

4. John Reese to Tissa Reese, Mar. 4, 1863, John Reese MSS.
5. Ibid.
6. Ibid.
7. Ibid.
8. John Mann to Mrs. Mann, Jan. 28, 1863, John Preston Mann MSS.
9. Ibid.
10. Eaton, *Grant, Lincoln, and the Freedmen,* 1–2.

ment's official stance that the reunification of the country was the only objective of the war, slavery, in the form of black contraband, bedeviled Union generals commanding armies in the South.

By 1863, the federal government had officially emancipated slaves living in areas in rebellion. Grant had gone into the war believing that once the conflict erupted, slavery could no longer exist. He thought as soon as Union forces scored a decisive victory, "negroes will depreciate so rapidly in value that no body will want to own them."[11] Time belied the notion that a little adversity would part Southerners from their slaves. For some time, Grant commented frequently on the possibility of a slave revolt in the South, but as his army moved deeper into the region, he learned that slaves much preferred fleeing their masters to fighting them.

Grant dealt with runaway slaves to some extent throughout his entire career as a Union officer. As was his habit, where policy existed concerning an issue, he faithfully upheld the federal government's dictates. When no policy guided him with black contraband, he improvised a system that proved to be more practical and comprehensive than that which the War Department finally articulated. Serving in Missouri under the government's policy of protecting the property of Southerners in the Border States, Grant had faced the unpleasant task of refusing protection to slaves who came into his camp. At the same time, stating that he had no desire to see the army "used as negro-catchers," he had also refused entry to slave owners seeking their lost property; they were referred to the civil authorities.[12]

In Cairo, Grant had encountered a different policy regarding the black refugees. When Federal flag officers began picking up a number of runaway slaves, Welles decided that naval officers must not encourage slaves to run away but they need not return them either. The secretary of the navy believed the black contraband would be capable of performing necessary duties on naval vessels in exchange for the cost of their maintenance. Foote, an ardent abolitionist, started signing contraband sailors to serve on gunboats. The blacks worked for eight dollars a month plus one ration per day. They enjoyed the status of freedmen as long as they were on the boats. Experiencing such a shortage of manpower that he had been forced

11. Grant, *Papers*, 2:22.
12. Catton, *Grant Moves South*, 92.

to release men from the guardhouse in order to make up sufficient crews for the gunboats, Grant condoned Foote's inclusion of black sailors.[13]

The idea of accepting blacks as soldiers met with much less enthusiasm; initially, the army treated black contraband with impatience and, sometimes, contempt. Army commanders, who never had enough supplies to provide properly for their soldiers, viewed the streams of runaways that sought their protection as a great burden. Providing food, clothing, and medical care for Federal soldiers had posed a challenge to the War Department and to commanding officers all over the Union. No surplus existed to provide for civilians.

The condition of runaways arriving in army camps varied greatly. Some arrived nearly naked. They were often weakened and demoralized, and many carried diseases that the fighting men could easily have contracted. The threat of infection combined with the chaos of sick and undisciplined throngs impeded the movements of military units that needed to move as quickly as possible and focus on military objectives.[14]

Having had very little experience with blacks in general, Union soldiers displayed a broad range of attitudes toward the runaways in their midst, ranging from concern and compassion to fear and mistrust. Many soldiers wrote of their first acquaintance with slavery. Subordinate officers under Grant's command assigned black contraband the role of servants, and, sometimes, slaves. Officers commonly secured black contraband to work for them or serve them. The blacks received very little pay from soldiers, if they were paid at all, and, generally, officers would require the services of numerous blacks.

Southern Illinois soldiers followed the common trend. Indulging his characteristic contempt for protocol, Michael K. Lawler gained a reputation for using the soldiers under his command as servants.[15] Once runaway slaves appeared on the scene, they quickly took the places of the white subordinates. In the minds of many northern men, blacks lent themselves naturally to that role. In a letter to his wife, Preston Mann complimented his contraband servant: "My

---

13. Boynton, *History of the Navy,* 28; Merrill, *Port,* 251; Catton, *Grant Moves South,* 103.

14. Eaton, *Grant, Lincoln, and the Freedmen,* 2.

15. Michael Kelly Lawler MSS, Aug. 3, 1863.

black boy (Charley Davis) is a pretty good cook as well as handy generally."[16]

Handy or not, the fugitives held little appeal for some Union soldiers. These Northerners perceived the runaways as indigent, undisciplined people.[17] Chaplains working with black contraband stated that the freedmen came in every imaginable state of dress and health, frequently displaying what Northerners referred to as the "vices of slavery: theft, licentiousness, and lying."[18] Contrasting sharply with the memoirs of white colonels who trained black soldiers later in the war, written records left by the chaplains indicated that a high percentage of the runaway slaves interpreted freedom to mean that they would never work again but would be allowed to live a life of idle indulgence.[19]

Some Union soldiers saw the freedmen in that light. William Onstat, a central Illinoisan, developed a negative view of the displaced population. He told his sister Lizzie that he had seen enough of slavery by 1862 to satisfy him. He also disdained the officers' appropriation of the blacks, stating, "We have several Nigger loving Captains who must have several of the peculiar institution with them."[20] Onstat assessed the blacks in his camp as lazy and mean.

William McLean, another central Illinoisan, shared Onstat's opinion. Seriously ill with tonsillitis, McLean expressed his disenchantment with camp life in a letter to his sister: "in the first place I should like to kill the officers and in the second place the negroes [sic] and third place I should like to go home and stay there."[21] McLean's illness no doubt colored his statements; however, his words contained some genuine sentiment that related to the relationships common soldiers witnessed between officers and blacks: "there is so many of them laying around here doing nothing I actuly [sic] do believe that the officers think more of the curses than they do of us."[22] Family members wrote back, scolding him for criticizing the blacks so severely.

16. Ibid., Feb. 26, 1863.
17. William Onstat to Sister Lizzie, June 27, 1862, William Onstat MSS; Adams, "Memoirs," 46.
18. Eaton, *Grant, Lincoln, and the Freedmen*, 3.
19. Ibid., 2.
20. William Onstat to Sister Lizzie, June 27, 1862, William Onstat MSS.
21. William McLean to Sister Jane, Feb. 14, 1863.
22. Ibid.; William McLean to Friends at Home, Mar. 2, 1863.

Displaying a more benevolent view of runaway slaves, Lemuel Adams concluded, "They all know more than one would think. [They] seemed to take great interest in everything that was going on and were always listening."[23] Adams's observation mirrored that of Lt. James Shirk, who in the previous year had picked up a load of contraband at Ashton, Louisiana. Shirk showed surprise at the amount of information possessed by the former slaves. General Grant also believed the blacks to be well informed. He consulted a runaway slave familiar with the Mississippi terrain around Vicksburg in order to get reliable information on a route for his army to follow when they marched below the Vicksburg fortifications.[24]

Whatever sentiments the soldiers harbored toward blacks, the presence of the fugitives in army camps tended to divide and distract the soldiers. Hoping to settle the black contingents before his army moved against Vicksburg, Grant conceived an innovative plan to care for those following his army. Grant's superintendent of contrabands, John Eaton, stated that although many commanders in different areas were applying various systems to deal with black contraband, Grant's plan was the most comprehensive and humane. Benjamin Butler had established a program in 1861 that showed some similarities, but at the time Grant conceived his system, commanders serving in different areas did not know what measures other officers were taking regarding the runaways. Eaton believed that, eventually, the federal government adopted the system that Grant had outlined in the field in November 1862.[25]

A top priority was separating the black contraband from the army. This idea reflected Grant's concern for both his soldiers and the runaway slaves. Grant could not afford to lose soldiers to diseases they might contract from the blacks. On the other hand, operating out of a sense of sheer humanitarianism, Grant thought the contraband should be protected from soldiers who tended to mistreat them. Grant first separated the ailing blacks from contact with the army. Then he decided the healthy runaways could do everyday tasks that would free soldiers from such work. Grant believed the able-bodied black men might someday even serve as soldiers; how-

23. Adams, "Memoirs," 46.
24. OR Navies, James Shirk to David D. Porter, Nov. 27, 1862, I:22:509; Catton, *Grant Moves South*.
25. Eaton, *Grant, Lincoln, and the Freedmen*, 15, 27, 47.

ever, Eaton recorded that most new arrivals appeared to be so dispirited they were unable even to care for themselves.[26]

On November 11, 1862, Grant appointed Eaton, an army chaplain, to organize the runaways into work details. The men would busy themselves with picking, ginning, and baling cotton. The women could cook and act as nurses. To ensure the safety of the blacks, Grant assigned guards to watch over the contraband work details. Soldiers served reluctantly as guards; most white men found the idea of spending time around the former slaves repugnant.[27] On November 12, Grant discussed his comprehensive plan with Eaton. The black contraband following his army would be cared for and gainfully employed. The sick would be separated out, and the workers would be paid for their labor.

On November 16, Halleck sent orders to Grant concerning the black runaways. The War Department wanted generals in the field to put the blacks to work but keep them with the army, providing for them by foraging. The first phase of Grant's system for the black contraband coincided perfectly with that of the federal plan. Once implemented, however, the system still bogged down the army in a way that Grant found unacceptable. So, he came up with an antidote to the problem. Protected under the auspices of the Confiscation Act of 1862—a measure that provided sanctuary for runaway slaves residing in Union states—Grant decided to settle the blacks in camps that would be separate and apart from the army.[28]

Reviving his tactic of commandeering the property of southern men in rebellion, Grant used abandoned homes of local Confederates to house the former slaves. Grant sent John Eaton to organize the first contraband camp at Grand Junction, Tennessee, while Gen. Grenville Dodge set up a similar site at Corinth. Stepping into untrod territory, Grant provided food for the destitute freedmen from the army commissaries and issued military tools for the blacks to use in performing their tasks. General McArthur's division provided one regiment to guard the camp.[29] Hoping the War Department would not frown on his decision to locate the contraband apart

26. Ibid., 13, 14, 15, 18, 19.
27. Ibid., 5, 22.
28. Eaton, *Grant, Lincoln, and the Freedmen,* 12.
29. Ibid., 16, 20, 21, 31.

from the army, Grant proceeded, aiming to house the blacks before colder winter weather overtook them.

In 1862, Grant began sending runaway slaves to Cairo. In the autumn of 1862, the army faced the daunting prospect of handling one more group whose needs strained the chronically insufficient resources of the Cairo district. Another army chaplain, James B. Rogers, drew the job of creating the contraband camp at Cairo. As the site of the northernmost contraband camp, Cairo became the center of operations. The Cairo post represented the most secure Federal territory in the western theater, and as a supply center, it was better equipped to offer refuge than any other in the West.[30]

In an effort to support the military officials at Cairo in the care of their destitute black campers, aid societies in the North gathered clothes and other supplies and sent them to the post.[31] In southern Illinois, particularly in Cairo, residents found the influx of black contraband alarming. As in their sentiments concerning the war, division existed among the white population. While some complained bitterly over the presence of the former slaves, others worried about the fate of the numerous runaways.

Mary Logan remarked that the hordes of refugees arriving at Cairo placed a great burden on the city. City editors repeated the claim. Displaced by the war, these people came to Cairo in need of everything: clothes, food, shelter, and protection. Military officers and some private citizens made a valiant attempt not only to offer the black fugitives protection, but also to provide them with some quality of life. Throughout Illinois, newspapers issued a call for citizens to donate necessities to the black contraband living in deserted army barracks in Cairo. The *Bloomington Pentagraph* tried to raise sympathy for the inhabitants of the camp by stating that many of the runaways were nearly white and couldn't be held responsible for the circumstances of their birth.[32]

Sisters at Mound City cared for large numbers of the camp residents until a contraband hospital opened its doors in Cairo. Those who were well enough attended the Freedmen's School that Chaplain Rogers started in December 1862. In addition to securing the

30. Ibid., 203; Edward Noyes, *Contraband Camp at Cairo, Illinois,* 204.
31. Eaton, *Grant, Lincoln, and the Freedmen,* 36, 37.
32. Noyes, *Contraband Camp,* 205, 211.

material necessities of life, army chaplains gave spiritual support by performing many marriage ceremonies. Newly freed men and women put aside the bondage of slavery and happily accepted the bonds of marriage that had been prohibited.[33]

The contraband camp in Cairo offered runaway slaves a better alternative to following the army, but problems arose. Late in 1862, chaplains still found it difficult to identify guards who would show kindness to the freedmen. Exacerbating that situation, residents of the border areas began abusing the black fugitives. Workers for the Western Sanitary Commission worried about the possible consequences of housing the blacks near whites who felt only disdain for the idea of freeing southern slaves.[34]

Expressing a negative concern over the presence of so many blacks in town, the editor of the *Cairo City Weekly Gazette* suggested that blacks be put to work on farms outside the city. Showing support for the editor's idea, Mary Logan hired a black contraband to work on the Logans' farm. The man proved to be an able worker, and his labor allowed Mary to keep the farm productive. Mary learned, however, that far from having a man about the place to protect her, she would have to confront local terrorists to protect him.

Just as Rebels used violence to persecute defenseless Unionists in the countryside, secessionists in Cairo threatened to drive black laborers from their jobs in rural areas. Mary Logan recorded that the Knights of the Golden Circle threatened to shoot her black farm worker. She could have gone to the provost marshal at the Cairo post for help, but she preferred to take matters into her own hands. Even though the Knights disguised themselves with masks, Mary recognized two of the men who rode out to her farm to threaten her. Wielding a gun, Mary held her ground, and in the end, the outlaws thought better of harming the wife of Gen. John A. Logan.[35]

By the close of 1862, fifteen hundred black contraband in the camp at Cairo were sent to work as laborers, but not all of them worked in the countryside of southern Illinois. News of the destitute blacks' arrival at Cairo aroused interest from other towns. Perceiving the refugees as potential labor, northern cities sought to alleviate what

33. Eleanore, *King's Highway*, 250; Pearson, *Historic Hospitals*, 28; Noyes, *Contraband Camp*, 212; Eaton, *Grant, Lincoln, and the Freedmen*, 35.
34. Logan, *Reminiscences of the Civil War*, 114, 81; WSC, 110.
35. Ibid., 204; Logan, *Reminiscences of the Civil War*, 84.

Cairoites considered the burden of the freedmen. Petitions deluged the officers at Grant's old headquarters requesting the dispensation of groups of blacks to serve as domestic help.

With the approval of Washington, Brig. Gen. J. M. Tuttle sent several groups of black contraband to northern cities.[36] The spectacle of large groups of blacks in predominantly white cities raised fear and anxiety among residents. Unlike the fanatical abolitionists, the majority of the white population in the North had felt only ambivalence toward the institution of slavery prior to the war. Marching through the South, northern soldiers tended to change their views of slavery after witnessing the institution firsthand, but the relatives at home had no such personal experience with the system.

In Illinois, exclusion laws, predating the conflict, had barred blacks from migrating into the state. City leaders who accepted black workers from the Cairo camp circumvented the laws by assuring citizens that the refugees would serve as temporary labor only and would not remain permanently in their cities.[37] Involving himself in the management of the contraband, Lyman Trumbull, a thorough abolitionist, attempted to reassure Illinoisans that the complexions of their societies would not be altered by the contraband. Trumbull stated that the blacks would return to the South as soon as possible since they could not acclimate to the cold northern climate.

Illinois residents took little comfort from Trumbull's statements. Cairo residents feared that the sea of blacks would settle along the southern borders of free states, where they would be shielded from their former masters and still enjoy a mild climate. Hysteria drove residents of the towns of Pittfield and Breadwell to draft resolutions calling for the enforcement of the Black Laws and the prohibition of black settlement in Illinois.[38]

Northerners were not very receptive to Trumbull's assurances, either. In Chicago, a few weeks after the city fathers requested workers from the contraband camp in Cairo, the mayor did an about-face. Explaining that under pressure from Democrats and the common council, he asked that the transfer of freedmen to Chicago cease. Shortly after this turn of events, Trumbull spoke at a mass meeting in the city, articulating a plan that continued to receive

36. Noyes, *Contraband Camp*, 211, 204; Bradsby, *History of Cairo*, 56.
37. Noyes, *Contraband Camp*, 206.
38. Logan, *Reminiscences of the Civil War*, 114; Noyes, *Contraband Camp*, 207.

attention from abolitionists until the end of Reconstruction in the South. If the federal government would institute a policy of confiscating plantations belonging to men who had waged war against the Union, the land could then be sold to loyal men. In accordance with the federal government's policy, Unionist planters would allow free blacks to stay on the plantations that had been their homes.[39]

This plan, adopted by the Radicals, never enjoyed serious consideration from lawmakers. The practicality of Trumbull's plan depended on implementing social revolution in the South, i.e., relocating rebellious planters to different areas of the country. Recognizing the impossibility of that option, even Trumbull believed that if free blacks remained in the South, living amongst Confederate planters, each one of them would need a gun to defend himself against his former master.[40]

During the existence of the contraband camp at Cairo, guns stayed in the hands of the Union army. Grant consistently expressed his concern to Eaton over the freedmen in the Mississippi Valley, but his attention, necessarily, centered mainly on the movements of his army. Eaton continued to work with the contraband at Cairo under Grant's direction and, later, under the auspices of the War Department. By the time the contraband camp in Cairo disbanded in the spring of 1863, Grant was thinking of Cairo mainly in terms of reinforcements. Once Federal troops had crossed the river below the Vicksburg bluffs, each day carried them closer to the siege that finally revealed Grant as the most capable commander in all the Union armies.

After the fall of the Vicksburg fortress, George Durfee assured his family that only the Union soldiers' great confidence in Grant had sustained them throughout the campaign. Logan's men showed similar devotion to a man who had proven himself an able general. At Vicksburg, Logan proved absolutely that he possessed a good measure of military skill while McClernand's incompetence became evident even to common soldiers. Grant relieved McClernand of his command before the final push to take the Confederate fortress.

The campaign against Vicksburg emphasized once again Grant's resourcefulness and appreciation for policy. He failed in his first attempt to take the fort but forged a new, ingenious strategy that

39. Noyes, *Contraband Camp*, 207.
40. Ibid.

kept him from retreating to Memphis at a time when such a move would have dispirited people in the North. In the success at Vicksburg, Grant accomplished Lincoln's first strategic priority in the war: he had given control of the Mississippi River to the Union.[41] Overlooked once again for promotion to a command in the East, Grant nevertheless gained Lincoln's undivided attention. Lincoln assessed the Vicksburg campaign as "one of the most brilliant in the world."[42] Ironically, Grant's defeat of the last Confederate obstacle on the Mississippi, at a time when Lincoln was casting about for a new commander in the East, convinced Lincoln that he needed to keep Grant in the West.

In October 1863, Lincoln elevated Grant to command of all departments and armies in the western theater. Grant relieved Rosecrans at Chattanooga, where he smashed the Rebel Bragg. Constantly maturing in his judgment of men, Grant saw Lagow's incompetence during that campaign and relieved him of command. To follow up the victory at Chattanooga, Grant sent Sherman to catch Longstreet near Knoxville, but the Confederate general robbed Sherman of a confrontation; he chose to retreat. Possession of most of east Tennessee now fell to the Union.[43]

At Chattanooga, Grant realized Lincoln's second most important strategic objective: he defeated the Confederates to open the entrance into east Tennessee. At long last, Lincoln rewarded Grant's great ability as a military commander with a commensurate position. The promotion required Grant's presence in the East. Eschewing an office in Washington, D.C., Grant stayed in the field with his army. Following this promotion, Grant expanded his plan for victory to include both theaters of the war, a process that forged the final link between his and Lincoln's strategic thought.[44]

41. Ibid., 275.
42. Ibid., 230.
43. Williams, *Lincoln and His Generals*, 290.
44. Ibid., 275, 285, 290.

Fifteen

Illumination

As the war dragged into 1864, Grant left an occupied West behind and moved steadily toward victory in Virginia. In Cairo, news of Grant's exploits in the East competed for attention with threats of marauding soldiers, guerrilla bands, and courts-martial that would plague the community until April 1865. On February 21 of that year, Cairo's *War Eagle* reported that the Union flag had been raised at Fort Sumter and the guns at "Fort Cairo" had fired a salute to mark the fall of Charleston.[1]

Although marauders never actually entered Cairo, the town had been grappling with another invader for two years. Close on the heels of battles, raids, and refugees, wealth had overtaken the village and created a boomtown. Unbridled audacity, clever entrepreneurship, and, in some cases, outright greed had allowed bold men to translate demand into supply. Consequently, they supplied themselves with vast amounts of disposable capital. Cairo's society had been unusual in the region before the war, and the wealth accrued during the war years gave the town a further distinction: of all the thriving communities in the tristate area, Cairo possessed the only bona fide elite class.[2]

Grant's presence and policies in Cairo had facilitated the development of an upper class, but another change in local society could also

1. *War Eagle*, Feb. 9, 1865; Edwin Loosley MSS, Feb. 13, 1865; *War Eagle*, Mar. 7, 1865; Lantz, *Community in Search*, 4.
2. Lantz, *Community in Search*, 4.

be attributed to the general. The contraband camp at Cairo introduced a large group of blacks into the town. Cairo's black population rose from only 7 black residents in 1860 to 2,083 in 1865 out of a total population of 8,569. At the war's end, ample evidence of the presence of former slaves appeared in Cairo. The military district continued to house a freedmen's mess hall and quarters, a freedmen's hospital, and a freedmen's school.[3] As the rich grew richer in Cairo, many blacks moved from facilities provided by the army into servants' quarters located on the grounds of mansions. The bulk of the new population worked as laborers and servants.

The presence of the military base had transformed Cairo into a community with the business opportunities and the cosmopolitan society of a metropolis. After Grant's campaigns opened the Mississippi River all along its course, the rivers that once had threatened to bring the enemy into Cairo instead brought trade. Great fleets of steamboats landed at the Ohio levee every day from the Mississippi, Ohio, Tennessee, and Cumberland rivers. Cairo's steamboat industry enjoyed unprecedented growth in the years 1864–1865. Railroads connected Cairo with all the major cities in the United States. Predating the war, a main thoroughfare had connected Cairo to Chicago. In the postwar era, several Chicago companies opened branch operations in Cairo.

Society, economy, and politics fell under the control of the nouveaux riches through interlocking directorates and a tight, internecine social circle. All over the country, the extravagant lifestyles of war millionaires seared the myth of the self-made man into the American consciousness. Scholars began debating the phenomenon. Economist Thorstein Veblen believed that the Civil War moved American society into a "predatory stage," manifested by a self-seeking pursuit of status in the form of material goods. Concurring with Veblen, Vernon Parrington concluded that war brings change, and the American Civil War changed society's devotion from democratic individualism into an elitist instinct for acquisition.[4] Preoccupied with acquisition, status, and material goods, the speculators in Cairo once again risked identifying themselves as treacherous, unpatriotic men.

3. Ibid.; Virginia B. Herbert and Ralph K. Gibson, Map of Military Installations in Cairo, 1866.
4. Veblen, *The Theory of the Leisure Class,* 42; Vernon Parrington, *Main Currents in American Thought.*

As Grant closed in on the Rebels in the South during 1865, celebrations erupted throughout the North. Ironically, in the town that had benefited so greatly from its association with Grant, local newspapers reported a lack of patriotic enthusiasm among the populace. No spontaneous festivities occurred in Cairo to mark the Union's victories; so, the editor of the military newspaper, *War Eagle*, prompted citizens to organize a patriotic display.[5] Reluctance to demonstrate support for the Union army lingered through January 1865, but, finally, a shocking event prompted a true outpouring of patriotism in Cairo.

Years after the war ended, rumors continued to circulate about the deep level of secessionist sentiment among Cairoites. One such story purported that so much southern sympathy existed in Cairo in 1865, the inhabitants rejoiced when they heard of President Lincoln's assassination.[6] Evidence shows, however, that the news of Lincoln's death brought an outpouring of genuine grief and a show of sincere affection for the slain Illinoisan.

Since the town was hosting a Union military base, a display of grief would be expected. But the level of mourning among Cairo's citizens went beyond expectation. Without any editorial urging, every public building and almost every home in Cairo displayed black mourning drapery. Black crepe festoons subdued the elegant mansions on Washington Avenue. Flags flew at half-mast on all public buildings and on all boats in port. Every bell in the city tolled in memoriam for a man few Cairoites had endorsed in 1860.

On April 19, while Lincoln's funeral services took place in Washington, D.C., many Cairo residents attended simultaneous services held in local churches. Prior to the memorial services, the Forty-second Wisconsin Regiment, then stationed in Cairo, marched through the streets with muffled drums and reversed arms. They passed through town and marched down to their camp at the point. There they listened to a sermon given by their chaplain.[7] Cairo's own Arab Rough and Ready fire companies followed the Forty-second, marching through the downtown to the Episcopal Church, where they attended a memorial service.

5. *War Eagle*, Apr. 8, 1865.
6. J. M. Howley, "Cairo and the News of Lincoln's Death," Oct. 1932, 25:3, 235–37, 236.
7. Ibid.

Remorse over the president's murder finally moved residents to hold a victory celebration. The jubilant event took the form of a grand illumination—a parade with fireworks. Reportedly, it lit up the entire Ohio levee, from the St. Charles Hotel to the City Mills. The *War Eagle* reported that Cairo's illumination was a blaze of glory. The brilliant spectacle not only honored the fallen president, but also symbolized the glorious era that the war had ushered into Cairo. The presence of an important military base had changed the residents' image of their town. The money that the war funneled into local business enterprises had transformed Cairo's society.

At the pinnacle of that society stood the men whose mercenary acquisitiveness had taken them down whatever road led to profit. By 1865, the five Halliday Brothers, Alfred Boardman Safford, H. H. Candee, Staats Taylor, William H. Green, Wood Rittenhouse, and Charles Galigher owned all of the major businesses and industries in Cairo. Hesitant to display patriotic fervor at the war's end, the successful entrepreneurs in Cairo fervently displayed their wealth through conspicuous consumption and philanthropy during the remainder of the nineteenth century.

Perhaps the wealthy men in Cairo possessed the same pioneer inventiveness that gave rise to so many significant innovations in the western theater during the Civil War, new concepts that originated in the West and migrated eastward. The first medical improvements in military camps appeared in the West and were later adopted by medical staff serving in the East. The first efficient system of transporting supplies moved from West to East. An efficient system for managing black and white refugees started in the West and followed the Western Sanitary Commission to the East. And, most important, the successful military strategies that ultimately wore the Confederates down were tested in the West and then implemented in the East by the man whose military genius had conceived them.

Militarily, the Mississippi Valley had played as important a role in Union strategy as had Washington, D.C., and Richmond, Virginia.[8] Unquestionably the town of Cairo served as headquarters to a military district that allowed Ulysses S. Grant to come into his own and redeem the tarnished reputation that had dogged him before the war.

8. Allan Nevins, *The War for the Union*, I:119.

In Cairo, Grant developed the strategic and administrative abilities that supported his campaigns throughout the war and allowed him to finally reclaim the entire country. The problems plaguing the base pushed Grant to realize his full administrative abilities. The nearness of the enemy prompted him to recognize and seize strategic opportunities. In command of a western district—far removed from the War Department—Grant was able to follow his instincts. The treachery and sabotage of the enemy in the midst of Union territory strengthened Grant's natural impulse for pressing on in the face of adversity. In campaigns that departed from Cairo, Grant and his volunteer troops had sent the Rebels back to their maps and manuals to search for new strategies. Having tasted a measure of defeat before the war, Grant finally realized great success through tenacity and quiet persistence. His moral fortitude, common sense, and steadfast loyalty led him to unexpected greatness.

Riding Grant's coattails into glory, the town of Cairo climbed back from the brink and achieved more success than its founders had ever imagined. Due, in part, to the persistence of Cairo's early residents and some of the trustees, the town stood ready to accommodate the needs of the Union army throughout the conflict. As Union and Confederate veterans made their way back to a greatly changed community, Grant's legacy in Cairo uplifted some and haunted others. Settling into civilian life, Confederate and Unionist alike found common ground in prosperity. For the newly wealthy in Cairo, money had replaced morals, clever entrepreneurship had eclipsed common sense, and loyalty lay with the highest possibility for the greatest profit. As the country turned away from military matters and steamed into the Industrial Age, those phenomena would provide the greatest challenges to Grant's ultimate legacy.

Epilogue

Cairo, 1880

Grant's carriage slowly churned its way through the muddy streets to the public platform, where Grant disembarked and mounted the steps. Men who remembered the slouching, introspective commander of Cairo saw a man little changed by two terms in the White House and a world tour. Innate modesty and natural shyness still characterized the hero who had led battles that fractured the Confederates' western line of defense. He sat quietly as Mayor Thistlewood welcomed the "great war hero" back to Cairo and delivered a short address.[1]

Following Thistlewood, the man whom Cairo residents had commissioned to welcome Grant on their behalf rose to speak. Judge William H. Green, a Democrat, stepped to the front of the platform so that everyone present might hear his carefully rehearsed speech. Veterans, local politicians, and people from near and far, pressed toward the stand.

Southern Illinoisans, in their enthusiasm to adulate the country's most popular public figure, seemed to forget the differences that had divided them so sharply during the sectional conflict. Among the multitude, another honorable Democrat who held vivid memories of Grant's command in Cairo listened intently. Judge William J. Allen, now a resident of Carbondale, had traveled to Cairo to attend

1. *Cairo Daily Bulletin*, Apr. 16, 1880.

a Democratic conference on April 15. His entire group had stayed over to see Grant.

Green opened by stating that, since the war's end, the Mississippi River had bound together "this now happy sisterhood of states."[2] Comparing past to present, Green remarked that goods of the merchant and crops of the planter had replaced the stores of the army's commissary on the Ohio levee. No longer did townspeople watch gunboats leaving Cairo to plague Confederates along the Mississippi River. Nowadays, the Ohio and Mississippi rivers presented only a spectacle of grain barges plying peacefully in trade.[3]

Green then turned his attention to Grant's achievements at Cairo. From that fledgling town, Grant had begun the arduous task of converting fiercely independent farm boys into disciplined, if somewhat spirited, soldiers. Echoing the conclusions of later historians, Green surmised that, drawing loosely from his prior experience in the Mexican War and greatly from his own personal strength and common sense, Grant had carefully shaped hundreds of unseasoned volunteers into competent campaigners who followed him into the first, and arguably the most, significant Union victories.

Gesturing toward the Ohio waterfront, Green recalled the dangerous situation that had faced Grant in the fall of 1861:

When your little army was marshaled on yonder levee, ready to leave us, and march to victory, it was almost literally true that—

Cannon to the right of them,
Cannon to the left of them
Cannon in front of them,
Volley'd and thunder'd.[4]

Concluding his remarks, Green could not resist acknowledging the town as well as the guest. He stated that Grant's time in Cairo had sharpened the general's own abilities: "Here, you planned the first campaigns, which resulted in decisive victories to the Union arms."[5]

Grant, a man who had taken on godlike dimensions in the nation's

2. Ibid.
3. Ibid.
4. John Lansden, "William Green's Speech to Welcome General Grant to Cairo in 1880," 8:423.
5. Ibid.

collective imagination, responded to Green's remarks with characteristic candor and succinctness. He began by stating that he believed the reunification of the country would last permanently and then deftly turned the oration from war to peace. He complimented Cairo's growth: "You are now in the full enjoyment of the pursuits of peace, a thrifty, promising little city."[6] Grant's remarks reflected his highest praise, considering that he had fulfilled his own promise in war, was still learning thrift, and had spent the last few years enjoying the peace of private life.

A short public reception followed the speeches. Grant interacted with the thousands of common people who had turned out to see him—an event that completely closed traffic between Ninth and Tenth streets. Then, succumbing to a long day first spent traveling and then shaking hands, a tired Grant expressed a desire to proceed to his lodgings.

Tucked into the carriage once again, the Grants passed several impressive public buildings as they traveled along Washington Avenue. The stately built environment epitomized Cairo's postwar development. In the First Addition, on the forty-eighth block, an attractive new courthouse graced the avenue. Initially, the town of Thebes had served as the Alexander County seat, but during the war, Cairo's growth had outpaced that of the rest of the county, and wealthy speculators had lobbied the legislature to make a change. Located at fashionable Washington Avenue and Twentieth Street, the classic revival courthouse rose to a majestic height of three stories. The imposing building displayed elements characteristic of its style and reflective of a democratic system that never took root in Cairo: columns, a pediment over the front doors and another over the end gables.[7]

Farther along, the Grants passed by another magnificent building. Designed in the Grant style in 1868 by Grant's own architect, A. B. Mullett, the United States Customs House covered all of block thirty-nine in Cairo.[8] The multipurpose building housed a U.S. Post Office on the first floor, the Customs House on the second floor, and federal courtrooms on the third floor. A mansard roof capped

---

6. Ibid., 425.
7. Alexander County Collector Book 1865.
8. Alexander County Assessor's Book 1867: 123.

bull's-eye windows on the facade, and an American eagle decorated the front entrance.[9]

Across the street, the Safford Memorial Library rivaled the U.S. Customs House in beauty and distinction. A privately endowed institution, the library benefited from the war millionaires' love of great literature and fine art. Stained glass windows depicting famous authors brightened the heavy chiseled sandstone facade of the building. A quintessential example of the Richardsonian Romanesque style, the library housed a large collection of books and hosted many social organizations.

At regular intervals along Washington Avenue, lampposts stood ready to flood the business district with crime-deterring electric light at nightfall.[10] Many saloons still sat on the riverfront; the order that Grant brought to the town left with the Union military. Beyond the public buildings, a very different type of structure covered residential blocks running from Washington Avenue to the river. The black community brought their own architectural style to town, and every type of shotgun cottage common to the American South and the Caribbean could be found in their neighborhoods.

At Twenty-eighth Street the carriage turned into the Fifth Addition. The lavish estates of war entrepreneurs claimed one end of Washington Avenue. As the carriage moved along Twenty-eighth Street toward its destination, Grant saw something that made his heart beat faster. Beautiful thoroughbreds trotted through their afternoon exercises at St. Mary's Park, the millionaires' private racetrack.

As the carriage clattered onto a brick-paved boulevard, residents of a classic Italianate villa frantically steered their staff through the many preparations essential to a presidential visit. During the Civil War, Charles Galigher had cultivated a warm friendship with Grant. Through supply contracts, Galigher had realized a vast fortune furnishing the Union army with flour.[11] Now, nineteen years after they had first met Grant, Charles and Adelia Galigher made ready to host the great man's homecoming to Cairo.

After a brief respite at the Galighers, Grant went out at 5:00 p.m. to start another round of receptions. At 10:00 p.m., amid swaths of

9. Ibid.; Mary Halliday MSS 21:7:1954; *Cairo Daily Democrat*, Oct. 3, 1868.
10. Alexander County Incorporation Record, 1872–1903.
11. *Attractions of Cairo, Illinois*, n.p., 1908.

colored tissue paper and scenes of Civil War battles, he and Julia reigned over an invitation-only ball at the St. Charles Hotel. Dignitaries from all over the Midwest waltzed to the music of an orchestra amid Spanish moss, evergreen festoons, and fresh flowers, but the beloved war hero, who disdained dancing, enjoyed a "feast for the gods" in a private suite and renewed old friendships. At 9:00 the next morning, the Grants left Cairo and headed north toward Bloomington, Illinois. Never again would Ulysses S. Grant return to the town so closely connected with his success in the Civil War.

Bibliography

Books, Articles, and Theses

Ackerman, William K. *Early Illinois Railroads*. Chicago: Fergus Printing, 1884.

Allen, John W. *Legends and Lore of Southern Illinois*. Carbondale: University Graphics, 1978.

Anderson, Bern. *By Sea and by River: The Naval History of the Civil War*. New York: Knopf, 1962.

Attie, Jean. *Patriotic Toil: Northern Women and the American Civil War*. Ithaca: Cornell University Press, 1998.

Attractions of Cairo. Cairo: People's Press, 1908.

Boynton, Charles Brandon. *The History of the Navy during the Rebellion*. New York: D. Appleton, 1867–1868.

Brinton, John H. *The Personal Memoirs of John H. Brinton, Major and Surgeon U. S. V.* New York: Neale Publishing, 1914.

Brown, Charles Leroy. "Lincoln and the Illinois Central, 1857–1860." *Journal of the Illinois State Historical Society* (March 1943) 36:1.

Brown, William H. *An Historical Sketch of the Early Movement in Illinois for the Legalization of Slavery*. Chicago: Fergus Printing, 1876.

Brown-Baker, Nina. *Cyclone in Calico: The Story of Mary Ann Bickerdyke*. Boston: Little, Brown, 1952.

Browning, Orville Hickman. *Diary of Orville Hickman Browning*. Springfield: Trustees of the Illinois State Historical Library, 1925–1933.

Burley, Augustus Harris. *The Cairo Expedition: Illinois' First Response in the Late Civil War*. Chicago: Fergus Printing, 1892.

Catton, Bruce. *Grant Moves South*. Boston: Little Brown, 1968.

——. *This Hallowed Ground: The Story of the Union Side of the War.* Garden City, N.Y.: Doubleday, 1965.

Chrichton, Jane Wallace. "Michael Kelly Lawler: A Southern Illinois Mexican War Captain and Civil War General." Master's thesis, Southern Illinois University at Carbondale, 1965.

Cole, Arthur Charles. *The Era of the Civil War, 1848–1870.* Springfield: Centennial Committee, 1919.

Comeaux, Malcolm. "Impact of Transportation Activities upon the Historical Development of Cairo, Illinois." Master's thesis, Southern Illinois University at Carbondale, 1966.

Dickens, Charles. *American Notes.* New York: P. F. Collier and Son, n.d.

Duncan, Louis C. *The Medical Department of the United States Army in the Civil War.* Gaithersburg, Md.: Olde Soldier Books, 1987.

Eleanore, Sister M. *On the King's Highway.* New York: Appleton, 1931.

Eaton, John. *Grant, Lincoln, and the Freedmen: Reminiscences of the Civil War, with Special Reference to the Work for the Contrabands and Freedmen of the Mississippi Valley.* New York: Negro Universities Press, 1907.

Eliot, William Greenleaf. "Western Sanitary Commission." *North American Review* (April 1864).

Fischer, Le Roy S. "Cairo's Civil War Angel, Mary Jane Safford." *Journal of the Illinois State Historical Society* 54.

Fuller, Melville W. "Biography of Sidney Breese." *The Early History of Illinois from Its Discovery of the Mississippi.* By Sidney Breese. Chicago: Myers, 1884.

Gates, Paul Wallace. *The Illinois Central Railroad and Its Colonization Work.* Cambridge: Harvard University Press, 1934.

Giesberg, Judith Ann. *Civil War Sisterhood: The U.S. Sanitary Commission and Women's Politics in Transition.* Boston: Northeastern University Press, 2000.

Glatthaar, Joseph. *Partners in Command: The Relationships between Leaders in the Civil War.* New York: Free Press, 1994.

Grant, Julia Dent. *The Personal Memoirs of Julia Dent Grant.* New York: Putnam, 1975.

Grant, Ulysses S. *General Grant's Letters to a Friend* New York: T. Y. Crowell, 1897.

——. *The Papers of Ulysses S. Grant.* Edited by John Y. Simon. Carbondale: Southern Illinois University Press, 1967.

———. *The Personal Memoirs of Ulysses S. Grant*. New York: Konecky & Konecky, n. d.

Haller, John S. *Farmcarts to Fords: A History of the Military Ambulance, 1790–1925*. Carbondale: Southern Illinois University, 1992.

Hattaway, Herman, and Archer Jones. *How the North Won: A Military History of the Civil War*. Urbana: University of Illinois Press, 1983.

Hicken, Victor. *Illinois in the Civil War*. Urbana: University of Illinois Press, 1966.

Holt, Earl K., and William A. Deiss. *William Greenleaf Eliot: Conservative Radical*. St. Louis: First Unitarian Church, 1985.

Howley, J. M. "Cairo and the News of Lincoln's Death." *Journal of the Illinois State Historical Society* (October 1932) 25:3.

Hughes, Nathaniel Cheairs Jr. *The Battle of Belmont: Grant Strikes South*. Chapel Hill: University of North Carolina Press, 1991.

Illinois Infantry, Thirty-first Regiment, 1861–1865. *History: Thirty-first Regiment Illinois Volunteers Evansville*. Indiana: Keller Printing & Publishing, 1902.

James, Edwin. *Account of an Expedition from Pittsburgh to the Rocky Mountains*. Ann Arbor: University Microfilms, 1966.

Jones, James Pickett. *Black Jack: John A. Logan and Southern Illinois in the Civil War Era*. Tallahassee: Florida State University Press, 1967.

Josephson, Matthew. *The Robber Barons: The Great American Capitalists, 1861–1901*. New York: Harcourt, Brace, 1934.

Kiper, Richard L. *Major General John M. McClernand: Politician in Uniform*. Kent: Kent State University Press, 1999.

Kircher, Henry Adolph. *A German in the Yankee Fatherland*. Edited by Earl J. Hess. Kent: Kent State University Press, 1983.

Kune, Julian. *Reminiscences of an Octagenarian Hungarian Exile*. Chicago: J. Kune, 1911.

Lansden, John M. "Cairo in 1841." *Journal of the Illinois State Historical Society*, vol. 5:1.

———. *History of the City of Cairo, Illinois*. Carbondale: Southern Illinois University Press, 1910.

———. "William Green's Speech to Welcome General Grant to Cairo in 1880." *Journal of the Illinois State Historical Society* (1915–1916): 8.

Lantz, Herman R. *A Community in Search of Itself: A Case History of*

Cairo, Illinois. Carbondale: Southern Illinois University Press, 1910.

Lincoln, Abraham. *The Collected Works.* Edited by Roy P. Basler. New Brunswick: Rutgers University Press, 1953–1955.

———. *Speeches and Writings of Abraham Lincoln.* Edited by Roy P. Basler. Cleveland: World Publishing, 1946.

Livermore, Mary Ashton Rice. *My Story of the War.* Hartford, Conn.: A. D. Worthington, 1888.

Logan, Mrs. John A. *Reminiscences of the Civil War and Reconstruction.* Carbondale: Southern Illinois University Press, 1970.

———. *Reminiscences of a Soldier's Wife.* New York: Scribner's Sons, 1913.

Long, E. B. *The Civil War Day by Day.* Garden City, N.Y.: Doubleday, 1971.

MacNaul, Willard Carey. *The Jefferson-Lemen Compact: The Relations of Thomas Jefferson and James Lemen in the Exclusion of Slavery from Illinois and the Northwest Territory.* Chicago: University of Chicago Press, 1915.

Maxwell, William Quentin. *Lincoln's Fifth Wheel: The Political History of the United States Sanitary Commission.* New York: Longmans, Green, 1965.

Merrill, James. "Cairo: Civil War Port." *Journal of the Illinois State Historical Society* (1983).

Miller, Henry H. "Ellesworth's Zouaves" in *Reminiscences of Chicago during the Civil War.* New York: Citadel Press, 1967.

Milligan, John D. *Gunboats down the Mississippi.* Annapolis: Naval Academy, 1952.

Monoghan, James. *The Man Who Elected Lincoln, by Jay Monoghan.* Indianapolis: Bobbs-Merrill, 1956.

Moore, Frank. *Women of the War.* Hartford, Conn.: S. S. Scranton, 1866.

Morrison, Marion. *History of the Ninth Regiment Illinois Volunteer Infantry.* Carbondale: Southern Illinois University Press, 1997.

Neely, Mark E. *The Abraham Lincoln Encyclopedia.* New York: McGraw-Hill, 1982.

Nevins, Allan. *The War for the Union.* Vol. 1. New York: Charles Scribner's Sons, 1959.

Noyes, Edward. *Contraband Camp at Cairo, Illinois,* 1972.

Pearson, Emmett F. "Historic Hospitals of Cairo." *Journal of the Illinois State Historical Society* (1984).

Perret, Geoffrey. *Ulysses S. Grant: Soldier and President.* New York: Modern Library, 1999.

Pitkin, William A. "When Cairo Was Saved for the Union." *Journal of the Illinois State Historical Society,* vol. 51.

Porter, David D. *Incidents and Anecdotes of the Civil War.* New York: D. Appleton, 1885.

———. *The Naval History of the Civil War.* New York: Sherman Publishing, 1890.

Pratt, Harry. "Lewis B. Parsons: Mover of Armies." *Journal of the Illinois State Historical Society* (Winter 1951): 44.

Simon, John Y., and Michael E. Stevens. "Forging a Commander: Ulysses S. Grant Enters the War." In *New Perspectives on the Civil War: Myths and Realities of the National Conflict.* Madison: Madison House, 1998.

Tap, Bruce. *Over Lincoln's Shoulder: The Committee on the Conduct of the War.* Lawrence: University Press of Kansas, 1998.

Trollope, Anthony. *North America.* Two volumes. New York: Harper & Brothers, 1862.

Trumbull, Lyman. "Lyman Trumbull Papers." *Journal of the Illinois State Historical Society* (April–January 1909–1910).

The United States Sanitary Commission: A Sketch of Its Purposes and Its Work. Boston: Little, Brown, 1863.

Walke, Henry. "Operations of the Western Flotilla." *Century Magazine,* vol. 29.

Walworth, Clarence Alvord. *Governor Edward Coles.* Springfield: Trustees of the Illinois State Historical Library, 1920.

Williams, T. Harry. *Lincoln and His Generals.* New York: Dorset, 1952.

Young, Agatha. *The Women and the Crisis.* New York: McDowell, Obolensky, 1959.

Government Documents

Alexander County Assessor's Book 1867: 123. Illinois Regional Archives Depository, Southern Illinois University Carbondale.

Alexander County Circuit Court Records, 1856. Illinois Regional Archives Depository, Southern Illinois University Carbondale.

Alexander County Collector Book, 1865. Illinois Regional Archives Depository, Southern Illinois University Carbondale.

Annual Report of the Adjutant General of the State of Illinois. Springfield: Baker & Phillips, Printers, 1863.

Appendix to the Congressional Globe 36th Congress, 2nd Session. City of Washington: John C. Rives, December 2, 1860–March 2, 1861.

Congressional Record. "Reports of Committees Made during the Second Session of the Thirty-Seventh Congress, 1861–1862." Report No. 2, House Select Committee on Government Contracts, I.

Eighth United States Population Census Report, Alexander, Bond Counties, Illinois. Microfilm, Southern Illinois University Carbondale.

Incorporation Laws of the State of Illinois, Passed at a Session of the General Assembly, Begun and Held at Vandalia the 6th Day of December, 1836. Vandalia: William Walters, Public Printer, 1837.

Laws Passed by the General Assembly of Illinois Territory at Their Sixth Session, Held at Kaskaskia, 1817–1818. Kaskaskia: Berry and Blackwell—Printers to the Territory, 1818.

Long, Henry C. "Report on the Site of Cairo, Illinois." United States Army Corps of Engineers, 1850.

Report of the United States Sanitary Commission, Chicago Branch, October 1861. No. 38. Chicago: Dunlop, Sewell, & Spalding, Printers, 1861.

Report of the Western Sanitary Commission. St. Louis: Western Sanitary Commission, 1864.

Twelfth United States Population Census Report, Alexander-Bond Counties, Illinois, 1900. Microfilm, Southern Illinois University Carbondale.

The War of the Rebellion: A Compilation of the Official Records of the Union and Confederate Armies. Washington, D.C.: Government Printing Office, 1880–1901.

The War of the Rebellion: A Compilation of the Official Records of the Union and Confederate Navies. Washington, D.C.: Government Printing Office, 1880–1901.

Manuscript Collections

Adams, Lemuel. Untitled. Typescript. Illinois State Historical Library, Springfield, Illinois.

Andrew Papers. Illinois State Historical Library, Springfield, Illinois.

Breese, Sidney. Papers. Illinois State Historical Library, Springfield, Illinois.

Cairo City Property Trust. Papers. Cairo Public Library, Cairo, Illinois.

Cullum, George. Papers. Illinois State Historical Library, Springfield, Illinois.

Dietschy, Joseph. Papers. Illinois State Historical Library, Springfield, Illinois.

Durfee, George S. Papers. Illinois Historical Survey Library, University of Illinois at Urbana-Champaign.

Fite, Hiram T. Papers. Illinois State Historical Library, Springfield, Illinois.

Grant, Ulysses S. Letters to Elihu B. Washburne, Illinois State Historical Library, Springfield, Illinois.

Halliday, Mary. Papers. Cairo Public Library, Cairo, Illinois.

Haynie, Isham N. Papers. Microfilm. Illinois State Historical Library, Springfield, Illinois.

Illinois Central Railroad. Papers. Cairo Public Library, Cairo, Illinois.

Lansden, John M. Papers. Cairo Public Library, Cairo, Illinois.

Lawler, Michael Kelley. Papers. Morris Library, Southern Illinois University Carbondale.

Loosley, Edwin. Papers. Morris Library, Southern Illinois University Carbondale.

McClernand, John A. Papers. Illinois State Historical Library, Springfield, Illinois.

McIlrath, James. Papers. Illinois State Historical Library, Springfield, Illinois.

McLean, William. Papers. Illinois State Historical Library, Springfield, Illinois.

Mann, John Preston. Papers. Morris Library, Southern Illinois University Carbondale.

Onstat, William. Papers. Illinois State Historical Library, Springfield, Illinois.

Parsons, Lewis B. Papers. Illinois State Historical Library, Springfield, Illinois.

Reese, John. Papers. Morris Library, Southern Illinois University Carbondale.

Skipworth, Joseph. Papers. Morris Library, Southern Illinois University Carbondale.

Swales, James. Papers. Cairo Public Library.

Yates Family Collection. Illinois State Historical Library, Springfield, Illinois.

Maps

Herbert, Virginia B., and Ralph K. Gibson. Map of Military Installations in Cairo, 1866. Cairo Public Library.

Long, Henry C. Topographical Map of Cairo, Illinois, 1850. United States Army Corps of Engineers. Cairo Public Library.

D. A. Sanborn National Insurance Company. Sanborn Maps and Publishing Company. American Fire-Insurance Maps, Cairo, Illinois, 1896.

Newspapers

Cairo City Times
Cairo City Weekly Gazette
Cairo Daily Bulletin
Cairo Daily Democrat
Cairo Sun
Cairo Tri-Weekly
Cairo Weekly Times and Delta
Chicago Daily Tribune
Harper's Weekly Journal of Civilization
Jonesboro Weekly Gazette
New York Illustrated News
New York Times
War Eagle

Index